VOTERS & VOTING

JOCELYN A.J. EVANS

VOTERS & VOTING

AN INTRODUCTION

SAGE Publications
Los Angeles • London • New Delhi • Singapore

Reprinted 2007

SAGE Publications Ltd
1 Oliver's Yard
55 City Road
London EC1Y 1SP

SAGE Publications Inc
2455 Teller Road
Thousand Oaks, California 91320

SAGE Publications India Pvt Ltd
B1/I 1 Mohan Cooperative Industrial Area
Mathura Road, New Delhi 110 044
India

SAGE Publications Asia-Pacific Pte Ltd
33 Pekin Street #02-01
Far East Square
Singapore 048763

British Library Cataloguing in Publication data

A catalogue record for this book is available from the British Library

ISBN: 978-0-7619-4909-1 (hbk)
ISBN: 978-0-7619-4910-7 (pbk)

Library of Congress control number available

Typeset by C&M Digitals (P) Ltd, Chennai, India
Printed and bound in Great Britain by Athenaeum Press Ltd., Gateshead

To my father and Margaret
Here's the answer.

Table of Contents

List of Tables and Figures

Preface

In writing this book, I have attempted to fill a gap in the voting literature. In teaching an undergraduate course on voting behaviour, it struck me that there was no single text which I could recommend to students as an introduction to the various theories and models which they would encounter during the course. It certainly struck the students that this was the case, and I'm sure some of them believed that, for some unfathomable and probably bizarre reason, I was hiding the existence of a textbook from them. To me, the bizarre reason why I was not providing this text was precisely because it did not exist.

Plenty of excellent texts on various aspects of electoral behaviour exist, but these are usually research monographs and articles addressing a specific element in the equation. Consequently they are aimed at an audience already versed in the subject. There are also a number of textbooks which consider voting behaviour in a country or a region, and which test theories of voting with copious empirical evidence. There are those texts which present the theories as part of a broader conceptual package. Lastly, there are texts which unpack a single theory in all its complexity, but which completely ignore theoretical fellow-travellers. I have no criticism of any of these approaches – but if only in their sheer quantity, complexity and often exclusivity of focus, they present an imposing obstacle to the student wishing to receive an overview of the voting theories on offer.

Add to this that the piecemeal nature of the various approaches often serves to hide the continuities in approach that particularly link much of post-war research into electoral behaviour, and students find themselves with not only a mountain to climb, but a contextual vacuum in which to accomplish this. Of course, the teacher should provide such a context in the classroom, but the non-existent text providing written support beyond the lecture theatre and seminar room would serve to reinforce this. Some might say that, precisely by dealing with electoral theories in a separate package, I am denying them their essential context (i.e. that they should be spoken of in the same breath as electoral laws, participation, social change, decision-making, etc.). They may have a point, and in my defence I would point out that I refer to all of these at various points in the book, to illustrate how voting theories relate more broadly. But an element in a system can be usefully studied in artificial isolation, as long as one never loses sight of its true functional position.

Lastly, for the postgraduate student embarking upon the *x*-year journey through methods classes, Stats 101 thru 199 and applied empirical testing in their own doctoral research, mastery of the models and equations characterising an increasing proportion of the electoral literature is a necessary part of the learning process. That voting theories are now tested in more sophisticated models is predominantly, to this author at least, a testament to their intellectual appeal and success. But for a Political Science undergraduate who requires grounding in voting theory, there is a tendency to give a cursory introduction to theories but leave to one side much of the best research simply because it is felt that undergraduates are unlikely to have the statistical tools necessary to understand it. I think this is largely fallacious. To carry out such research demands a high level of statistical know-how. To read the research and understand the basic concepts which drive the models does not. Deciphering what the models are getting at is not the same as knowing exactly how they work. To this end, I have provided what I regard as a suitable minimum of explanation which can get non-statisticians started with appreciating – but not carrying out – such quantitative research.

It was with all these aims in mind that this book was written. It is intended as an introduction to the wide array of voting theories for students with little or no previous exposure to these concepts, and no statistical training. I have made sure to select readings which provide clear and concise explanations of their findings, and which do not rely on the reader to decipher these from the models. I certainly do not expect it to present anything new for experts in psephology (the study of voting), nor do I present any extensive primary research. Given the vast range of literature on offer, it does not pretend to present every major text on a given subject, but rather the key texts which I think get across to the reader the main thrust of a subject. Some texts are used more copiously than others precisely because they stand out as benchmarks. As a textbook reviewing and presenting existing research, I would not try and pass off any of the ideas as 'mine', with the exception of parts of Chapter 8. They are the good ideas of others which I want to bring to an audience which too often shies away from them.

Acknowledgements

A number of people and institutions should be acknowledged in the production of this book. I would like to thank Robert Andersen, Eva Anduiza Perea, Tor Bjørklund, Martin Bull, Elisabeth Carter, David Farrell, Steven Fielding, Jonathan Simon and Peter Ucen who have all provided information at various times or commented on drafts. Given that Chapter 8 is derived in part from my doctoral thesis – this chapter includes the only previously 'seen' work in the book – I should thank my thesis jury, Anthony Heath, Yves Mény, Pascal Perrineau and my supervisor, Stefano Bartolini, for their comments which have now belatedly found their way into this book. Usual disclaimers as to responsibility for accuracy and errors herein apply.

Various colleagues have provided encouragement along the way, expressing a desire to see the finished product, which is always incentive for an author. I am certain there are more, but three spring to mind in particular – Tim Bale, Ben Clift and John Garry. I would also like to thank Ed Page for helpful suggestions made early on when I was considering writing the book. The students who took my 'Voting Behaviour: Theories and Empirical Testing' course at Salford deserve thanks for their feedback on much of the material which has been used here – and also for being willing to take a module with what is, on reflection, a monstrously off-putting title. (I promise future cohorts that I shall change it to something less stodgy.) At Sage, I am particularly indebted to Lucy Armitage and David Mainwaring who provided patient encouragement throughout the writing of the book.

Institutionally, I acknowledge the support of the ZA-Eurolab in Cologne for having given me access to the NSD 1993 Norwegian electoral data during my stay there in 1998, the original analysis of which provided two of the figures used in Chapter 5. A similar acknowledgement to the *Centre d'Informatisation des Données Socio-Politiques* (CIDSP), Grenoble, for providing the SOFRES 1995 French post-election survey which was also used in that chapter. I should also thank this institution and its staff for very kindly hosting me during a period of research leave from Salford University during which I completed the book. I am similarly grateful to the French *Centre National de la Recherche Scientifique* (CNRS) for partially funding this leave. Finally, I should thank Salford and its Politics and Contemporary History department for allowing me sufficient time to conceive of this project and start the writing process.

1

Introduction

Looking at the vast literature dedicated to the analysis of voting behaviour and its context, it is sometimes difficult to work out exactly what kind of activity voting is. On the one hand books on democracy and democratic theory present voting as a unique activity which forms the bedrock of political equality and civic rights in our society. People have fought and died for the right to vote, and in some countries continue to do so. As the pinnacle of power in democratic societies, would-be prime ministers and presidents devote much of their lives in pursuit of office, spending time and money to win the support of the voting public. The apparently increasing failure of many individuals to participate in this selection of leaders and their parties leads to indignant and outraged accusations of apathy, and calls for measures to address the decline in interest in precisely the activity which allows all citizens access to the political process. From this perspective, voting is unique and of paramount importance.

Yet if we turn to much of the literature on how voters make up their minds whom to vote for, the impression we receive is far from the hallowed responsibility that the previous literature provides. Many of the theories present voting as an activity much like any other. In particular, the way individuals make up their minds how to vote is linked to how individuals make up their minds and take decisions in many other spheres. Which car should I buy? Which football team should I support? Which TV programmes should I watch? Which party should I vote for? Of course, the first literature is referring to the activity of voting itself, whereas the latter is referring to how people make their minds up when engaged in that activity. However, precisely the fact that analyses of vote decisions suggest that we use common processes to decide whom to vote for itself suggests that the activity is far from unique. Moreover, the fact that many people do not vote, and that many people express opinions which suggest they do not find voting important, or spend more time over other decisions, reinforces the view that, whilst voting may be an institution of inestimable importance, it is also one which is of little value for many.

In this book, we aim to set out the various explanations of why people vote the way they do, and in one chapter why they vote at all. Its principal intellectual motivation is precisely to present the various theories of voting in such a way as to explain how an activity which has such resonance as a part of democratic life is also based upon very mundane elements in voters' personalities and contexts. The educational motivation of the book is to present such theories in an accessible way for students. The books and articles relating to voting research are immense in number and span over 60 years. As with any academic discipline, this literature can be overwhelming and confusing for the newcomer. Which books and articles to read? How do the different approaches to the subject relate to each other? What themes to be aware of? In this book, we present what we feel to be the main topics which a newcomer to the area should be aware of, and in a way that conveys the salient points in each.

Given the timespan of this research, the newcomer is also often lost as to the evolution of electoral analyses. Where did psephology – the study of voting – develop from, and what have been the main features of its development? From another point of view, it is often confusing for newcomers to find that, despite the widespread predictions and proofs of the decline of social indicators of voting preference, many contemporary models continue to use such theories, and with great success. What have been the main social changes which have apparently heralded the demise of such sociological theories, and why have these latter instead remained very useful perspectives in approaching voting behaviour? In the following chapter, we will look at the developments in voting analysis to provide initial answers to such questions, and then follow up on each approach in the relevant chapters.

The mode of analysis has also changed from qualitative analysis and basic descriptive statistics to sophisticated multivariate models requiring ever-increasing levels of computing power. Many if not most students who are looking at voting theories for the first time encounter this technical sophistication as a problem. Given that we are often interested in numerically-based questions (such as how many votes a party has won or will win, the likelihood of a voter choosing one party over another, or the relative strength of different indicators in predicting vote), such techniques are vital to rigorous analyses of voting, but they do provide a daunting barrier to readers not versed in their use. Consequently, another aim of this book is to provide readers with enough information for them to see what the statistical techniques are doing in such analyses.

We should emphasise immediately that this book does not provide sufficient instruction in statistical techniques for readers to carry out analyses themselves, or to know exactly how these techniques work. This is the subject of other books. But it is not necessary here. With just a few simple pointers as to what the empirical analyses employing the statistics are doing, and the benefit of the explanations of findings by the authors themselves in their analyses, even someone with no training in statistics can still appreciate another researcher's findings. For those with the time and inclination, however, there is absolutely no substitute for learning the statistical techniques involved, particularly if they want to carry out analyses themselves.

This chapter, then, has two distinct purposes. Firstly, we will look at the nature of voting as a decision-making procedure and why it is out of the ordinary, together with a brief consideration of the influences on this decision which will be developed in subsequent chapters. Secondly, we will look at the main methodological elements and statistical techniques which will be encountered in the literature.

What is voting?

Voting is clearly a choice, but is it a choice like any other? Certainly in terms of the motivations which drive individuals, electoral choice is very similar to other choices we make in our daily lives. As all the subsequent chapters will show, voters choose parties and the candidates on the basis of the benefits they think or are told they will derive. The nature of such benefits vary according to the theories in question – it may simply be an affirmation of identity, or conversely a concrete calculation of material benefit – but just as in any choice that an individual makes, voters have a set of criteria which they wish their choice to satisfy. What these criteria are may vary according to the voter.

However, in looking at voting choice, the different theories either try to find criteria which best characterise as broad a number of voters as possible, or they try to find characteristics of voters which indicate that they are likely to share similar desires and consequently similar voting choices. We will look at some of the broader categories of motivation in the following section. For the moment, however, what differentiates this choice from other choices we make? A common analogy which is drawn with voting is that of the market. A number of candidates and parties present their products (political programmes for government) and voters pick from amongst these, 'paying' their vote to the party offering the product which best satisfies their criteria. Whilst some theories have developed this analogy as their theoretical basis (Chapter 4), we need to be careful to acknowledge the differences which obtain between the political market and the economic market.

The first thing to notice about voting is that it contributes to a *collective outcome*, rather than affecting us purely as individuals. Many of the market choices we make in life are designed to have a tangible effect only on ourselves – which food to eat, which film to see at the cinema, and so on. Of course, such choices will also have an effect on others. For instance, choosing to go to see a film will contribute to the financial well-being of the cinema and the film-makers (and the opposite effect for those connected with a film we opt not to see). However, this is not usually the primary motivation, if at all, of going to see a film. In a vote of any kind, however, we precisely make a decision conscious that, if we get what we want, this will be imposed upon others too.

Who those 'others' are depends on the nature of the vote. In this book, we concentrate almost entirely on national elections. In this case, 'the others' would be the population of a country electing a president or the constituents in one parliamentary constituency electing their representative. But it is instructive to remember that voting occurs in more than just general elections. Committees which run all manner of organisations vote on a range of proposals. Even in the most anodyne of situations, voting matters – for example, the members of a tennis club deciding whether to build a new club-house or not.

Indeed, the large number of contexts in which voting occurs is reflective of the broad nature of politics itself – individuals' decisions having an effect on others. When we look at other decisions which individuals take in everyday life and which, having repercussions beyond the individuals themselves, *do* affect others, we often refer to them as being 'political'. Consumer goods boycotted because of their manufacturers' employment practices; employees appointed because of a managerial agenda; university places rejected because of the institution's selection procedures – all can be and are termed political even though none is directly related to politics in its narrow sense, in other words the job of running government.

Consequently, when people make their voting choices, the decision is made on the basis of what is the best choice for them. But this will include a statement of values which implies what is 'best' or 'right' for others. The nature of what is best for others will vary widely, from a highly interventionist state managing the lives of all its citizens, to a society left largely to determine its own course without state intervention. At the limit, it may be support for a regionalist party which proclaims no interest in many of the 'others', and a separation of one territory from the rest. Even in the case of a voter motivated by nothing more than self-interest, the practical outcome – if her vote is influential – is an effect on other individuals.

As well as providing collective outcomes, voting is also a *collective activity*, unlike many of the other choices we make in our lives. When we make an individual choice among alternatives, the results are often clear. For instance, when we pick a brand of biscuits to buy, we are sure to get those biscuits.[1] In voting, however, we are far from certain about getting what we want. We may vote for a candidate, but if a majority of other voters choose a different candidate, then my attempt to buy my candidate's 'product' fails. Voting is not the only example where individuals group together to engage in activity, market-oriented or otherwise: the professors using a common room in a university department may take it in turns to buy biscuits for tea break; lottery syndicates in offices and social groups pool funds to buy tickets; and groups of parents share the school run to drop off and pick up their children. In such cases, individuals derive benefits from engaging in the activity with others – fewer trips to the supermarket; a wider range of potentially winning numbers; or fewer return trips to school every week. However, in all these cases, individuals are able to withdraw their participation if they are not happy with the outcome – the tasteless brand of biscuits colleagues buy; the unlucky lottery numbers which the syndicate keeps choosing; or some of the other parents' bad driving.

However, in voting, withdrawal is rarely if ever an option. I can withdraw from the common room biscuit pool and buy my own, but I cannot ask my favoured but losing candidate to set up his own personal government for me. Moreover, if I refuse to take part in the election and do not vote, I am still unable to withdraw from the system, having the victorious party/parties foisted upon me in the government. The reason for this is clear: government and the state form the institutions which regulate the public sphere and aspects of the private sphere in which individuals live. Thus, the decision-making procedure to which citizens are allowed to contribute implies an acceptance of the rules of the game which determine the state's right to manage society and how the managers are chosen. Given that the managers (governments) and potential managers (parties and coalitions) are drawn from within this society, the majority decision can be seen as the largest aggregation of similar views as to what form this management should take. Those who desire alternative forms are free to do so, but in the short term agree to accept the majority decision with the proviso that at subsequent elections their favoured candidate or party may win, but also that via various institutional routes they may still influence the government.

Thus, individuals agree to abide by the rules of the game, even where their favoured outcome is not reached, because the game continues.

In short, the following quote from *The American Voter*, a book we will subsequently refer to a number of times, sums up our book's overall take on voting:

> In the contemporary world the activity of voting is rivaled only by the market as a means of reaching collective decisions from individual choices. (Campbell et al., 1960: 3)

What then are the motivations which drive individuals' vote?

What influences vote?

Amongst the desires which may motivate vote are:

- group benefit (e.g. a class-related party working in this class' best interests)
- material gain (e.g. lowering of taxes)
- managerial competence (e.g. the successful running of public services)
- focus on relevant issues (e.g. environmental policy to reduce pollution)
- another party's defeat (e.g. voting for a Conservative party to keep out a Socialist party which the voter despises).

It would be very easy to extend this list to thousands of different motivations, some of them very particular and not widespread at all. Consequently, the characteristics of voters which indicate the likelihood of sharing similar desires also become useful. Such characteristics include:

- age
- gender
- social class/occupation
- religious group
- ideological group.

It is clear that the first four of these all come under the heading of social characteristics, and one of the most influential schools of thought on how people vote has been the sociological approach, which we will consider in Chapter 3. What is an ideological group, however? Unlike the social categories, ideological groupings cannot necessarily be identified by overt characteristics such as age or occupation. Instead, these describe individuals according to their different views on political issues such as the ones listed earlier. Researchers have tried to find patterns which apply to these issues so that one can group voters from different parties into different ideological categories – for instance, Left-wing and Right-wing voters or libertarians and authoritarians. We will look in more detail at what these mean in later chapters. However, the point again is that individual voters are not unique in their preferences and motivations. Indeed, to look at electoral behaviour scientifically, we have to be able to discern common elements in voter choice, otherwise we can never hope to explain people's motivations. As with all social scientific analysis, we are trying to identify a 'parsimonious' number of indicators which explain people's behaviour.[2] From our theoretical perspective we posit the motivations which determine vote choice, and in order to test these hypotheses to find out which are accurate and which are the stronger/weaker explanations, we need to construct causal models using empirical data.[3]

Methodological and empirical perspectives

Probably the main obstacle to students coming to theories of voting for the first time is the methodological complexity which the more recent literature employs. As the subsequent chapters will show, the basic theoretical elements are not complex at all. Indeed, many of their arguments are ones which have passed into everyday usage – class voting, the role of issues, governments losing votes when unemployment rises, to name but a few.[4] However, because researchers wish to test these as completely as possible, and look at the relative strength of different theories in accounting for vote, they employ statistical models. In focusing on the methods behind such models, what are the key elements we should be aware of in their construction and application to data?

Dependent and independent variables

In testing hypotheses as to the relationship between voting and individual's social and attitudinal profiles, economic and political context, we are implicitly placing these different elements in a causal relationship. In other words, we are searching for an effect and a number of causes, which can also be referred to as the dependent and the independent variables. For some reason, people often confuse dependent and independent variables. To remember it: the effect *depends* upon the causes.

In a single model of voting, we will find one dependent variable and a number of independent variables. Given that we are interested in voting, we will normally find that the dependent variable relates to vote. It may be the vote for a specific party, the vote for a party family (Socialist parties,

Christian Democrat parties, etc.), vote for a Left-wing (or indeed a Right-wing) party or vote for the incumbent (or for the opposition). In each case, it depends on the range of hypotheses that the model is testing. For instance, one analysis may be interested in analysing which elements of voters' social profile most strongly predict a vote for the French Socialist party. Consequently, its dependent variable will measure French Socialist party vote and contrast this with other party votes in terms of their electorates' social characteristics. The most common way of testing such a hypothesis would be to take survey data of the French electorate, divide the respondents in the survey into Socialist party voters and non-Socialist party voters, and run a *group-membership model* (see below) to compare the two in their social profiles.

Another analysis, however, might be interested in analysing the relationship between unemployment and the incumbent's vote in all elections (analyses of this type can be found in Chapter 6). Here, researchers will collect unemployment data for all the countries they are interested in including in the analysis, together with the level of vote for the incumbent party/parties in the same countries, and include these in a *linear model* (see below) to see if the levels of unemployment before an election have an effect on the level of vote for the incumbents.

Moreover, in studies exploring broader aspects of the voting process, the dependent variables may be a variable related to vote but not actually vote itself – for instance, party identification (which we will encounter in the next two chapters) or popularity of a political candidate (which we will study in Chapters 5 and 6). As can be seen from the above descriptions, there are a number of different variables which can be used in voting models, both as dependent and independent variables. The nature of what these variables are measuring has an effect on how they can be measured, and consequently which statistical technique can be used to test hypotheses including these variables. We turn to these elements below.

Measurement and variables

There are essentially three types of variables used in empirical research – continuous (interval-level) variables, and two types of categorical or 'discrete' variable, ordinal-level variables and nominal variables. Continuous variables can be most simply thought of as measuring concepts which can be placed along a numerical scale. Everyday examples of continuous variables are temperature, height, depth and weight. Given measuring instruments accurate enough, we can measure these to as tiny a fraction of a degree or a metre or a gram as we wish. There is thus the possibility of constructing a continuous scale, whence the name. In voting, there are few variables which can be measured in such a way. The actual level of vote for a party in an election is one of them – granted, it is unlikely that we need to measure it to 10 decimal places, say, but by social science standards the measurement is continuous. Similarly, amongst independent variables, age is regarded as continuous, as is level of income.

The main set of independent variables which are included under the 'continuous' heading are attitudinal variables. Here, researchers construct scales measuring levels of authoritarianism for example, made up of a number of questions tapping a survey respondent's attitudes towards various relevant topics, such as the death penalty, homosexuality, abortion and the like. They then construct a scale from a range of possible scores – at one end 'completely authoritarian' and at the other 'completely libertarian', and place each respondent on this scale. Similar scales include economic ideology, xenophobia, political satisfaction and so on. A similar technique can be used to assess a candidate's popularity, using a so-called 'thermometer scale', whereby survey respondents give a score between 0 and 100 to assess their view of a candidate: 0 = 'I despise him/her', 100 = 'my ideal candidate'. Alternatively, researchers can use opinion poll data to measure a candidate's popularity or a government's approval rating amongst the population at certain points in time. This is usually measured as a percentage ('65 percent of the population approve of the government at this time') and again this constitutes a continuous variable.

However, not all variables can be measured in such a way. For instance, in social profile an individual's religion could not reasonably be ranked along a scale. One could not allocate a meaningful score to 'Protestant', 'Catholic', 'Jewish' and 'other'. Similarly, gender cannot be scored along a scale – one is either male or female. In these cases, the data are said to be discrete (or categorical) – one can allocate individuals to categories. Such variables are also often referred to as 'nominal' if there is no implicit ordering to the categories. Other independent variables which use such measurement are: occupation (blue-collar worker, white-collar worker, farmer, etc.); region of residence; and union membership. For voting-related dependent variables, vote for a Socialist party (rather than for another party) would be a categorical variable.

Where there are only two categories (for instance gender or union membership) the variable is known as a 'dummy'. When they function as independent variables in a statistical model, their interpretation is very simple – as we move from one category to the other, what is the associated change in the dependent variable? In essence, we are comparing the two categories – 'men are more likely to vote for the Extreme Right than women' or 'union members give the Socialist candidate six more points on a thermometer score than non-members'. Moreover, when multiple-category variables are included in models, a similar comparison is used when looking at their effect. For instance, if we have a three-category variable for religion – 'Catholic', 'atheist' and 'other', then its effect in a model might be described thus – 'Catholics are 30 percent more likely than atheists to support the Right-wing rather than the Left-wing party, but other religions are only 14 percent more likely than atheists to do so.' In this case, the atheists are being used as the 'reference' category.

Returning to the issue of measurement, variables may fall between the continuous and nominal types, being categorical but having an element of order to the categories. Education is a good example of this – a person having completed secondary education has more education than a person having completed primary education; a university degree is higher than secondary and so on. However, in such cases, the question to ask is, 'Can I be sure there is a meaningful underlying scale whereby each of the categories is equally distant from its neighbours?' In other words, if we measure education as 'primary', 'secondary' and 'tertiary', is the amount of education (and what that actually means in our model) which accrues between 'primary' and 'secondary' an identical amount to that which accrues between 'secondary' and 'tertiary'? The answer is likely to be no. Similarly, if one is measuring religious practice, one may have 'non-practising', 'occasionally practising' and 'regularly practising'. Here again, there is a hierarchy, but a scale with just three discrete points is unconvincing as a continuous scale.

This example illustrates a type of variable 'in between' the categorical and continuous types, which is known as an ordinal variable. There *is* a level of hierarchy, but this is a fairly rough grouping with no underlying scale. Generally such groups will be treated the same as nominal variables in statistical models. Conversely, however, in the attitudinal scales mentioned above, many analyses use a single question to construct such a scale, and this may be made up of a question to which there are only four responses. For instance, to measure authoritarianism, researchers might ask respondents to answer 'I strongly agree', 'I agree somewhat', 'I disagree somewhat' and 'I strongly disagree'. From these four answers, they then construct a continuous scale scored 1 for 'I strongly agree' up to 4 for 'I strongly disagree'.

The point to understand is that allocating variables is as much a matter of what one believes is a reasonable assumption to make and the statistical technique one is using. In the literature, researchers always state how they have coded variables, and the importance is then in how they test such variables – in other words, which statistical technique they use. For the newcomer to voting theories and their testing, it suffices to be aware that different variables are coded in different ways and how that affects the testing.

Macro/aggregate and micro/individual approaches

As well as the measurement of the variables themselves, the level at which these are being measured also influences how one can analyse the data and what one can infer from the analysis. There are two main types in the voting literature – macro or aggregate-level analyses and micro or individual-level analyses. The former concentrate on aggregations of individuals, usually at the national level, and consequently employ aggregate data.[5] For instance, the example above looking at unemployment and vote for the incumbent in all countries is a classic example of a macro-analysis. The data points which the researcher collects refer to a country at a specific election, the vote for the incumbent and the unemployment rate at that time. Thus, we have two continuous variables measured at the aggregate level: we are looking at the overall vote and its relationship with the national level of unemployment. As this only gives us one case, the researcher adds more countries at more elections across time and looks at the relationship between these. This allows any underlying relationship to be discerned, but it does not tell the researcher anything about individual voters' actions – all he/she knows is that, for example, the more unemployment rises between elections, the more the incumbent's vote drops.

To be able to look at individual voter's motivations, the researcher must use a micro-analysis. Here, the analysis looks at the lowest level of disaggregation, namely individual voters. Because it is impossible to look at every single voter, these individual data will consequently be a representative sample drawn from the electorate in a survey.[6] The researcher can then look at each individual and test hypotheses regarding their vote – to continue the economic example, whether being unemployed makes a voter more likely to vote for an Extreme Right party, for instance, or to abstain. Clearly here, the national unemployment level used in the macro-model cannot be used, as for each voter in an election the unemployment level will be identical (a percentage of the workforce). But individual economic variables such as being unemployed or not, or how the respondent would rate the government's management of the economy, can be used instead. Overall, macro models usually try to account for actual vote in an election (and hence are popular with researchers trying to predict elections) whereas micro models concentrate on explaining individual vote-decisions.

Cross-section and times series

What the researcher wishes to test will determine what type of data he/she uses. For instance, in the above example of a macro-model, the researcher was interested in national unemployment figures and their effect on incumbent's vote. To test this relationship across countries and across time periods, a number of observations from different countries and elections were pooled. Such an analysis would be comparative (as opposed to country-specific) but also a time series analysis – the data points consist of a number of observations across time.

When dropping down to the micro-level of analysis, looking at individual voters, the researcher may just look at a single election in a single country, using a single survey. In this case the researcher is using a 'cross-sectional' design. However, in some studies, researchers may want to retain the time series element as well as looking at individual-level vote motivations. For instance, they may hypothesise that the degree to which class affects vote will diminish between the 1950s and the 1990s. One way of testing this would be to take a number of cross-sectional surveys from that time period and pool them – in other words, use the individual respondents from each of the surveys at different points in time as a separate case. This hybrid form of analysis is known, appropriately, as a 'pooled cross-sectional' design. For shorter time periods, where researchers wish to look at changes in individuals' profiles, panel data can be used, whereby the same individuals are interviewed on a number of occasions.

As with all of the methodological considerations, which type of data researchers use depends on which questions they wish to answer (and which type of data is available of course). Looking at the effect of unemployment irrespective of time or national context will involve aggregate time series analysis. Looking at the declining effects of a social indicator across time may use pooled cross-sections. Looking at how different individuals change their intended vote in the six months preceding the election would imply the use of panel data. Again, researchers will state what type of data they are using, and how this allows them to test the hypotheses in which they are interested.

Statistical techniques

It is impossible in this chapter to consider all the statistical techniques which can be used. Instead, we will limit ourselves to highlighting the two most common 'families' of techniques which we shall refer to as *linear models* and *group membership models*. All we wish to do here is to give a very basic outline of why they are used, and how a statistically untrained reader may get a very simple handle on what they are saying.

Linear models

'Linear' models, as their name suggests, are based upon the assumption that there is a linear relationship between the dependent and independent variable. That is, as the independent variable increases in value, so the dependent variable either increases or decreases in value. The most common technique is ordinary least squares (OLS) regression, also sometimes referred to as multiple regression. Taking the same example again, as the level of unemployment rises, so the level of incumbent vote will drop. A linear model assumes the change will occur at a constant rate, so that if a change of 2 percent in unemployment rate (from 4 percent to 6 percent) results in a drop in the incumbent vote of 3 percent (65 percent to 62 percent), we can infer that a change in unemployment rate from 4 percent to 8 percent – a 4 percent change – will also result in double the change for the incumbent, thus a drop from 65 percent to 59 percent. As a good rule of thumb a linear model will only be used where the dependent variable is continuous.[7] Consequently it is particularly appropriate for use in macro-models looking at incumbent vote, for example, or at popularity ratings for governments.

How are the findings of a linear model likely to be presented? Looking forward to Tables 2.2a and 2.2b in the following chapter shows the two most common formats for findings. Table 2.2a provides the 'equation' form, Table 2.2b the 'tabular' form. In the equation form, the first thing to notice is the dependent variable to the left of the equals sign (in this case, G, the governmental popularity rating measured by a Gallup opinion poll). No value is given for G, because, as the dependent variable, this represents the effect for which we have a range of values, and to which we wish to see how the independent variables contribute. The first value to the right of the equals sign is known as the 'intercept' or 'constant', which for our purposes here can be ignored (though its role is crucial in the mathematics behind the model). Each subsequent value in the equation represents the coefficient of each independent variable. For example, in equation 1, 'Ut-6' indicates the unemployment rate six months before the election in question, and its coefficient is –0.02. This can be interpreted as follows: for every unit change (in this case, one percentage point) in unemployment six months before the election, there is an associated change of 0.02 in the governmental popularity rating. So, if unemployment rose by 1 percent, then the popularity of the government will change by $1 \times -0.02 = -0.02$, i.e. a drop of 0.02 percent. If unemployment rose by 4 percent, then the change would be $4 \times -0.02 = -0.08$ percent. A similar calculation can be made for each of the subsequent coefficients in the equation, and together these will give an estimate of support for the government.

If we look at Table 2.2b, we can see the more common tabular output (the equation format is less used in more recent research). This is a different model, clearly, but the logic is the same. Firstly, at the bottom of the table we notice the constant or intercept. Then, instead of listing each variable in the equation, variable names are given down the left-hand column, and the coefficients in the subsequent columns. Here, the researcher has run five different models, one for each country. The dependent variable has not been included, because the researcher realises this is explicit from the original text which accompanied the table. However, for the sake of illustration, let us say for the moment that this was the thermometer score which respondents gave to the incumbent party.[8] In this case, then, we could interpret the 'government on economy' coefficient as follows: for every unit change in a respondent's rating of the government's management of the economy, the thermometer score for the government will change by 0.14 units in the case of Britain, 0.11 in the case of Germany, and so on.

What do the asterisks referring to the 'p-values' at the bottom mean? Very simply they indicate the 'significance' of the coefficient, meaning how strongly the data which we are using to test this hypothesis support the finding regarding this coefficient. The *smaller* the p-value, the better – it indicates a lower probability that we might find something different using other data, or indeed that the relationship might not hold for the population from which the sample data were drawn. Usually if the p-value is larger than 0.05, then the hypothesis is rejected. In the example in Table 2.2b, the researcher has used a value of 0.1, which is also sometimes acceptable as a cut-off point. So, looking at the coefficent for social class in France, the value is 0.04, and we can be 90 percent (1 – 0.1 = 0.9) certain that this relationship holds.

In Table 2.2a, no p-values are given. Instead, the standard error is given – the figures in brackets below the equation. In fact, the p-value is calculated using the coefficient and the standard error, and so the researchers could have given the p-values. However, standard errors can also be used in conjunction with the coefficient to assess the confidence we can have in the model's findings. More recent research generally tends to list the p-values, however. If not, accompanying explanations will tell the reader which values are significant and which can be disregarded.

The last elements to consider at this basic level are the model statistics. In both the at tables, an 'R^2' (R-square) statistic is given. In linear models, this or an alternative coefficient will always be given. Normally, the value for these will always lie between 0 and 1 (if not, authors will indicate this, and how to interpret it). The R-square tells the reader the variation in the dependent variable which the model accounts for. For our purposes, dependent variable being the vote, how well do these variables account for vote? A score of 0.1 means 10 percent; 0.9 means 90 percent. Obviously, then, a larger R-square score is better than a lower one. However, it is in the nature of social science statistics that we very rarely get large R-squares. Depending on the model, we can be very happy with scores of 0.4 or 0.5. Indeed, if we get a score of 0.9, we should be very suspicious – this often indicates that our model is a self-fulfilling prophecy, for instance we are using vote as our dependent variable and party membership as our independent variable (and, unsurprisingly, there is almost a perfect relationship between which party you belong to and how you voted). One sensible use of the R-square is to see how much models improve as we add more variables. For instance, if we test a model which includes just class and find an R-square of 0.3, then we include religion and the fit of the model improves to 0.6, this would tell us religion very much improved the fit. If the R-square only increased to 0.31, then we would be less enthused about religion.[9]

These constitute the principles of how to read a linear model. Remember the following steps:

- How are the dependent variable and independent variables measured (i.e. what scales or categories are being used)?
- Is the relationship between the independent variable I am focusing on positive or negative (i.e. when one increases, does the other increase or decrease)?
- How strong is the relationship (i.e. the size of the coefficient)?
- Is the relationship significant (i.e. the size of the p-value)?
- How well does the model fit (i.e. the size of the R-square)?

Group-membership models

In statistical training, the linear model is the first one which is encountered when students move to multivariate techniques. This is because it is one of the easier techniques to learn, and it is relatively common in social sciences and other disciplines using statistics. Unfortunately for newcomer psephologists, it is probably not the most useful technique for testing vote. The reason is simple: as we have seen in the sections on variable coding, one of the most fundamental questions we wish to ask is, 'Why do people vote the way they do?' For instance, why do they vote Socialist (rather than Christian Democrat or whatever)? This normally implies categorical measurement – those who voted Socialist in one group, those who did not in another. Or three groups – those who voted Socialist, those who voted Christian Democrat and those who voted for any other party. Given that linear models should use a continuous dependent variable, they are ill-suited to incorporating these group variables.

Instead, researchers tend to use what may generally be called 'group-membership models' (most commonly logistic regression and logit models, but also probit models, ordinal models and discriminant analysis). The main characteristic of these models is that their dependent variables consist of groups, rather than a score on a continuous scale. The best way of thinking about the interpretation of the model is that, instead of predicting the dependent score as linear models did, they calculate the probability of belonging to one group rather than to another.

This is the end of the bad news. Table 2.1b gives an example of a 'binomial' (two-category) logistic regression. As we can see, the tabular format is almost identical to that of the linear model. The variable names are listed in the left-hand column; the coefficients, standard errors and p-values are all given; even the constant is present (and again, we should ignore it). Fit statistics are also given, although these are different to the linear model because the model is calculated using a very different mathematical approach. Very often, however, a so-called 'pseudo-R^2' is given which, although calculated in a different manner to the linear R^2, can be interpreted by the newcomer in exactly the same way.

In the second footnote in the table, we are informed that Democrats are coded '1' and Republicans are coded '0'. These figures should not be interpreted as meaningful in themselves – this is simply a two-category dummy coding which we looked at in the variable measurement section. This means that survey respondents were allocated to the two groups according to their vote. The model consequently tests how well the values of the independent variables can allocate Democrats and their Republicans to the correct group. Interpreted another way, given a certain profile as provided by the independent variables, what is the probability of belonging to the Democrats rather than the Republicans (or vice versa)? The p-values tell us which coefficients are worth looking at, and the coefficient itself tells us the strength of the relationship. At this point, we should be wary of interpreting the coefficient any further, however. Unlike the linear model, which posited a simple linear relationship between cause and effect, the same does not apply to logistic coefficients. In essence, this is because the relationship, being based on probability, is not linear, and so the coefficients need to be transformed before they can be interpreted in 'real-world' terms. However, this does not prevent us from seeing the significant terms, their direction (positive or negative) and the relative strength of the relationship. Any transformations for the sake of real-world interpretation will be provided in the accompanying explanations.

Lastly, it is worth noting the interaction terms (which can equally be used in linear models). Interactions have a very simple theoretical basis, although again, interpreting the coefficients is more complex and again will usually be done in the accompanying text. In the case of the example in Table 2.1b, an interaction between the 'professionals' occupation category and racial attitudes (measured using a question asking about support for civil rights for African-Americans) is used ('professonals x racial attitudes'[10]). We can see that professionals are significantly more likely to vote for Republicans than Democrats from the single-variable effect under 'class categories'. We can also see that those with greater support for civil rights are more likely to vote for the Democrats (the first variable under 'social issue variables'). The interaction tells us that, amongst professionals, there is a stronger effect than amongst other class categories on the basis of racial attitudes – professionals with support for greater civil rights are more likely to vote for the Democrats than any other occupation with similar levels of support for civil rights.

In causal terms, then, the effect of an independent variable on the dependent variable may vary according to the value of another independent variable. Once the researcher is able to look at such interlinking between different causes of voting, the true relationship between vote and its predictors can begin to emerge.

This provides what we would regard as the very minimum needed to start to look at the voting models which we find in the literature. Not all articles and books use such statistical techniques, but suffice to say that the most influential pieces of work in recent years generally do so, and so it is essential even for the non-statistician to be able to get some handle on this work. To emphasise once more – the above explanations are in no way sufficient for the reader to be able to carry out statistical analysis themselves. For this, and indeed to be able to understand the models fully, a throrough grounding in statistics is vital. However, for those who do not have the time or opportunity to undertake such training, we believe that the above should make the literature that little bit more accessible.

Having given our own interpretation of what voting theories and models are trying to achieve, and a few pointers as to how they do that, we can now turn to the essence of the book – which are the principal theories which researchers have developed and tested in the history of psephology?

Notes

1 Even here, though, our choice contributes to a collective outcome – our choosing a brand of biscuits over another has financial implications for the companies involved, and may also contribute to effects on other consumers. The price may change as a result of brand popularity, or indeed the brand may be taken off the market because it does not sell well. Of course, the effect here is tiny and for an individual cannot be measured.

2 Parsimony is the scientific principle that one should choose the simplest explanation and/or smallest number of variables that can explain the greatest number of observations of a phenomenon.

3 We expect readers to be familiar with the notion of causality. For those unfamiliar with it, we would recommend in particular Babbie (1998). For a more applied use of causal modelling and statistical techniques, see Pennings et al. (1999).

4 One should be wary of the 'common sense' arguments too, however. Many of the accepted layman's truths about voting are often simplistic, if not wrong. For instance, the claim that 'modern politics is all about personalities, not about policies' would not find much support in this book, given the copious space we give to policies and related concepts. There *are* personality effects, certainly – but there is a lot more besides.

5 Disaggregated analyses looking at regions or constituencies, and hence falling short of total disaggregation to the individual level, are sometimes known as 'meso-level' analyses.

6 For a good overview of sampling, we would again refer the reader to Babbie (1998).

7 There are very high-profile arguments in the literature over this, which the newcomer should feel free to ignore.

8 We should note that this was not the dependent variable in the original model, but to use the true dependent variable – a dummy variable indicating actual vote – would constitute an immensely confusing example in the context of separating linear models from group-membership models. Considerations of space force us to use this example, however.

9 As more variables are included, the R-square can only go up (or stay the same, although this is very unlikely). The question the researcher needs to ask is – 'Up by how much?'

10 The interaction being indicated by the multiplication sign explains why interactions are sometimes also called 'multiplicative' terms (whereas individual effects can be referred to as 'additive').

2

The Historical Development of Voting Studies

Summary box

- Historical perspectives on theory development
- The roots of voting studies
- Formalising a voting model
- *The American Voter* and the Michigan model
- Re-balancing long- and short-term vote determinants
- Social change and theoretical development
- The survey tool
- Technological and statistical advances.

Introduction

When we study theories in political science, and in the social sciences more generally, there is often an unfortunate tendency to learn about the theory but to ignore where it comes from. We look at the assumptions and implications of the theory, we operationalise it and test it using empirical data and we criticise the results – but we rarely delve deeply into *why* this theory exists in the first place. This is not true of all fields within political science, of course: political theorists, for instance, tend to rely upon the historical and epistemological contexts of theories precisely because part of their goal is to identify the roots of thinking pertaining to the theory they are interested in – the context of Marxism, for instance, or the individualisation of society leading to post-modern approaches. But once we start to apply theory empirically, so the risk is that the initial roots of the theories become more and more distant.

This book too could simply present a series of different theories and how to use them, spending little or no time on where these come from in the first place. However, such a 'balkanised' approach would be inappropriate for three reasons. Firstly, it risks alienating the reader from the theories: there is nothing drier than a stand-alone concept which apparently relates to nothing. Interest in a subject derives largely from having the bigger picture to hand.

Secondly, voting theories are linked to each other intellectually because some developed from others either as complements or as critiques. We need to know who is revising whom and why if we are to understand what the different theories are trying to do.

Thirdly, the historical – and intellectual[1] – context of each theory's development is crucial because it allows us to see the all-important assumptions that are being made by the theorists themselves. As we shall see in Chapter 4, for example, rational choice theories are derived from earlier economic theories about markets. In this case, one of the key assumptions must have been that in some respects voting behaviour could be seen as a 'political market' – an assumption that can certainly be challenged. Similarly, the model which this chapter will spend some time presenting – the Michigan socio-psychological model – relies upon the concept of 'party identification', whose roots are firmly planted in the inter- and post-war US political context. Yet, party identification is a concept which has been applied in a whole range of countries in recent electoral research. Despite our desire to find common concepts which can be applied cross-nationally, the performance of a concept in one country may not be as good as in another – and in the case of party identification, the US assumptions are by no means a given in all other countries. But unless we know what these assumptions are, we risk applying this and other theories and models willy-nilly and coming to erroneous conclusions.

Consequently, to avoid these problems, this chapter will do four things. It will firstly provide a brief introduction to electoral research prior to the appearance of the Michigan model, essentially the first formalised model of voting behaviour. Secondly, because of the seminal nature of the Michigan model, it will explain this and illustrate how its components provide a benchmark for most, if not all of the theories which this book goes on to consider. Thirdly, we will consider why many of these theoretical elements in the Michigan model have been developed as theories in their own right. It would be wrong to think that all theories of voting are derived directly from the Michigan model. However, it is true to say that, as a full model of voting, the Michigan model does contain most of the principal elements included in all theories of voting, and as such it provides a useful starting point in looking at their historical development. Lastly, the chapter will consider the technological progress which has enabled more comprehensive theories *and* a more comprehensive testing of theories in increasingly sophisticated models. Three advances stand out as having revolutionised voting studies: the development of survey research; the growth of statistical techniques for empirical testing; and advances in computer technology.

It should be emphasised before we proceed that the separation of these elements is artificial. For instance, it will become clear that the Michigan model itself would have been impossible without the advent of survey research. Consequently, these developments should not be regarded as entirely independent of each other, but rather part of a broad evolution in voting studies. The separation is designed simply with clarity in mind, to allow the reader to understand the part played by the different developments in the overall process.

Early voting studies

As in many new fields of research, early voting studies were characterised by their piecemeal nature and narrowness of scope. Until the early 20th century, there are virtually no examples of studies of voting behaviour *per se*. Voting is mentioned in many of the classic works of political philosophy and commentary from Aristotle to De Tocqueville, but only as one element in broader considerations of political theory and behaviour. No studies focus on voting itself. At the turn of the century, extensions of the franchise across classes and to women was the focus of much debate, but only to the extent of qualitative discussion of how the working class or women would and should vote, in the former case Marxists widely predicting the victory of Socialist parties and in the latter case early feminists looking to gender-oriented candidates to win greater support from women.

The extent to which such predictions were not borne out and in particular the extent to which working-class parties largely failed to predominate in government despite apparent numerical superiority pushed commentators to search for reasons behind the actual voting patterns of the fully enfranchised electorate. However, an absence of quantitative data comparable with modern sources meant that initial studies were either qualitative in their approach and essentially anecdotal, or relied upon those scant data that did exist, namely national voting figures with, in some cases, regional and local breakdowns. Such figures only allowed the analysis of very basic divisions between, say, urban and rural voting behaviour or regional differences, but this did allow electoral geographers such as Siegfried, who studied voting patterns in the West of France before the First World War (1913), to identify general stability in regional voting patterns. Another of the more productive lines of analysis was of voting turnout, as exemplified by Gosnell's *Why Europe Votes* (1930), which compared the US, France, Germany and Britain in an attempt to understand why turnout was declining in the US whereas it was remaining stable in Europe. Even this, however, relied upon linking institutional and economic factors to levels of turnout, without being able to look at the all-important voter profiles which could give a direct explanation rather than inferential speculations over levels of turnout. At best, census data could be linked to electoral data to provide ecological estimates of voting, for instance linking social class or levels of income with party support at the district level. In some countries, such techniques have remained the norm, with more sophisticated ecological analyses of gender, class and religion being used, for example, in the classic study of Italian electoral behaviour (Galli et al., 1968). However, such ecological inference risks being fallacious – just because regions with high proportions of workers have high levels of Left-wing voting does not necessarily mean that workers are more likely to vote for Left-wing parties. To make such a claim requires the use of individual-level data.

The main advance in this respect came with the introduction of surveys by commercial polling companies in the 1930s, and their subsequent use in particular by Lazarsfeld and Berelson's Columbia voting studies based at the eponymous New York university.[2] The first of these, *The People's Choice* (Lazarsfeld et al., 1968, 3rd edition[3]), was originally published at the end of the Second World War and was based upon the 1940 US presidential election. It used Erie County, Ohio, as its sampling district largely because it was small enough to be logistically manageable and was as close to a 'typical American county' as could be found. However, as Lazarsfeld and his colleagues emphasised, '[It] was not the "typical American county" but for the purposes of this study it did not need to be. We were not interested in *how* people voted but in *why* they voted as they did.' (1968: 10, authors' italics). In other words, rather than taking an interest in the breakdown in proportions of Republican and Democrat voters to extrapolate to the national level, the authors of *The People's Choice* were interested in studying the processes leading up to the vote, but with the vote itself almost as an after-thought. In particular, they emphasised preference formation via radio and other media, and the role of the campaign in shaping voters' views.

The second improvement on previous analyses – and one which a surprising number of national survey institutes have yet to take up, or at least to implement successfully – was the use of panels, interviewing a number of respondents on successive occasions in order to measure changes in their attitudes, consistency of voting preference and the like. For the first time, the individual bases to vote choice could be examined as well as looking at social group belonging, political events and macro-level context. However, the study was still largely exploratory in its use of the data, looking at all aspects of preference formation and change throughout the electoral year. Also, it only concentrated on a single county, rather than being a national study.

In 1948 a second study was done, this time in Elmira, New York, and published in *Voting* (Berelson et al., 1954), which was more formalised in its approach to the vote. Rather than concentrating on the campaign, it concentrated more on preference formation – the 'social' side to voting – and then looked at the electorate's political behaviour *per se*. Again, it was based upon a panel study, but most importantly it provided a synthesis of the decision-making process in voting under the title 'The Social Psychology of the Voting Decision'. The principal finding, and one that would guide the subsequent Michigan model, was that overall voting preference remained remarkably stable, and all the more so when social context was mutually reinforcing – an absence of what *The People's Choice* had already referred to as 'cross-pressures'. People belonging to homogeneous social networks tended to vote for similar parties, and to do so consistently across time.

Yet, again, this study was also largely inductive in its approach, only providing its formalisation of voting preference formation on the basis of the data exploration. Moreover, it was focused on a single locality and thus could not be reliably used as a guide to national voting preferences. Such a national survey and a deductive formalisation of vote preference formation was only provided on publication of the University of Michigan's Survey Research Centre's studies, most famously *The American Voter*.

The Michigan revolution: formalising a socio-psychological model

Perhaps no other model in voting studies has proved more influential than the Michigan socio-psychological model. Both the structured approach to a formalised account of voting choice, the key concept of party identification around which the model is based and the primary elements influencing both identification and political affiliation of voters have provided subsequent researchers with a foundation for their own theories and models. The model also proved to be a methodological watershed in that its use firmly established the survey tool as a means of looking at individual voters' social profiles and attitudinal predispositions at the national level not just in cross-section, i.e. at a single point in time, but also longitudinally, i.e. across time.[4] Consequently, the act of voting could be studied and conceptualised not just as a discrete act at a single election, but as a dynamic process extending to a series of votes across a voter's (political) lifetime, and, using retroprospective questions, stretching back to the voter's childhood and formative experiences.

The main study cited as the cornerstone to the Michigan project is *The American Voter* (Campbell et al., 1960)[5] and was based upon survey data collected between the presidential victory of Harry Truman in 1948 and the re-election of Dwight Eisenhower in 1956. In this, the authors assert that the principal motivation behind voting in the US is party identification, being a long-term stable psychological affinity for one of the two major parties. This does not mean that individuals all join the party or even take part in political activity connected with the party. Instead, such an emotional or 'affective' attachment develops initially during the socialisation process in childhood and adolescence, when individuals pick up the attitudes and values of their parents, family and peers, and are often explicitly directed towards being a Democrat or a Republican (in the US context). The authors go as far as drawing a close analogy with religion in this respect – children are taught from an early age to 'believe' in one of the parties and what it stands for.

This core concept of party identification subsequently serves a number of purposes both as a pivot for explanations of party choice and as a grounding for the subsequent development of theories of voting. Firstly, it provides a very powerful explanation of why the vast majority of voters across their lifetime vote for one party with few variations. One persistent problem which we will encounter in a number of voting theories is the marked lack of knowledge and interest that a large proportion of the electorate manifest towards politics. Finely honed intellectual theories as to the reasons behind individuals' voting preferences continually collide with the blatant fact that large numbers of voters understand next to nothing about individual policies, about parties' positions on these policies, even about the very basic functioning of their country's political system. When Converse, one of the authors of *The American Voter*, looked at the attitudes of voters on an array of policies, he found that most people's views on most issues fluctuated wildly across time, almost seeming random in their response (Converse, 1964). And indeed, this was partly due to respondents giving 'top-of-the-head' responses to questions they did not understand, or simply 'yea-saying' – blithely agreeing with statements made by the interviewer simply (albeit unconsciously) to win approval.

As we shall consider shortly, great debate has ensued over whether or not voters have recently become politically more knowledgeable. Whatever the changes that *have* occurred, however, it is clear that there still persists a large group of voters with very little political information. Consequently, it is difficult to reconcile this lack of political cues and knowledge with patterns of essentially stable voting. In essence, if many people's political views are effectively random, would one not expect their voting choice also to be random? Party identification, however, provides a potential map of reality, given that voting does not appear in any sense to be random. Simply, from one's socialisation experiences in early life and the social situation that one finds oneself in throughout life, a basic psychological affinity with a certain party provides sufficient cues to at least vote for that party. At the extreme, one need not understand any of the party's policies or anything about how the system works – to return to the religious analogy, one simply puts one's 'faith' in the party. As such, if one's socialisation provides any sort of partisan cue, this should provide for a voter's default setting in terms of voting.

But some have challenged this concept as being tautological. If someone possesses an emotional or psychological attachment to a party, their consequently voting for it might seem to be a given. It could be akin to someone explaining that they read a certain newspaper 'because I enjoy it'. Indeed, some commentators who have criticised the concept of party identification maintain that many people will profess to identifying with a party simply because they have voted for it. Continental European research has been particularly sceptical of the appropriateness of party identification in countries where the conditions of the stable two-party environment that are met in the US are notably absent. For the European contributors to *Party Identification and Beyond*, social groups and ideological position are more appropriate determinants of vote than any notion of psychological affinity to a party (Budge, Crewe and Farlie, 1976). In terms of the Michigan model's voting 'equation', then, the socialisation process and individuals' social context provides the psychological predisposition towards a certain party. Other researchers prefer to bypass the party identification mediation and look at the direct effects of social context on voting behaviour. In this book, we will consider the broad arrange of theories and models associated with these *sociological* determinants of voting in Chapter 3.

But people evidently *do* change their vote, otherwise any notion of political competition and indeed the very concept of elections themselves would be meaningless. One reason for this might be that social context changes. At one point in time, a voter might find him/herself in, say, a lower social class and hence vote for a party of the Left or a working-class party. Across time, however, this voter might find him/herself moving up through society's ranks and hence might abandon the Left-wing or working-class

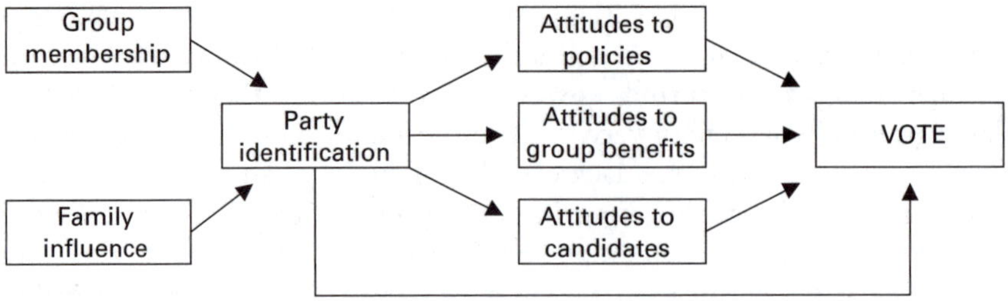

Figure 2.1 *Michigan socio-psychological model*
Source: Harrop and Miller (1987: 132, Figure 6.1)

party and vote for a Right-wing or middle-class party. Undoubtedly this dynamic does occur, but two factors mean that this would be an unsatisfactory explanation of all voting change. Firstly, as we shall consider in more detail in Chapter 3, the socialisation process is particularly strong during childhood, and hence one tends to hold onto an initial political predisposition. Granted, someone whose social situation changes across time will be more likely to see their early socialisation changed, but this is relative rather than absolute – the initial formative experience remains dominant for most people. Secondly, social mobility is a long-term process which does not happen with sufficient speed or frequency to account for the sometimes dramatic changes which are seen between two elections. In the following section we will look at the extent to which the structure of societies has changed since *The American Voter* was written, but neither before nor since its development has social change been sufficiently rapid to account for all voting change.

More realistic sources of immediate voting change, however, are the short-term intervening factors which condition – if not change – a voter's choice. In a very helpful diagram depicting the Michigan model, Harrop and Miller categorise these short-term intervening factors into three groups – attitudes to candidates, attitudes to policies and attitudes to group benefits (see Figure 2.1).

'Attitudes to candidates' is fairly self-explanatory. In any election, the personalities of candidates and their perception by the voters play an important role in pulling votes or turning votes away from parties. As such, a voter may identify with a party but may particularly dislike the candidate on the ballot paper at a certain election, and thus not vote according to their identification. Al Gore in the United States and Lionel Jospin in France are both leading party candidates widely held to have 'turned off' some of their own parties' potential electorate. Conversely, they may be particularly attracted to a candidate who is standing for another party, and hence vote against their identification on these grounds: Bill Clinton in the United States and Tony Blair in Britain would fit the profile of candidates whose personal qualities as politicians have won over otherwise unwilling support.

'Attitudes to policies' concerns the individual elements of the party programme which a party presents in its manifesto and more broadly which the voter perceives as forming part of the party's ideological baggage. If a particular issue associated with the party of identification is viewed negatively by the voter, or again if another party is promoting a policy which the voter supports very strongly, then this may cause the voter to change their vote in that election. For instance, I may identify with a Left-wing party but if, during a period of economic downturn, this party decides to cut spending on healthcare in order to shore up unemployment benefits and spending on education, I may reject this prioritisation and turn elsewhere to bestow my vote.

Lastly, 'attitudes to group benefits' concerns the effect that the party will have upon politically relevant groups that a voter is a member of, for instance trades unions, employers' associations, an ethnic, religious or linguistic group, or indeed any social grouping which may benefit or suffer according to a party's programme. Despite identifying with the conservative Gaullist Party in France, French farmers may turn away from this party if they feel that it is not doing enough to represent their interests by fighting for continued Common Agricultural Policy subsidies from the EU. Clearly, there is an overlap between 'attitudes to group benefits' and 'attitudes to policies'. However, the latter does not necessarily imply that the voters feel the policies will have an adverse (or beneficial) effect on themselves. Under the policy heading, a single male may still support a party on the basis of its promotion of paid maternity leave, despite being unlikely to be directly affected by such a policy.

Given that the model emphasises stability in voting, it is important to note that these three sets of factors are partially determined by the party identification and thus indirectly by the same socialising factors, as indicated by Figure 2.1. Indeed, in the post-war period, the attitudinal factors were seen as being overridingly determined by the party component. And this would make sense – of course one is more likely to be predisposed towards candidates, policies and group benefits representing the party with which one identifies. However, such factors may also exercise an independent effect on the vote and, in the short term, may change a voter's preference away from that predicted by their party identification, for example a particularly unpleasant candidate, or a policy with which the voter simply cannot agree, either because it goes against the voter's own values or because it disadvantages a group to which the voter belongs.

This explanation of voting change has a number of important implications. Firstly, it implies that voting change is a deviation from a stable or loyal norm. The model works on the basis that such factors causing a move away from the party of identification will occur infrequently, when particularly issues or the personality of a candidate become salient. For most voters, Michigan tells us that issues remain largely beyond their cognitive scope. For the Michigan model, voting is thus a predisposition first, and only a consciously deliberated act second. Secondly, it portrays parties as imperfect actors who, despite having a pool of potentially loyal support, need not only to mobilise this group but will also inevitably take policy positions and field candidates who to a greater or lesser extent will alienate some of this support at any given election. Parties are thus not organisations starting from a *tabula rasa* in collecting an electorate, but instead actors striving to actualise potential support.[6]

Social change as theoretical catalyst

Theoretical developments in any discipline rarely emerge simply from a researcher's inspiration. One of the most common sources of change is the interdiscplinary exchange of ideas. Perhaps the most famous example of this in the field of voting is the implantation of rational choice theory (Chapter 4) from older economic market theory. More recently, critiques of rational choice theory have produced the directional spatial theory (Chapter 5) which comes from older emendations of economic theory by Simon and psychological studies by Tversky amongst others.[7] Even the original theories of social structural voting are themselves derived from the classic sociological approaches of Marx, Weber and more recently Parsons (Parsons and Smelser, 1956).

Yet the applicability and dissemination of these theories generally seems to accompany changes in the topic of study which gives the new – and by definition competing – theory an apparent value added over its older 'rival' which the rejection of one theory in favour of another demands. In the case of voting studies, it is noticeable for example that rational choice theory in voting studies did not immediately take off in 1957 after the publication of Anthony Downs' *Economic Theory of Democracy*: the first explosion of rational choice literature occurred in the late 1960s and early 1970s, followed by a second burst during the 1980s.[8]

Far from coincidentally, the late 1960s and 1970s are generally seen as representing the beginning of the principal restructuring of industrialised societies away from their industrial period frameworks towards the modern setting characterised by less clearly defined and generationally more unstable social strata, a less differentiated occupational hierarchy, greater economic, social, territorial and educational mobility and a broader range of social and political values. As we will see in Chapter 3, Inglehart's *The Silent Revolution* (1977), itself introducing the psychologist Maslow's 'hierarchy of needs' concept (1954) saw that the generation of voters coming of age in the late 1960s had been socialised under substantially different contexts to their parents. The latter had been struck by the Great Depression of the 1930s, in Europe they had experienced perhaps the most exacerbated of ideological opposition – between Communism and Fascism – in democratic history, and of course they had lived through the Second World War. Their children were born into a period free from economic recession, and indeed one which enjoyed massive economic growth, and would instead be concerned with the post-materialist raft of issues – environmentalism, feminism, pacifism, sexual equality – which the traditional parties did not address.

More broadly, the changes in the post-war period concerning standard of living brought on by increased affluence and the expansion of education, pushed many commentators to posit that the old view of the voter as a politically ignorant and uninterested individual with unclear, unstable views on policy was an anachronism. A larger group of more educated voters would be likely to have greater political autonomy and savvy, and not need to rely upon party identification as the signpost for voting and for political orientation more generally. Voters, in short, would be increasingly able to choose for themselves. The changes in the economic structuration in post-industrial societies, with the decline of the traditional Marxist working-class/middle-class dichotomy and the growth of the 'new middle class' or 'white-collar workers' in the service sector, increasingly released European voters from the close party ties to Left- and Right-wing parties.

Lastly, such structural changes were not restricted to economic class, but also to cultural groups. In particular, growing secularisation in Europe meant that the traditional secular/Catholic divides in many nations was becoming relevant for decreasing numbers of voters and increasingly to the older, female category – the hard core of practising Catholicism. The traditional ideologies associated with the religious Right also fell prey to the new libertarian issues characteristic of post-materialism. Just as economic classes could be seen converging on a predominant white-collar mass, so European societies generally became culturally secular.

Such developments are to a large extent overlapping and depend as much upon the analyst's theoretical perspective as upon their empirical verifiability. Books such as *The Changing American Voter* (Nie et al., 1976) claimed to demonstrate that the rise of new issues and 'protest politics' throughout the 1960s which largely crosscut traditional partisan lines in the US and the coming of age of a new, politically mobilised generation fighting against the old-fashioned stance of the Democrat and Republican parties represented an electorate increasingly coherent and educated in its political views and decreasingly conforming to the passive identification of their 1950s counterparts. However, later research cast doubt on the extent to which this increased sophistication on the part of the US electorate was methodological artefact – in other words, it was not so much a phenomenon being measured by the authors of *The Changing American Voter* so much as a phenomenon of how they were measuring it. Similarly, the embourgeoisement thesis for European electorates falls down amongst working-class families where relative inequalities in fact increased despite the absolute rise in affluence. Equally, class may have declined in its traditional working-class/middle-class format, but new and more appropriate class categorisations indicate that class structure still counts in vote preference.

These concerns, although important to the interpretation of political change, are less relevant in this respect to the development of voting theories. Instead, the importance lies in analysts' perception of potential changes within politics and electoral behaviour, and hence their favouring of some theories and explanations over others. In particular, the 1970s and 1980s saw the rise of those theories which favoured individual decision-making and choice in the voting decision. In Figure 2.1, the left-hand side of the diagram – sociological determinants and the product of childhood socialisation – began to be seen as increasingly anachronistic. Why would an educated, politically knowledgeable voter simply defer blindly to a party loyalty passed down to her? Moreover, given the decline in structural clarity and the increased blurring of the traditional lines of political conflict, the end result of socialisation would be equally unclear in terms of the values imbued. How to predict the socialisation end-point for children in mixed ethnic, religious, cultural and even class marriages, for instance?

Thus, the Michigan model provides us with a useful starting-point from which to view the rise in the 'individual' theories of voting – rational choice, economic theories, issue voting and spatial theories – as the increasing dominance of the right-hand side to the voting diagram in Figure 2.1. Instead of voting being a predisposition occasionally mediated by short-term concerns, voting theories now concentrated on the short-term concerns *ab initio*. Today, as ever-greater emphasis is seemingly placed on personalities, issues and social dislocation in mediatised 21st century politics, so the shift in balance towards the right-hand side of the Michigan model proceeds apace. However, it is noticeable that the major studies of voting behaviour still include the sociological left-hand side of the equation in their explanation, and the concept of party identification itself.[9] Indeed, as we shall see in the following chapter, social structural explanations of voting have enjoyed somewhat of an intellectual and methodological renaissance precisely in response to the modernist conceit that all is individual and fragmented, and nothing is social and collective.

Yet, one by-product of this shift in emphasis needs to be fought against. Because such theories have been applied to modern voting contexts, it is sometimes tempting to believe that only traditional theories are relevant to the older electoral periods. Too often one may write off pre-war politics as epitomised by social divisions and nothing else. In his conclusion to *The End of Class Politics?* – precisely one of the books that goes against the social structural decline hypothesis – Evans argues that '[i]n the absence of historical survey data rather than aggregate statistics, we might be inclined to believe in the monolithic electoral class struggle – [...] this is probably a myth; the product of an over-fertile sociological imagination' (1999a: 334). The development of issue models in the latter half of the 20th century threatens a similarly blinkered view – but it does *not* mean that no-one prior to this point voted on the basis of an issue. Economic theories may have begun with Goodhart and Bhansali's study of post-war political economy in 1970, but this does not mean that economic conditions did not temper voters' actions in the 1930s.

Despite the greater array of policy areas and issues which now constitute politics, and the greater information available to voters upon which to make their choice, the bases to this decision can still be reconciled surprisingly well with the basic patterns presented by *The American Voter*. The shift in the focus of voting theories does not *necessarily* now make the voting choice more complicated. However, it is often difficult to apply these theories retrospectively because of the relationship between theoretical advances and the techniques which are developed for its use. Modern theories are premised on modern tools and data sources which generally do not exist for historical periods by definition. The following section looks at these tools in more detail.

The effects of technological progress

The advent of survey research

Without the appearance of mass surveys in the 1930s, it would simply be impossible to test and develop any of the individual theories of voting. Analysis of social structure or of association between vote for a party and a macro-economic indicator such as unemployment or GDP can be performed using national or regional data taken from censuses or basic government statistics. At the opposite extreme, in-depth interviews can help to reveal the nuances in a small group of individuals' political views and motivations.[10] However, to be able to assess the effects of various attitudes and political knowledge on voting whilst controlling for social variables, only sufficient cases can be provided via a national sample. How survey data are used in testing voting theories will be explained in the subsequent chapters.

However, it is useful to be aware that survey data are certainly not without their problems. Looking at national electoral survey data across the world, it is surprising how many encounter significant sampling biases in terms of voting levels, for instance. One can use weighting to correct for this, but this may hide the fact that certain subgroups of voters are being ignored. For instance, it is almost always the case that the proportion of voters for an Extreme Right party will be underestimated in an electoral survey. But simply weighting the voting figures to reflect the actual election result assumes that there is no variation within the sample bias for Extreme Right voters, for instance a heightened proclivity for under-reporting amongst former Left-wing supporters.

A second problem which is more pertinent to the Michigan model is the risk of eliciting unreliable responses from survey respondents, either by prompting respondents to select answers which they do not understand or by conditioning their response by the nature and order of the questions. In the first case, asking a respondent a 'closed' question as to whether they identify with the Democrats or Republicans might prompt some to pick one of the parties when, had the question been 'Do you identify with a political party? If so, which?', their answer would have been 'No'. However, if the latter 'open' question format is used, the rate of non-response and variation in response climb dramatically. Question conditioning has been cited by critics of the party identification concept: those who say they 'identify' with a certain party may be saying this simply because they have reported voting for that party earlier in the survey, and hence they want to appear consistent. This problem can be reduced by arranging the order items are asked in the survey, but it cannot be eliminated entirely.

Similarly, in panel studies, conditioning can occur across the period of the survey. For instance, a respondent who failed to answer any of the political quiz questions used to test political knowledge in the first wave of a survey might, despite being politically disinterested, still read about politics before the second wave so as to be able to answer at least a couple of the questions. The survey is thus conditioning its sample in a way that will not be found in the population at large – and hence the sample will no longer be representative. Again there are ways of reducing this – using a rolling panel, whereby a proportion of the respondents are replaced at every wave, or duplicating each wave with a cross-section control group who by definition cannot have experienced conditioning – but these are costly measures which cannot always be employed satisfactorily.

In fact, there is great variation in the use of electoral surveys across countries. For instance, Italian electoral research has relied far more upon ecological data at the national and regional level than upon individual survey data, for reasons of sampling and very high non-response rates in its survey data. Norway, however, has enjoyed the use of a rolling panel survey at every election since 1965. Belgium and France have based election studies to date on cross-sectional post-electoral surveys. The last major obstacle in survey usage for the comparative researcher lies in the use of cross-national surveys, theoretically at least the best opportunity of testing theoretical concepts beyond a single country case. A number of these exist – Eurobarometer, the World Values Survey, amongst others – but, given the cost of performing such large-scale projects, the sample sizes tend to be smaller, the number of questions included is often similarly reduced or focused on a particular topic, and lastly but perhaps most importantly, the question of 'What does a concept mean?' across countries may invalidate or at least hamper comparison.

In mapping social characteristics, level of education is difficult to standardise across countries – how to compare countries where technical and classical educations are given separate but equal streams with countries where a 'comprehensive' education system exists? Similarly occupation in countries characterised by large primary industrial production may be difficult to categorise in a way comparable with a primarily service-sector economy. Even more problematic is attitudinal measurement – does 'liberalism' mean the same thing in France and Germany? Is a policy of 'tax reduction' in the US equivalent to that policy in Denmark? Or, to return to our previous example, does party identification mean the same thing in all countries, if it even exists? Such questions have occupied and will continue to occupy comparative researchers for many years.[11]

However, despite such problems, survey data solves far more problems than it causes. Again, without this resource, voting studies would not have been able to advance past the ecological research of the immediate post-war period. In addition to its theoretical value, this resource has also spurred on the development of other tools necessary for its full exploitation, namely the statistical techniques to analyse multivariate data, and has also exploited the advances in computer technology to be able to do this to full effect.

Statistical and technological advances

There is no doubt that the advent of the computer and the massive increases in computing speed have done as much for all scientific enquiry as any other development. In the pre-IT era, every calculation had to be done manually, a daunting task even if aided by a mechanical adding machine or calculator. Even the most basic univariate calculation, such as an average age, would have taken a significant amount of time to produce. Bivariate calculations which are taken for granted today – a cross-tabulation

Table 2.1a ***Class voting within selected demographic groups, four Anglo-American countries surveys between 1952–1962 (means)****

Country	Age groups				Religion		Region		Cities
	20–30	30–40	40–50	50–60	Protestants	Catholics	Highest	Lowest	over 100,000
Great Britain	39	36	37	42	46	44	47	23	41
Australia	30	28	35	39	36	29	47	22	36
United States	13	13	22	13	21	16	31	4	20
Canada	5	9	13	9	10	2	26	−12	11

* Figures given here are means of a number of index figures for each country, 5 in Britain and Australia, 4 in the United States, and 6 in Canada. See Robert R. Alford, *Party and Society*, 1963, Appendix C, for the definition of regions used.

Source: Alford (1967: 83)

or a correlation coefficient – could be major undertakings. The advent of computers in the post-war period – gigantic room-sized machines with information coded onto a punchcard – meant that the arduous task of going through each survey response, and summing and cross-referencing the responses, was eliminated. All information from each survey respondent could be coded on a single card, and the computer programmed to produce a certain range of combinations and calculations involving all or a subset of responses. However, punchcards were flimsy and wore out; diagnostics for wrongly coded responses were very difficult to perform; the range of calculations that the computer could carry out was limited, and often took days to perform; and computing time cost a fortune, with only a handful of computers accessible to a few people at a small number of universities.

In other words, highly complex procedures, and in particular the multivariate models mentioned earlier, existed on paper but it was impossible to carry them out in practice. Only with the advent of the microcomputer and electronic data storage did computing time become quick, cheap and accessible enough to allow such techniques to be used and refined sufficiently to allow the more complex models to be tested. With such testing procedures now possible, theories could be revisited and revised much more effectively, and consequently theories themselves became much more sophisticated.

This is best illustrated using two examples from the voting literature, one looking at sociological determinants of vote (Chapter 3), the other at economic theories of voting (Chapter 6).

Tables 2.1a and 2.1b compare a four-country comparison of mean levels of class voting by different sociodemographic groups by Alford (1967) and a pooled cross-sectional analysis of US class and class-related voting by

Table 2.1b ***Logistic regression coefficients[1] (s.e. in parentheses) for explanatory model of vote outcome, 1972–1992 (N = 3971)***

Independent variables	Coefficients	(s.e.)
Constant	−1.53*	.32
Class categories (reference = non-labor-force participant)		
Professionals	−2.04*	.44
Managers	−.02	.15
Routine white-collar employees	.21	.12
Self-employed	.04	.16
Skilled workers	.20	.17
Nonskilled workers	.13	.14
Class-related independent variables		
Household income (in 1,000s of dollars)	−.01*	<.01
Union membership (reference = non-member)	.65*	.11
Economic satisfaction (category 1)	.37*	.09
Economic satisfaction (category 2)	1.03*	.10
Class consciousness (working-class identification = 1)	.07	.08
Welfare state attitudes	.29*	.02
Other sociodemographic variables		
Age (years)	<.01	.01
Race (African-American = 1)	1.81*	.20
Gender (women = 1)	.14	.08
Region (South = 1)	.05	.09
Employment sector (Public / nonprofit = 1)	−.01	.12
Education (years)	−.04*	.02
Social issue variables		
Racial attitudes	.43*	.07
Gender attitudes	.10*	.02
Political alienation		
Care about outcome of election	.14	.08
Interactions		
Economic satisfaction (category 1) × 1980	−.33	.21
Economic satisfaction (category 2) × 1980	−1.12*	.18
Professionals × racial attitudes	.77*	.19
Professional × gender attitudes	.33*	.08
Fit statistics		
−2LL (d.f.)	4404.38 (3945)	
BIC	−28,287	

An asterisk next to a coefficient indicates significance at the .05 level (2-tailed test).
Dependent variable is coded '1' for Democratic and '0' for Republican vote choice.

Source: Manza and Brooks (1999: 76, Table 3.3)

Manza and Brooks (1999). There are some similarities between the two. Both sets of data look at a number of social variables including class; both are interested in class voting in more than a single election year – 1952 to

1962 in the Alford table, 1972 to 1992 in Manza and Brooks' table; both want to present a picture of the effect of class on voting in broader contexts, including region, religion and age in their calculations of the effect of class on voting. However, there the similarities end. Firstly, the definition of class for Manza and Brooks is much more nuanced: they use a modified six-category adaptation of the Goldthorpe schema rather than the single index used by Alford.[12] Thus, even without necessarily understanding the meaning of the coefficients in the tables, we can already see that the Manza and Brooks table provides a more nuanced and comprehensive approach to class.

Secondly, however, the information which Manza and Brooks provide is in the context of a single model whereas Alford is in fact providing a number of different models. To include as many variables as Manza and Brooks, Alford would have had to provide a vast number of similar tables. More importantly, Manza and Brooks are able to control for the effects of all the different variables they have included in their model simultaneously to see the actual effect that, say, being a professional has on the likelihood of voting Democrat rather than Republican (the dependent variable referred to at the bottom of the table). Conversely, Alford's table tells us the index of class voting for Australian Protestants or Canadians between the ages of 30 to 40, but we have no way of knowing how much of the effect is due to the Australians being Protestant, or how much is due to the Canadians' age. Without knowing the prevalence of both religious groups amongst the two age categories, and vice versa, we are unable to adjudge the strength of the relationship between the different factors and class voting. Lastly, as we explained in Chapter 1, Manza and Brooks are able to include interaction effects, in this case between gender and racial attitudes and the professional class category. Alford's approach is simply unable to do this.

Similarly, looking at Tables 2.2a and 2.2b, the differences between Goodhart and Bhansali's analysis of determinants of political popularity (1970) and Lewis-Beck's (1993) full model of economic voting are apparent. Again, there is a different geographical focus for each model and the older analysis uses an aggregate time-series design. Unlike the last 'older model', Goodhart and Bhansali also use a multivariate model to look at the different determinants of incumbent popularity and to control for each one's effects. However, their data are aggregate. The variables shown are national-level economic data on unemployment and inflation, together with three variables looking at the effect of the electoral cycle – the changes which occur in a government's popularity during the period immediately preceding or following an election. This model cannot account for individual

Table 2.2a *The Basic Determinants of Political Popularity*

(1) Gallup data: January 1947 – June 1968						
G =	12.73	−0.02Ut-6	−1.25*d*P	+0.75EU	−0.16TR	+1.60BA
	(1.86)	(0.005)	(0.15)	(0.17)	(0.03)	(0.28)
R2 = 0.15		D.W = 0.40.		249 degrees of freedom.		
(2) Gallup data: July 1956 – June 1968						
G =	25.78	−0.016UG	−2.42*d*P	+0.94EU	−0.19TR	+2.36BA
	(3.23)	(0.002)	(0.37)	(0.24)	(0.04)	(0.38)
R2 = 0.58		D.W. = 0.74		132 degrees of freedom		
(3) Gallup data: November 1951 – October 1964						
G =	12.02	−0.004UG	−1.37*d*P	−0.52EU	−0.28TR	+2.51BA
	(2.30)	(0.002)	(0.23)	(0.34)	(0.04)	(0.35)
R2 = 0.47		D.W. = 0.57		144 degrees of freedom		
(4) N.O.P. data: February 1961 – June 1968						
G =	46.05	−0.077Ut-6	−3.42*d*P	+0.67EU	−0.24TR	+2.38BA
	(3.78)	(0.007)	(0.50)	(0.20)	(0.04)	(0.38)
R2 = 0.81	D.W. = 1.52			82 degrees of freedom		

Ut-6 = unemployment rate 6 months before survey
UG = unemployment rate at time of survey
*d*P = six-monthly rate of inflation
EU, TR and BA = three dummy variables approximating electoral cycle of governmental popularity
D.W. = Durbin-Watson test for serial correlation of residuals

Source: Goodhart and Bhansali (1970: 62, Table 3 abridged)

views on the economy at any single point in time. Moreover, the approach is ungainly: the authors employ almost 70 similar equations to look at various time periods and breakdowns of party and governmental support based upon this small array of independent variables.

Conversely, Lewis-Beck's model is precisely able to look at a wide array of independent variables *and* at the individual level, using the individual survey respondents' views on: their own finances; how the government has affected the national economy; its likely future effect; the state of the national economy as viewed by the respondent; and the level of affective response to how the government was handling the economy ('anger'). Moreover, he controls for social class, religiosity and ideological position,

Table 2.2b ***Full Single-Equation voting model (OLS), all nations, 1984***

	Britain	France	Germany	Italy	Spain
National economy	.03*	.01	.03	.04**	.04**
Government on self	.04*	0	.03	.01	.03
Government on economy	.14***	0	.11***	.07***	.05*
Future policies	.13***	.06*	.12***	.03	0.11
Anger	.08***	.04*	.04*	.02	.06***
Social class	−.09***	.04	−.01	−.17***	.07
Religiosity	.00	.00	.03**	.09***	.00
Ideological ID	.06***	−.15***	.10***	.08***	−.06***
Constant	−.80***	.97***	−.89***	−.33***	.95***
R2	.56	.53	.48	.39	.31
N	454	411	435	332	400

*p < .10, **p < .05, ***p < .01, in the expected direction

Source: Lewis-Beck (1988: 62, Table 4.4)

also derived from the survey data. This allows him to test, for instance, how much of the evaluation of governmental economic policy is based upon the ideological position of the voter rather than simply a 'neutral' observation of how the government has done, irrespective of ideological views. Such models rely extensively upon reliable individual level survey data, rather than simple aggregate figures, but consequently provide much more robust and informative findings.

As we shall see in Chapter 7, macro models are still used to test economic voting, although they are similarly more sophisticated than Goodhart and Bhansali's work. The micro-analysis is a new development, however, and the advance in statistical techniques has also allowed far more complex interactions between the different variables to be tested, using techniques such as path analysis which rely precisely upon the advances in computer speed and accessibility to which we have referred.

These examples are meant merely as illustrations of how the discipline has advanced in a relatively short space of time. This is not to say that those working in the 1950s and 1960s were not aware of such considerations, but simply that the means of testing such possibilities were not open to them. Alford, Goodhart and Bhansali would simply have been unable even to begin to test their hypotheses with the same sophistication as Manza, Brooks and Lewis-Beck. What one should not fail to notice, however, is how the basic elements which are deemed to have determined and determine voting behaviour have not changed, even if the sophistication in their testing has.

Conclusion: similar theories, changing techniques

This chapter has presented an overview of the basic trends in the development of voting studies in order to put the theories explained in the subsequent chapters into their historical context. As we noted at the beginning, such theories can be seen in isolation and tested in a similar manner. However, in striving to explain voting behaviour in all its complexity, it makes far more sense to consider each theory as one perspective among many on how voters make up their minds which party to vote for. Although we may strive for the perfect model of voting behaviour, this is ultimately a Holy Grail. There is no single 'correct' answer as to why people vote the way they do. Despite its formidable contribution to voting studies, not even the Michigan model can provide a 100% accurate prediction or indeed explanation of how American voters behaved in the post-war period: there will always be individuals who do not follow the explanatory 'rules' defined by a theory; and even when the explanatory rules are followed, it is not always possible to predict which of them will be responsible for determining vote in cases of conflict. Precisely how much a Democrat has to dislike the Democrat candidate before refusing to vote for him or her in spite of party identification is not necessarily knowable. All one can know is that, *ceteris paribus*, the more someone dislikes the candidate, the less likely they are to vote for that candidate. Consequently, strongly disliked candidates have a habit of losing.

This example may seem to be verging on the self-evident, and hardly worthy of a magisterial model of voting. However, as with the various theories and models which have appeared in the history of voting studies, none bases itself upon complex concepts of the type encountered in the natural sciences: the theories' tenets may seem self-evident simply because they are based upon the 'common sense' rules which govern our everyday decisions whether political or otherwise. The complexity derives from interweaving these rules and testing them as rigorously as possible. We may not know the absolute levels of candidate dislike responsible for certain voting patterns, but in a good voting model, we can judge the relative importance of candidate dislike when weighed against dislike of a certain issue.

But given that these rules have remained essentially constant for voters, even if the context has changed, it is important to recognise the different theories of voting for what they are – as much changing perspectives on a consistent act, as a series of perspectives appropriate for one stage in a changing act. Social structural models can still inform us about individuals' actions in the way that they did half a century ago; issue models could potentially inform us about historical voting, data permitting. Awareness of the range of theories, however, gives us the most complete perspective on voting.

Summary box

You should now be able to:

- place voting theories in their historical context
- explain the initial perspectives on voting
- understand the key assumptions of the Michigan socio-psychological model
- distinguish between short-term and long-term vote determinants
- explain the basic improvements in theory-testing across time
- identify theoretical components in models of voting.

Related reading

Berelson, B. and W. McPhee (1954) *Voting: a Study of Opinion Formation in a Presidential Campaign*, Chicago: University of Chicago Press.

Campbell, A., P. Converse, W. Miller and D. Stokes (1960) *The American Voter*, New York: John Wiley.

Converse, J. (1986) *Survey Research in the United States*, Berkeley: University of California Press.

Galli, G. et al. (1968) *Il comportamento elettorale in Italia*, Bologna: Il Mulino.

Heath, A. et al. (1993) *Understanding Political Change. The British Voter 1964–1987*, Oxford: Pergamon Press.

Inglehart, R. (1977) *The Silent Revolution: Changing Values and Political Styles among West European Publics*, Princeton: Princeton University Press.

Lane, R. (1962) *Political Ideology. Why the American Common Man Believes What He Does*, New York: Free Press.

Lazarsfeld, P., B. Berelson and H. Gaudet (1968) *The People's Choice. How the Voter Makes Up His Mind in a Presidential Campaign*, 3rd edition New York: Columbia University Press.

Michelat, G. and M. Simon (1977) *Classe, Religion et Politique*, Paris: FNSP.

Miller, W. and J. Merrill Shanks (1996) *The New American Voter*, Cambridge (MA): Harvard University Press.

Notes

1 We shall generally leave the intellectual context of each theory to the relevant chapter, limiting ourselves here to presenting the historical development.

2 For an overview of survey research in the United States, see Converse (1986).

3 In our opinion, later editions of the work are superior to the original because they contain additional prefaces which add a significant amount of contextual information about the surveys and methodological updates.

4 Since the initial Michigan work in 1948, the US National Election Studies have provided consistent survey data for each election.

5 Other works by the same authors built upon this and extended the study, for instance Converse (1964) and Campbell et al. (1966).

6 This concept of latent support within the electorate is developed by Converse (1966).

7 See, for instance, Simon's *Models of Thought* (1979) and Tversky's contributions in *Judgement Under Uncertainty* (Kahneman et al., 1982).

8 We base these figures upon those reported for the *American Political Science Review* by Green and Shapiro in their critique of rational choice theories (1994: 3, Figure 1.1).

9 See for instance, Heath et al. (1993), Miller and Merrill Shanks (1996) and Boy and Mayer (1997).

10 For a classic example of this approach, see Lane (1962).

11 See, for instance, van Deth (1998).

12 For a definition of how Alford calculates this voting index, and the drawbacks of this method, see Chapter 3.

3

Social structural theories of voting

Summary box

- The political sociology context
- 'Sociology of politics' and 'political sociology'
- The origins of political cleavages
- Measuring cleavages: the class example
- Absolute and relative class voting
- Dealignment and realignment
- What does 'social structure' mean today?
- Recent tests of structural voting
- Party identification and social structure.

Introduction

'A cross on the ballot is an implicit statement of social identity.' (Harrop and Miller, 1987: 173). If there is one view which characterises early voting studies, and continues to motivate much contemporary psephological research, this quote encapsulates it. As we discussed in Chapter 1, voting is certainly a unique activity in terms of the role it gives all enfranchised individuals in the political process, but at the same time it is also a remarkably ordinary activity in terms of the elements which drive the decisions underlying the vote these individuals cast. As in choosing a career, a partner, a car and a brand of toothpaste, whom we vote for is influenced by a range of attitudes, values, desires and beliefs – and which career, partner, car, toothpaste and political candidate or party we choose reveals the elements upon which such choices are based.

However, we have also seen that there are distinct differences amongst researchers as to which elements matter the most in the voting process. Indeed, we have already emphasised that it is perhaps more helpful to think of voting not as a decision-making process *per se* but as a predetermined expression of the important political elements which predispose the voter to a party or candidate: the element of choice should be eliminated by social science theory. As we shall see in this chapter, the elements which political sociologists and supporters of social structural models of voting would underline are the basic predispositions which are passed to us by our position in society.

'Why does society matter?' is an implicit question which this chapter will begin to answer in the case of voting. But to provide some initial bases for the study of society and voting, here are some possible answers:

1. The social context in which we grow up imbues us with a set of beliefs, values and attitudes, including that subset which relates to politics. As such, our electoral choice will be based on this subset, and its social origins are consequently important.
2. We belong, consciously or unconsciously, to different groups in society: age, gender, education, occupation, to name but a few, can all be used to categorise us. Because of belonging to certain categories, we experience certain events and interactions with other individuals which may be common to others in the same category. As such, the attitudes mentioned above will develop in similar ways, and so each group of individuals will manifest common attitudes on some matters which delineate them from other groups.
3. Political parties use these social groups which individuals belong to as a basis for mobilising support. Parties have limited resources and cannot provide tailor-made arguments and policies to mobilise each and every voter. So they appeal to those views which are common to social groups. Such appeals correspond to their ideologies and the view of society that will appeal to their targeted social groups.
4. Key social groups define the major lines of division opposing sections of society which are in competition for scarce economic, social and cultural resources. In mobilising these groups by prioiritising their preferences, parties engage in a zero-sum game in the competition for such resources.

As one can see from these four examples, the role of society and of the different groups within it can move from basic assertions about its role in shaping individuals' attitudes and preferences – usually referred to as socialisation, and political socialisation more specifically – to quite specific assertions about the interaction between social groups and the political system, and the results of this interaction. The last example clearly bears a strong resemblance to elements of Marxist thinking on the class conflict in society, but has broader relevance to other fundamental divisions in societies along lines of conflict – 'political cleavages' as they are often known.

Thus, in this chapter we need to look at how these different interpretations have been used in the social structural voting literature. We begin by looking at the early uses of social bases in studies of voting, for instance the Columbia studies, and then concentrate in particular on the study which is widely regarded as the founding comparative framework for the origins of social bases to vote, and to the patterns of political supply in nation-states more generally, *Party Systems and Voter Alignments* (Lipset and Rokkan, 1967). We then consider how one can test the relationship between social group structure and vote empirically; how these tests reflect researchers' assumptions about the nature of this relationship; and the implications that such methods have had for conclusions about the validity of the relationship, particularly in the case of class voting. This particular cleavage has been focused on in the light of changing social structure in comtemporary societies, and so we look subsequently at the arguments for realignment and dealignment and the extent to which they have affected the shape and validity of the social structural account. Finally, we consider the continued use of sociological models in the voting literature.

The political sociology context: different approaches to social structure

In a famous article written in the late 1960s, Sartori posited that too much research into social structure was based upon what he called 'the sociology of politics' and not on 'political sociology' (1969). In other words, when analyses looked at voting behaviour or the structure of a party system, for example, they relied too heavily upon ideas taken from sociology and then imposed upon political systems, rather than showing how the two relate and how political systems might equally impose themselves upon social structure. Similar to the fourth example in the previous section, Sartori notes that the 'chief impetus of the sociology of parties [and by extension voters] goes back, ultimately, to Marxist assumptions' (1969: 72). The reference here is to class differences, which as we shall see have dominated the social structural accounts of voting across the years. But a similar statement could be made about other social bases to voting which have traditionally been studied – religion, language, urban/rural dwelling, *inter alia*. How does social structure relate to voting? A Marxist has his assumptions about the nature of conflict between different classes, the importance of this in orienting political conflict, even the final result of such conflict. But similarly, an analysis of how religion affects vote must make similar assumptions about why religion matters, how it affects individuals' views of politics, and how this relates to the party for which people vote.

Sociology of politics explanations

In early studies of voting, the 'sociology of politics' approach can be seen. Studies such as the Columbia school look at a range of social indicators such as age, gender, occupation, religion and ethnicity and look for associations between these groups and Republican or Democrat vote. In what the latter of these studies terms 'the social transmission of political choices', the authors highlight three fundamental processes by which certain indicators – socioeconomic classes, defined using occupation, income and education, religion and ethnicity – maintain longstanding associations with vote choice (Berelson et al., 1954: 73–5). These are:

- *differentiation*, whereby individuals with shared characteristics also share a common interest in terms of how government policy affects them. Conversely, those belonging to a different group will also have a different, often opposing interest, in policy.
- *transmission*, whereby there is a handing down of values and attitudes, notably from parents to child, which remain with the voters for their entire lives and condition their vote. This is one of the most important tenets of traditional sociology, namely that there is some level of intergenerational transmission of values which ensures continuity in social structure, other things being equal.
- finally, *contact*, whereby individuals must spend more time in the presence of members of their own social group, rather than members of other social groups, to ensure a reinforcement of the attitudes and values which characterise this group. Contact with other groups could provide dissenting views which weaken a voter's socialised beliefs, by producing so-called 'cross-pressures', whereby an individual receives different cues as to what action to take or what to believe.

These factors have been replicated and confirmed by many studies of socialisation and the role of social group belonging and identity both in the US and elsewhere (Langton, 1969; Jennings and Niemi, 1968; Percheron and Jennings, 1981). As individuals grow up, they receive sets of values and beliefs or interests which enable them to function within their social group and in society more generally. They find these values confirmed and challenged according to the milieus in which the individuals move. Where groups with specific profiles and defined interests surround the individual, the likelihood of the group interest corresponding to the individual's own perceived interest is higher. For the most part, the influences later in life build upon the foundations laid in the formative years – there may be counter-influences which present other perspectives and interests, but these must be very strong if they are to challenge, if not displace, earlier perspectives. Indeed, research has shown that the beliefs and values imbued at an early age withstand changes in context which offer competing perspectives. In France, for instance, parental ideology may often predict an individual's vote, no matter what their own ideological position is (Boy and Mayer, 1998: 77; Evans, 2003). Assuming that this is not due to people voting to keep their parents happy, we can assume that parental socialisation influences are playing a role in determining vote that values adopted in later life and perhaps influenced by cross-pressures do not.

This helps explain why some social indicators do not have much of an effect on vote – age for instance. Given the primacy of transmission and the role of the family environment in socialisation, cues received later on are unlikely to have as great an effect on an individual and, given the stability in social group belonging assumed by the contact condition, most cues are likely to be reinforcing anyway. Additionally, age groups do not divide society as clearly as socioeconomic conditions. Policies affecting old people differently than other age groups, for instance, are but a small minority of policies. Greater differentiation will be seen on the other policies, consequently rendering them more important in how an individual votes. A similar argument could traditionally be used about gender, although as we shall see later this is perhaps no longer the case.

As important as individual characteristics is individuals' integration into society according to their explicit social group belonging – that is, the organisations they belong to and in which they may discuss politics or simply engage in social interaction which generally reinforces their beliefs.[1] Thus, trades unions have been seen as playing a particularly strong role in mobilising individuals on a class basis and hence contributing to the stability of this group's vote (Berelson et al., 1954: 125; Lipset, 1959a: 262). Similarly, religion may provide the basis for a cleavage in society but an active participation in church can reinforce the likelihood of a voter supporting a religious or conservative party (Berelson et al., 1954: 67–9). In both cases, the evidence for these organisations actively pressuring members to vote in a certain way was scant however – the mobilisation was seen as more an influence derived from social belonging and participation reinforcing ideas.

This leads us finally to consider context. As well as considering the social characteristics of individuals and the social groups to which they belong, others have looked at the social context in which individuals find themselves irrespective of their own profile or proactive group belonging. In class voting, contextual effects have been seen over time which vary according to the 'class profile' of the area in which an individual lives (Butler and Stokes, 1971: 174ff; Andersen and Heath, 2002). The neighbourhood effect provides an 'experiential source' (Marsh, 2002: 209), that is an invisible communicative network between inhabitants which influences social and political values and behaviour. Moreover, the strength of contextual effects can be considerable: for example, in Italy the effects of regional subcultures – historical allegiance to political traditions – used to be more important in how people voted than their individual characteristics (Galli et al., 1968; Mannheimer and Sani, 1987: 66). The Italian peasantry did not have a single party preference, varying between Communists and Christian Democrats according to region (Barnes, 1977: 57).

However, as Sartori notes, this may confirm a reflection of social groups but it does not confirm that political parties are *representing* the different social groups.[2] In voting as democratic *representation*, we want to know whether parties are representing their voters, as well as knowing that voters are voting for their parties out of a perception of interest.[3] Why is this important? The principal reason that simply looking for associations between social structure and vote is only a partial explanation is that there is considerable variation in which social divisions matter, according to which country we look at and in which time period. The Columbia studies were only concerned with America, and their finding was that socioeconomic status, religion and ethnicity affected vote. But if we look at the UK, the traditional view was that only class mattered.[4] In France, religion and class mattered (religion more than class, in fact) (Michelat and Simon, 1977). In Switzerland and Belgium, class, language and religion all counted, but class was well back in third place (Lijphart, 1980). Why, then, do some social divisions matter in some countries but not in others?

Political sociology explanations

The first comparative analysis to provide a framework linking social structure to party system format and electoral behaviour, and the one which remains central to political sociological explanations of voting, was provided by Lipset and Rokkan's introductory framework to *Party Systems and Voter Alignments: Cross-National Perspectives* (1967). Instead of taking a micro-sociological approach – that is, identifying the main patterns in individual voters' social profiles and their party choice – the work adopted a historical macro-sociological approach.[5] In other words, their analysis is based on the premise that the party arrays and voting patterns that could be identified in post-war Europe, could be found in the nation-state building and democratization processes which placed different social groups in opposition to each other as a developing centralised and secular state challenged existing territorial, cultural and economic loyalties. Institutional structures, competing alliances and the resolution of conflicts were crucial in deciding which social divisions became relevant in the structuring of political competition of a nation. Thus, political elites mobilised groups on the basis of their potency of support, and obviously the level of such potency would depend precisely upon the social divisions which existed.[6]

In this way politics, rather than being the simple reflection of social structure that Sartori objected to, became a dependent and an independent variable (Allardt, 2001: 19). In electoral terms, social cleavages which were present in society could be used for mobilisational purposes by elites, but not always – '[C]leavages do not translate themselves into party oppositions as a matter of course: there are considerations of organizational and electoral strategy.' (Lipset and Rokkan, 1967: 26). How, then, did they identify social cleavages and how did they account for those which became salient as a political cleavage in one society but not in another?

In their analysis of social cleavages, just because their overall framework gives equality to the 'political' as much as to the 'sociological' does not mean that their starting point was not quintessentially sociological. Lipset and Rokkan adapt Talcott Parsons' theory of differentiation, which looked at how different sub-systems within society – economic systems, political systems, the family, and so on – serve to orient individuals in their decisions and behaviour. These sub-systems are linked to functions that the system must fulfil if it is to survive, and of which there are four (Table 3.1).

Lipset and Rokkan took these four functions from the A–G–I–L system and hypothesised that, in order to understand how the social structure of a society contributed to the shape of the political system via the process of nation-state building and democratization, one should look in particular at the I, G and L elements and their interaction (Table 3.2).

In terms of mass electoral behaviour, the I–L and L–G interactions are clearly of the greatest importance. How ready are individuals to be mobilised by political parties as an organisational element? And what is their relationship with the political leaders of the newly forming nation-state? But the relationship between parties and the polity is important in that it represents the interchange between organisations for the loyalty of individuals. That is, in the democratization process there is competition between the 'new' national polity and the 'old' groupings which exercise influence and power at the local level.

Two dimensions matter in the tensions which this new nation-state produces. Firstly, the elite is based in the capital – the symbolic and territorial 'heart' of the new nation, normally characterised by greater urban

Table 3.1 ***Structural-functional sub-systems***

Function	Description of function	Sub-system examples
Adaptation (A)	The system must provide resources by adapting to and shaping its environment	The economy
Goal attainment (G)	The system must decide which aims are to be given priority in its maintenance and development	The polity
Integration (I)	The system must arrange and regulate the interactions between its different components	Communities, associations, churches, legal frameworks, etc.
Latency (L)	The system must ensure that individuals maintain the values and motives which sustain it	Families, schools, etc.

Source: Lipset and Rokkan (1967)

Table 3.2 ***Key interactions between sub-systems***

Interaction	Elements in interaction	Political relevance
I – G	Political leaders and organisational groups	Party formation
I – L	Organisational groups and individuals'involvement	Individuals' group identity and mobilisation
L – G	Political leaders and support of individuals	Elections

Source: Lipset and Rokkan (1967); Flora (1999: 278)

development and higher levels of secularisation. It therefore challenges peripheral areas – those areas separated from the centre by geographical distance – and their characteristic social groups. Such groups are not always immediately allowed access to representation: one need only think of the early years of post-revolutionary France and the Jacobins' murderous treatment of dissent, for example. However, one can contrast this with, for instance, Norway, where the Constitution of 1814 allowed for representation of burghers, the rural and peripheral peasants and the *embedsstanden*, the centrally based official estate (Rokkan, 1967: 369–71).

However, it is clear that not only territorial divisions matter: irrespective of one's position in geographical relation to the centre, one's ideological relation to the centre may also matter. Thus, Lipset and Rokkan hypothesised a cross-cutting functional axis to emerging cleavages. This axis stretched from specific material considerations characteristic of economic concerns (to become relevant after the Industrial Revolution), to more encompassing cultural and moral *Weltanschauungen* (world-views or ideologies) which influenced an individual's entire lifestyle and choices. In particular, competing allegiances beyond the nation-state territory proved especially divisive. In Counter-Reformation countries where the Catholic church had retained dominant influence against the Protestant Reformation begun in the 16th century, the formation of a secular state challenging Papal authority led to deeply entrenched divisions between Catholic and secular groups. Thus in Italy, France and Austria, for instance, religion 'counted' in cleavage terms, and consequently in the basis for people's vote. However, in the Reformed Nordic countries, such as Norway and England, state religion was an integral part of the state itself, and consequently no separate religious cleavage developed.[7]

These two cleavages – centre-periphery and Church-State – are said to derive from the critical juncture of the National Revolution.[8] The very formation of the state promotes conflicts within its territory which until that point have remained latent, but which are integrated into the system as a means of resolving differences peacefully, allowing individuals access to the economic and power resources of the state via political parties, and consequently the state being legitimised by these individuals who benefit. However, Lipset and Rokkan note that such parties (in the modern sense) can only form once they are allowed to manifest opposition without threat of state repression – the first 'threshold of democratization' – and then the extension of suffrage to allow such groups to compete electorally – the second threshold. In some cases, these thresholds are surpassed in quick succession, as well as the third – representation in Parliament.[9] This would characterise the Norwegian case. In other cases, the access to representation is more drawn out – the British case, for instance.

More fundamentally, the access to representation may be contingent upon the timing of the second critical juncture, namely the Industrial Revolution. Two further social cleavages become salient after this: a primary/secondary sector division between the agricultural and industrial sectors, falling towards the specific-interest end of the functional axis; and of course the workers/employers division or the class cleavage. The first of these is a characteristic of those countries – essentially the Scandinavian states – where there was a close alliance between the centre-based elite and an urban economic elite (Lipset and Rokkan, 1967: 44). Where the peripheral agrarian economies felt threatened by industrially led growth, agrarian parties developed. Why, however, did such parties not develop in other countries with large primary sectors such as the UK, France or Italy?

The answer lies in the distribution of the sectors and the presence of established elites. In the UK, the division between country and town corresponded to the pre-existing division between the Tory and the Whig parties, the former representing the landowning rural gentry, the latter representing the urban bourgeoisie. There was no room for a separate agrarian party to mobilise in this context. In the case of France, Italy and other Counter-Reformation countries, the geographically dispersed peasantry were already mobilised by the Catholic parties, or were subsequently mobilised by anti-clerical Communist and Socialist parties. In the French case, the more conservative Catholic vote would be associated with the larger farmer, the Left vote with independent smallholders (MacRae, 1958: 292). Consequently we can see that established parties have generally resisted the arrival of new challengers where a previously unenfranchised group does not exist. This also helps explain why the religious cleavage has generally outweighed class, where this former cleavage exists.

But throughout all these processes, the reaction of elites – both central, nation-state building elites and the 'protest movements' against this established elite which then became integrated in the national centre (Lipset and Rokkan, 1967: 23) – was key to the mobilisation and strength of cleavages. In this regard, Belgium provides a good example. In this country, the religious cleavage between Liberals and Catholics did not initially give rise to the same harshly divisive dynamics that it did in France because of the liberal constitution of 1830 guaranteeing the right of the Church to develop freely. Greater conflict occurred from the late 1850s onwards because of growing anti-clericalism on the part of the Liberals and the threat this posed to the Catholic influence in schooling. However, as Kalyvas shows, the reactionary 'ultramontane' Catholic groups which developed as a result, and could have destabilised Belgian democracy, were prevented from doing so by the reaction of an *external* elite – the Vatican – in supporting the more moderate Catholic camps in joining with secular Conservative forces (Kalyvas, 1998). Moreover, the resolution of the religious divide via compromise opened the way for the linguistic cleavage to emerge as a force, itself being resolved by the restructuring of the party system into two regional and linguistically homogeneous sets of Flemish and Walloon, rather than Belgian, parties (Deschouwer, 2001: 212).

Thus, when we look at social structure and vote, we should never lose sight of the role parties and elites play in activating social divisions as vote determinants, particularly in establishing the array of parties which for the most part still compete today. As we shall see, many of the developments in social structural theories have returned to the micro-sociological approach, rooting voting behaviour in the Columbia tradition. Whilst from the demand side – which of course is what we are principally interested in from this book's perspective – the hypothesised relationship can be explained persuasively, we should not lose sight of the need to test this from the supply side as well.

Measuring social structure and vote: the example of class

As Flora notes about Rokkan's work,[10] most of the variables which he uses in his accounts of democratisation and nation-state building are dichotomies – presence/absence of a certain system property; high/low levels of another; and most importantly, the dyadic oppositions across political cleavages (Flora, 1999: 4).[11] This is understandable, given the vast edifice that constitutes his work on nations and democratisation, and consequently his use of an array of basic oppositions to define these.

This approach has continued into the empirical testing of the effects of cleavages, but not always with beneficial results. Looking first at the country and area analyses following Lipset and Rokkan's theoretical introduction, many authors employ basic cross-tabulations looking at the size of class voting in terms of a working-class/middle-class split; or a 'Catholic/others' religious split. For example, Alford's study of class voting in Anglo-American systems provides a detailed breakdown of occupations in the UK, Australia, US and Canada, but in testing hypothetical dimensions of class party relationships, dichotomises class into manual and non-manual categories, and parties into Left and Right (Alford, 1967).

Let us take a number of hypothetical examples to illustrate how such figures can be used to look at class voting. There is no reason that these approaches cannot be used to look at other cleavages such as religion and language. However, class is by far the most common topic studied in the literature, for reasons we will consider afterwards. The first measure that can be used is *absolute* cleavage voting, in this case absolute class voting. Here, simply the number of individuals who vote for the party of their class are given as a proportion of the total electorate (Sarlvik and Crewe, 1983). For instance, if there are 10 million voters in an electorate, spread equally between two classes, and 3 million from each of these 5 million classes vote for the 'correct' party, then the absolute class level will be 60 percent. Using this measure, the focus of attention is on what proportion of the electorate vote the 'correct' way.

However, other researchers have claimed that we should take into account the individual parties' electorates, and their composition in cleavage terms (e.g. Heath et al., 1985, 1993). There are two related reasons for this. Firstly, if a party loses or gains votes in an election, which sections of the electorate it loses these votes from matters in how we interpret these losses. In class terms, does the party principally lose votes:

(1) from its 'natural' class, for instance working-class voters from a Left-wing party? or
(2) from all classes? or
(3) from 'deviant' cases, in this case middle-class voters for the Left-wing party?

Table 3.3 ***Hypothetical Alford index example***

	Manual workers	Non-manual workers
Left	75	45
Right	25	55

In case (1), absolute class voting would decline; in (2), class voting might decline – the Left-wing party would have lost a proportion of its working-class vote – but if the middle-class vote moves to the Right-wing party, this could offset the decline; in (3), class voting would rise, as the 'deviants' move back to their natural party on the Right. (2) emphasises that it matters where voters go – the defectors might all choose a third party, in which case class voting would still decline, despite the losses from *both* classes suggesting that class was not the reason for the decline. Rather than look at the proportion of 'correct' votes and nothing else, then, critics of absolute class vote suggest we should look at the propensity of the different classes to vote for their natural party.

One solution to this has been to look at *relative* class voting. In early research, the Alford index was the favoured measure of relative voting. Rather than looking at a single proportion encompassing the 'natural electorates' of both parties, the Alford index subtracted the proportion of 'deviant' cases from the proportion of 'correct' cases (Alford, 1963, 1967).

For instance, in the example in Table 3.3, we can see that 75 percent of manual workers vote for Left-wing parties (the traditional representatives of manual workers) and the remaining 25 percent vote for Right-wing parties. Conversely, 55 percent of the non-manual class vote for the Right, and the remaining 45 percent for the Left. According to Alford's index of class voting, one subtracts the percentage of non-manual workers voting for the Left ('deviant' cases not following the expected relationship) from the percentage of manual workers voting for the Left. In this case, then, the Alford index would be 30. The logic is clearly to identify the level of preponderance of the expected class in the party's vote. By itself, the figure does not give us much information – if it were negative, this would be an indication that a greater proportion of the middle class were voting for the working-class party than from the working class itself – but comparing two countries using the indicator, or looking at a single country across time would give us two indices which could be compared. We could then judge whether class voting had gone up or down.

However, as Heath et al. (1985: 40–1) noted there is a problem with this index and gave the following example. Take two consecutive elections, and measure class voting using the Alford index. At the first election, 62 percent of manual workers and 28 percent of non-manual workers vote for the

Left party. Consequently, the Alford index is 34. At the following election, the Left party loses all its non-manual voters and its manual vote drops to 33 percent of that class. The Alford index is therefore 33. In this case, the Left party now has an entirely working class electorate, and so in balance terms class voting should have increased. And yet the Alford index has dropped.

Both the absolute class voting measure and the Alford index are sensitive to the changes in the size of the class or of the party electorate. The methodologically more satisfactory alternative they suggest is the 'odds ratio'. In effect, this calculates the odds of a member of one class voting for one party rather than another. In a two-party system – Left and Right parties – with two classes – manual and non-manual – and assuming that the manual workers should vote Left, the non-manual workers Right, the odds ratio is calculated thus:

$$\frac{\text{[Proportion of non-manual Right-voters/proportion of non-manual Left-voters]}}{\text{[Proportion of manual Right-voters/proportion of manual Left-voters]}}$$

Taking the example from Table 3.3 again, the odds ratio would be:

$$(55/45)/(25/75) = 1.22/0.33 = 3.66$$

We can also see from the above equation that, if the odds ratio is 1, this means that there is no class voting. For instance, if 50 percent of each class vote for each party, then:

$$(50/50)/(50/50) = 1/1 = 1$$

The 'odds ratio' comes into its own in real-world situations where two classes do not split perfectly between two parties. Indeed, the proponents of its use illustrated how votes for third parties – in this case, the Liberals and SDP/Alliance in Britain – could cause misleading conclusions using the Alford index. To take a hypothetical example, as illustrated in Table 3.4, we use the same assumptions as we did above but include a third, Centre party which we assume has no class basis to its vote.

Between two elections, the Right-wing party's vote remains constant, but the Left-wing party loses votes to the Centre party. If we calculate the odds ratios for both of these elections, we find they are the same: 7. Relative class voting has remained the same. Looking at the distribution of votes, this makes sense – the Right-wing party has remained stable, and the Left-wing party has not lost from one class but from both. In terms of proportions, the Left-wing vote remains the same as well, even if the total number of votes is smaller. However, had we used the Alford index on the Left-wing party,

Table 3.4 ***Hypothetical odds ratio example***

	Election 1		Election 2	
	Manual worker	Non-manual worker	Manual worker	Non-manual worker
Left	60	20	30	10
Centre	10	10	40	20
Right	30	70	30	70

we would have calculated 40 for Election 1 and 20 for Election 2. Similarly, the level of absolute class voting would have decreased.

Some authors have criticised the use of odds ratios (Crewe, 1986; Dunleavy, 1987) claiming that stability such as that shown in the example above hides clear changes in class voting, and also conversely that the odds ratio is very sensitive to small changes. As such, they argue the odds ratio is an unsatisfactory indicator. In fact, the sensitivity of the indicator is precisely a property of the odds ratio which is a benefit – the changes may be small in absolute terms, but in relative terms they may not be. For instance, in a system with a tiny Left-wing party a change from 3 percent to 6 percent manual workers voting for it may be 'small', but it represents a 100 percent increase. In a situation where the Right-wing party's vote amongst the manual workers remains stable at 90 percent, this represents a change in odds from 30:1 to 15:1. The logic behind the use of the odds ratio also allows its extension to the multivariate setting, where the likelihood of different social groups voting for a party can be tested in a logit model.

The question, then, is not whether the odds ratio index is satisfactory methodologically – it is – but whether the theoretical justification for its use is strong. Particularly in a situation where the class traditionally of interest – blue-collar workers/the manual class – is declining in size, the odds ratio may allow us to exclude that dynamic from our assessment of relative class voting, but at a certain point the size of the class will precisely be an issue. Working class voting may still be strong for a Left-wing party, but if this represents a tiny percentage of the electorate, so what? Other factors will presumably be needed to account for voting amongst the non-working class majority.

However, the Alford index has continued to be used as evidence that class voting in society is declining (Dogan, 2001: 102). Moreover, as Hout, Brooks and Manza argue, the index can only be used on a two-class society (1993: 265). Testing class from the Lipset and Rokkan perspective might imply a simple dyad. However, given the changing and more complex social structure of post-industrial society which we consider below, to write off class because an empirical measure based upon a situation which no longer pertains indicates decline, is a very weak basis for such a conclusion.

The challenges of dealignment and realignment

From the Lipset and Rokkan 'ideal type' of voters aligned with their socially defined parties, a number of analyses looking at the period since the 1960s have hypothesised that this alignment has gradually been eroded by a number of phenomena. Particularly in the case of class, but also in the case of other cleavages, clear links between party and vote according to traditional social structure have disappeared. Either voters have become more individual in their voting choices, due to a rise in sophistication, political knowledge and a blurring of issues at the policy-level, and hence are likely to be more selective and hence potentially more volatile at successive elections (the dealignment hypothesis) or lines of division still exist in politics, but they have evolved from the traditional cleavages.

The context to socio-political change

The key to change in the post-war period in industrial democracies is the context of changes in social structure and the social context, and consequently to the changes in electoral behaviour seen from the late 1960s onwards. Firstly, societies became notably more affluent in the period between the 1950s and the 1970s – France's *trente glorieuses* (thirty glorious years), the German *Wirtschaftswunder* (economic miracle), and similar changes across Europe. As a result, standards of living rose, the consumer revolution took off and prosperity altered many of the political priorities that had become entrenched in particular by the Great Depression of the 1930s and the war. At the elite level, fear of inflation may still have oriented German economic policy, for instance, but at the mass level feelings of economic insecurity were lessened.

Secondly, as a result of this affluence, the development of new infrastructures and the beginning of the growth of the service economy, geographical mobility grew. Increasing numbers of individuals moved geographically to take up new jobs, as well as changing milieus: the decline in the agricultural sector saw many moving from the countryside to the cities in search of employment. The decline in the traditional industrial sector as the powerhouse of Western economies saw the shrinkage of the locally based and geographically immobile blue-collar class. Social mobility was also more common: instead of the highly stratified societies of the prewar period, the nature of employment and particularly advancement and promotion in white collar jobs meant that class divisions became much less entrenched.

Thirdly, and vital for such changes to become implanted, was the increase in education. Larger numbers of youngsters staying on at school for longer and attending universities supplied labour for the growing white-collar sector. Education provided an increasing proportion of the electorate access to a wider range of employment possibilities. Thus, not only did the rise of the service sector produce a growing white-collar worker electorate, which was impossible to classify according to the traditional Marxist dichotomy, but many of those who traditionally would have entered the blue-collar electorate now moved into this new class.

Lastly, the cultural and moral divisions engendered by religion declined as the number of people attending Church declined. The secularisation of post-war society would consequently engender a decline in the importance of the religious cleavage. In virtually all nations, the proportion of the electorate proclaiming a religious affiliation has decreased, and the number professing to practise their faith has similarly declined. That said, for those who still proclaim active religious affiliation, particularly in Catholic countries, religion is still a strong predictor of Right-wing vote (Boy and Mayer, 1998). Again, this reflects the theoretical concerns highlighted with regard to class above: at what point does a strong predictor from the cleavage structure perspective lose its importance because of the decline in size of the group in question? There is no easy answer to this. To the extent that one acknowledges other more widespread explanations, the more marginal predictors remain relevant.

The decline of cleavages structures

Perhaps the most radical hypothesis advanced is that voters have become decreasingly aligned with traditional cleavage structures, and that they will not realign with new social divisions, but will instead choose on the basis of political issues and at each election, rather than deciding on the basis of social group cues and developing lasting attachment to a single party (Nie, Verba and Petrocik, 1976; Habert and Lancelot, 1996; Popkin, 1991). This sees the electorate as an increasingly sophisticated set of individuals with access to political information and the ability to make well informed decisions as a result. In many ways, these would resemble the ideal 'rational' voter whom we will consider in the following chapter. However, whilst such individuals may exist, there is little evidence that such voters characterise the entire electorate any more than in the past (Smith, 1989) and as such it would seem unwise to assume on this theoretical assumption alone that increasing numbers of voters are less reliant on social cues. Levels of political information vary, and whilst higher levels can allow voters to make more informed political choices (see Chapter 8) there are still many who do not have such information upon which to rely. Moreover, the bulk of the testing of such hypotheses has been restricted to the US to date – convincing evidence for Europe is scant.

The embourgeoisement hypothesis

As the authors of *Electoral Change in Advanced Industrial Democracies* drily noted, '[European workers ...] spend Saturdays washing their cars and Sundays driving into the countryside – clearly not the makings of a Marxian class struggle' (Dalton, Flanagan and Beck, 1984: 16). Due to the rising affluence of post-war democracies, the working class has not seen its standard of living drop but rather increase, with access to consumer goods, housing and educational possibilities for their children which had previously been denied to them. In being able to aspire to a middle-class lifestyle, the working class were consequently likely to take on middle-class values, distancing them from the ideals of the more radical Left-wing parties, and thus reducing the class-vote link.

However, given increased affluence amongst middle-class groups as well, such an absolute measure may not see a decline in prosperity, but in relative terms the gap is still large. It is also not true that blue-collar workers are enjoying unprecedented affluence. In many countries, the improvement in the working class' lot began prior to the Second World War and the Depression, with no apparent decline in class affiliation. Moreover, in the modern post-industrial economy, it is precisely traditional blue-collar groups which suffer from insecurity, a lack of value in the service-oriented jobs market and long-term unemployment as a result.

Finally, from a theoretical point of view, it places heavy emphasis on a basic indicator of material wealth as the motivation in class voting. In terms of socialisation, why should the possession of consumer goods override values imbued amongst workers in their childhood and adolescence when the pre- and inter-war were still largely confined to their traditional pattern.

New sectoral cleavages and the new middle class

The rise of the private sector and the expansion of public services in the post-war period has seen the growth of a large occupational class which does not conform to the working class/middle class dichotomy. Increasingly, traditional blue-collar workers are a minority compared to white-collar workers. It has been suggested that a more relevant cleavage may now divide society along a public/private employment divide, whereby those working in the state sector will gravitate towards the parties of state involvement – the Left – whereas those relying upon private firms, dependent upon competitivity in the market and freedom from state shackles, will move to the parties of free enterprise – the Right.

A more generalised hypothesis of private and public consumption hypothesises that those who own their own houses, have private healthcare arrangements and use their own means of transport, will vote for the Right, whereas those living in rented or state-subsidised accommodation, relying on public healthcare provision and using public transport, will vote for the Left (Dunleavy, 1979). This also emphasises the possible mirror image of embourgeoisement, namely the 'proletarianisation' of workers nominally in the middle class, but with low wages and low job-security. Systematic testing of this cleavage being rare, the extent to which such a new cleavage can be found fundamentally dividing contemporary democracies is unclear. Also, some have criticised it for being unclear in explaining the mechanisms by which these sectors are linked to vote (Franklin and Page, 1984).[12] However, elements relating to house ownership and financial holdings have continued to be introduced into voting models as part of the class explanation (Heath et al., 1985, 1993). It also refocuses our attention on the fact that characterising non-manual work as 'middle class' is much too simplistic to be effective if we are trying to characterise social conditions as causally related to vote. Variation within this 'middle class' is enormous.

The new value cleavage

Arguably no other theory in political science has had more influence than Inglehart's theory of post-materialist value change (1977). Due to the economic affluence of post-war democracies and the rising levels of education, the post-war generation, socialised under such conditions, have different value-priorities to their parents. Instead of worrying about financial matters and material concerns more generally, they could afford to concentrate on 'quality-of-life' issues such as the environment, pacifism, gender equality, equality of ethnic groups, *inter alia* – the 'post-materialist' value set. Consequently, they would be less likely to be mobilised by the traditional cleavages and associated values rooted in the conflicts over resources and legitimacy, and more by issues connected with their own values. But, because these new issues were precisely nowhere to be found on mainstream political parties' agendas, such post-materialists would be less likely to vote at all, and would instead engage in unconventional direct political action such as strikes, demonstrations, occupation of public buildings, etc.

It rapidly became clear that such individuals were also the ones who were more likely to vote, as well as engage in direct action; and parties such as the Greens sprang up to represent environmental issues, whilst other post-materialist issues became characteristic of the New Left influence which gradually found its way into Left-wing parties' agendas (Kitschelt, 1994). Consequently, these issues have become integrated into the mainstream. That post-materialist issues may not always be directly related to class structure or other social structural indicators is evident, and as such they have become important short-term indicators, either in a model such as the

Michigan model, or in the issue and value dimensions used to operationalise the spatial models we will look at in Chapter 5. These values are now firmly part of the political process. However, the extent to which post-materialists may be influenced by elements of social structure is still a valid analytical question: just because their values may be different does not mean that they are not constructed in similar fashion. More broadly, the fundamental division in society, that the post-materialist 'value-cleavage' was meant to represent, is far from clear in contemporary society. Some authors see post-materialism as closely related to the libertarian-authoritarian dimension which has been an important dimension of political space for far longer than post-materialism as a concept (see Chapters 5 and 8).

Recent sociological accounts of voting

For many, such varied challenges to the traditional social structure represent an end to the usefulness of social structural accounts of voting – 'the sociological account of electoral behaviour is clearly obsolescent' (Whiteley, 1986: 98). But in general these conclusions have been reached either using the basic indicators of change which we looked at earlier – for instance, absolute measures of cleavage voting or the 2-by-2 Alford index – or simply taking it as read that social structure could not matter anymore, and proceeding from there to look for alternatives. Despite this, somewhat of a renaissance has occurred in sociological studies of vote, and these suggest that whilst the social structure has in all likelihood evolved, it is simply not the case that the social structure no longer matters.

As we have already noted, the vast bulk of work concentrating on the testing of vote and social structure has focused on class. In part, this is certainly due to the ubiquity of class divisions in democracies. It also relates to the nature of class as a structuring variable. In the case of, say, language or religion, the division is fundamentally dyadic. In the Belgian case, people either speak French or Flemish. Many Belgians may speak both; for some there may even not be a natural 'first' language. However, if it is to be related to vote, one or other language counts. Similarly with religion, secular/Catholic or Protestant/Catholic are the principal divisions. One can introduce religiosity – the regularity of religious practice – but then the variable becomes something substantively different: a fluid scale, rather than a clear division. In the French case, some researchers have used this as an attitudinal scale, rather than a social structural indicator *per se* (Grunberg and Schweisguth, 1998).

What about the case of class? The general consensus amongst sociologists is that a simple manual/non-manual dichotomy is woefully inadequate in describing the occupational class structure in modern societies, and consequently any proof of class voting which uses this dichotomy is no proof at all. The premise for this is simple. If political science is going to employ sociological measures such as class, it is blinkered in the extreme to rely upon a Marxist division which may have characterised class conflict in the initial period of working-class enfranchisement, but which in contemporary post-industrial societies is now anachronistic.

In their criticism of the Alford index, Hout, Brooks and Manza make the problems with the two-class account very clear: 'By lumping together all persons employed in non-manual occupations in one "class", and all persons working in manual occupations into the other "class", the Alford index creates artificially high levels of cross-class voting among both groups. For example, secretaries, low-level clerks and service-sector employees, who may have very similar class interests to manual workers, are counted as deviant if they vote for left parties. It has been apparent for some time that the two-class model [...] does not capture the full complexity of class voting.' (1993: 265)

Consequently, if we are going see secretaries as having interests in common with manual workers, for instance, the criteria for classification must differ substantially from those used to define the two-class dichotomy. The criteria for the most common class model which has been adopted are based upon studies by Erikson and Goldthorpe (1992) and Wright (1985). These schemes were not developed specifically to look at class voting, but rather to look at social mobility and the relationship between social position and income. The number of different classes which can be identified vary, but four principal classes form the basis for most versions – the salariat, the petty bourgeoisie (self-employed and owners), the routine non-manual class and manual workers. These can be further sub-divided into a higher and lower salariat, skilled manual workers, unskilled manual workers and foremen and technicians. Some authors have also distinguished between professionals (self-employed and salaried occupations such as lawyers, doctors and accountants) and managerial occupations (Manza and Brooks, 1999: 57).

The different categorisations illustrate the principal improvement that this classification provides over the old dichotomy. Instead of basing the political relevance of class on two blocs with mutually exclusive interests, the multi-categorisation bases its analysis on the employment characteristics of each occupation. In particular:

- Is the individual an employer or an employee?
- In their occupation, does the individual exercise authority over other employees?

- What is the nature of the work contract – short-term wage-base for manual employees, or career-oriented salariat?
- What is the promotional structure?
- What is the nature of the work carried out – creative/intellectual or standardised and repetitive?
- What level of job security is provided, and/or to what extent are skills transferable?

The combination of these different profiles can then be used to identify different categories. Consequently, the routine non-manual class can be seen to be close to the manual class because of the lack of promotional opportunities and low pay. However, the nature of the work separates these two classes.

For empirical testing, the different categories cannot be used as a continuous scale. Clearly, the income disparities between different classes are likely to exist, but they do not form a single scale along which one can array them. For instance, skilled blue-collar workers may well earn more than some routine non-manual workers. More importantly, however, the above classification is concerned with far more than just income disparities. Consequently, models employing such classifications always include them as categorical variables, comparing the effect of belonging to one class to that of another (the 'reference' category mentioned in Chapter 1). The inclusion of these, then, allows a robust testing of social structural effects on vote, and used on time series analysis, can also allow the charting of changes in the relationship between these variables and vote – decline (or not) of class and religion, and in addition, the growth of new cleavages such as gender and ethnicity. The country examples we have used so far in this chapter provide the most complete testing of such hypotheses to date.

A role for party identification?

As we highlighted in Chapter 2, with the exception of the UK, European research has often tended to see party identification as an unnecessary variable between social structure and vote. Indeed, some have even seen it as an impediment, providing 'evidence' of psychological attachment motivating vote which simply does not exist, or in some cases proving a weak predictor of vote (Thomassen, 1976). One of the principal theoretical criticisms of party identification outside the US is that the notion of party and the relationship which voters have with parties varies differently from country to country. In France, for instance, most parties were traditionally small club-like groups of politicians, warily perceived by the electorate and constantly fragmenting and amalgamating – hardly a likely source of political cues for French voters (Evans, 2003). Moreover the socialisation process excluded the overt political influence which we often find in the US (Pierce, 1995: 45).

Thus, from the sociological perspective, the partisan cues which proved so influential in the social networks which enabled voters to make up their minds about which candidates and parties to support in wartime and post-war America are simply not as strong in Europe – and just as influential will be other group belonging, such as Church, trade union, region, neighbourhood and family. If we take the more deterministic Lipset and Rokkan macro-sociological approach, then the mobilisation of voters according to their social group by parties means that an identification variable becomes redundant. If I vote for a party because of my belonging to a community which has, across generations, supported one party to the extent that voting for it is more akin to a tick on a census form ('male', 'between 29 and 35 years old', 'Protestant', 'Socialist') than an electoral choice, a sense of party loyalty or identification may well exist, but this does not provide any added explanatory value.

Of course, not all members of social groups do vote for a macro-sociologically defined party and, given the changes in social structure considered above, the clear dividing lines that such a model provides are increasingly simplistic or anachronistic.[13] We are thus faced with two scenarios regarding social structure and party identification. Either the social influences will cross-cut increasingly, providing cross-pressures which should reduce the levels of identification; or new social structures will provide identification to the levels of the old cleavage structures because their influence is different but as strong. The former, which as we have seen has been used to challenge sociological models, would also predict a declining influence in party identification. The latter would see party identification as stable, but consequently its explanatory role would be cast into question – if party identification is shifting in close coordination with social structure, then how does identification provide added explanatory value to vote?

The last criticism of party identification's use as an intervening variable between social structure and vote is whether we can trust it as an indicator taken from survey data. Quite simply, when we ask a voter if they identify with a party, or more worryingly in translated versions of the question in non-anglophone countries whether a voter feels *close* to a party, what proof do we have that her answer will indicate a true identification with the party, rather than just a recall of past or statement of intended future vote? Just because I answer does not mean I am answering the question.

In sum, despite the widespread use of the concept in the voting literature, and its fundamental position in the Michigan model's explanation, we think that much care and some suspicion is necessary when confronting its explanatory role in European countries. If it exists, vote outcome is evident – but the more interesting question is where the identification derives from. That all said, this does not mean that party identification does not have its uses. For instance, from a methodological point of view it can act as a very useful control variable before looking at some of the individual explanations of vote which we are about to look at in the following chapters. Given that the social structural variables we have talked about in this chapter will not pick up all of the contextual effects in a model, no matter how many of them we include, party identification can be included as a way of tapping all vote predispositions, before we include other individual aspects which may vary vote.

Secondly it can be used as a useful indicator of 'core' vote or intended future vote. If we want to try to identify a party's stable electorate for use as a dependent variable, for instance, we can be more confident that party identification represents this than a simple vote recall question. Lastly, from an explanatory point of view, party identification can be useful in looking at the role of parties in determining attitudes. As the Michigan model showed, support for and identification with a party provides cues as to which policy positions to hold. The bulk of research to date, however has concentrated on how policy positions and attitudes determine vote. In looking at voting as a dynamic interaction between parties and voters, then, this endogenous relationship is important to discern to understand how parties mobilise, as well as how voters choose.

Conclusion: social structural flexibility and resilience

That social structure still matters to vote must be taken as a given. How it matters and the extent to which it determines vote relative to the past remains the principal explanatory goal of sociological accounts. As much contemporary work on class in particular notes, both political scientists and sociologists have been guilty of misrepresenting social structure in the past – sociologists have often asserted its strength to too great a degree, political scientists have assumed its disappearance in recent times too easily (Evans, 1999a). In a happy irony, the micro-sociological 'revival' has caused many sociologists to ask precisely the question which Sartori accused them of ignoring 40 years ago. Whilst finding that social structure is still important, even if the structural bases to voting have changed significantly across time, Manza and Brooks, for example, note that looking at the social structure in its present format begs the question – given the inequalities and differences which still exist today, why have these not resulted in *more* entrenched cleavages than they find? (1999: 239–42).

Critics would argue that this demonstrates that social cleavages do not matter: cleavages and vote correspond in the past; structural change occurs, and we consequently expect to see radical vote change; radical vote change does not occur; therefore cleavages cannot matter (e.g. Zuckerman, 1982). The response to this remains similar to the Lipset and Rokkan approach: cleavages and social divisions matter to a certain extent where elites decide they will. Organisational and institutional effects need to be brought into the equation.

It is not sufficient to look just at the demand side. Political supply needs to be included too. But this aside, from purely the demand perspective, the social context plays a vital role in accounting for the preferences of voters and their eventual policy views. As we shall see in the subsequent chapters, despite Michigan asserting the primacy of party identification in giving policy cues, even the most uninformed voter will still have basic attitudes and values which influence their political leanings. They may not be informed on a certain policy, or have even heard of it, but this does not mean that they are not more open to some political arguments than others. Where do such values and attitudes comes from if not from social context? Media are often held up as playing an increasingly important role. But media vary in their political bias – so who reads which newspaper? Who watches which TV news? How do voters respond to the information presented? If the answers cannot be derived at least partially from social context, past and present, then it is unclear where they *can* be derived from.

Summary box

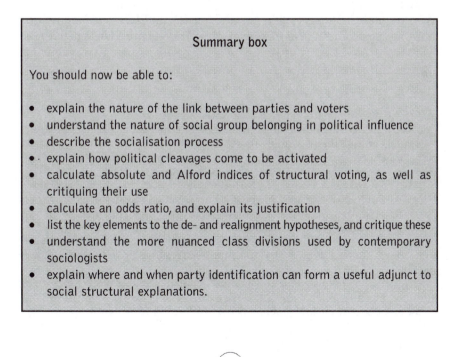

You should now be able to:

- explain the nature of the link between parties and voters
- understand the nature of social group belonging in political influence
- describe the socialisation process
- explain how political cleavages come to be activated
- calculate absolute and Alford indices of structural voting, as well as critiquing their use
- calculate an odds ratio, and explain its justification
- list the key elements to the de- and realignment hypotheses, and critique these
- understand the more nuanced class divisions used by contemporary sociologists
- explain where and when party identification can form a useful adjunct to social structural explanations.

Related reading

Alford, R. (1963) *Party and Society*, Chicago: Rand McNally.

Berelson, B. and W. McPhee (1954) *Voting: a Study of Opinion Formation in a Presidential Campaign*, Chicago: Chicago University Press.

Butler, D. and D. Stokes (1971) *Political Change in Britain: Forces Shaping Electoral Choice*, Harmondsworth: Penguin.

Erikson, R. and J. Goldthorpe (1992) *The Constant Flux: A Study of Class Mobility in Industrial Societies*, Oxford: Clarendon Press.

Evans, G. (ed.) (1999a) *The End of Class Politics? Class Voting in Comparative Context*, Oxford: Oxford University Press.

Flora, P. (ed.) (1999) *State Formation, Nation-Building and Mass Politics in Europe*, Oxford: Oxford University Press.

Heath, A. et al. (1993) *Understanding Political Change. The British Voter, 1964–1987*, Oxford: Pergamon Press.

Langton, K. (1969) *Political Socialization*, New York: Oxford University Press.

Lazarsfeld, P., B. Berelson and H. Gaudet (1968) *The People's Choice. How the Voter Makes Up His Mind in a Presidential Campaign*, New York: Colombia University Press.

Lipset, S. M. and S. Rokkan (eds) (1967) *Party Systems and Voter Alignments: Cross-National Perspectives*, New York: The Free Press [esp. Introduction].

Manza, J. and C. Brooks (1999) *Social Cleavages and Political Change. Voter Alignments and US Party Coalitions*, New York: Oxford University Press.

Notes

1 This is also sometimes referred to as 'social encapsulation'.

2 As another commentator states in the case of class voting, '[T]he existence of class voting of itself does not imply that there is a consistent link between class and party, or between class and a bloc of parties, or between class and a type of party. Hence as long as a class votes as one, there is class voting ...' (Mair, 1999: 310)

3 As Przeworski and Soares note, Sartori was not the first person to realise this – Marx too emphasised the need for political organization mobilising class interests (1971: 63). However, Sartori's comment does provide a useful reminder in the face of much sociological research which sweepingly assumed – and, in some cases, continues to assume – that differences between social groups and associations with certain parties must be indicative of a close functional relationship between the masses and elites.

4 This text will follow a long and glorious tradition in studies of class and voting in Britain by citing Peter Pulzer's famous adage, 'class is the basis of British party politics; all else is embellishment and details' (1967: 98).

5 Much of the work looking at how individuals are influenced by their social context provides aggregate figures according to class or other social group belonging. However, the explanation adopts an individual, and thus micro perspective. However, Lipset and Rokkan never interest themselves in the influences at the individual level – they are concerned exclusively with the political divisions between groups as an outcome of the interaction between elites and masses and historical events.

6 Many commentators draw attention to the conceptual similarities this shares with Schattschneider's concept of 'mobilisation of bias' (1975).

7 In such countries, we do find religious parties, for instance the Norwegian Christian People's Party. However, these are based upon peripheral counter-cultural concerns, rather than a challenge to the nation-state's legitimacy itself.

8 In fact, they also subdivide between two 'critical junctures' – the first being the Counter-Reformation, dividing between a national and supranational religion (Protestantism v Catholicism) and the second being the National Revolution when the state asserts its right to the latency function, namely a secular education. However, the National Revolution is often used to conflate the two.

9 The fourth threshold is defined as access to executive power.

10 Lipset worked on the early Colombia studies, and hence has links to the US micro-sociological tradition (Manza and Brooks, 1999: 13). Rokkan on the other hand had worked on a framework of historical analysis for the formation of democratic states, which led up to the cleavage structure analysis we have looked at here. Consequently, as Allardt says of the Lipset and Rokkan framework, '… the Parsonian thoughts played a much greater role for Rokkan than for Lipset.' (2001: 19).

11 The term cleavage has been defined in many ways by many researchers. However, one thing is evident – it must include a clear division between groups.

12 Taylor-Gooby goes some way towards explaining the mechanism by linking the elements of sectoral belonging to subjective perceptions of differences between state- and market-oriented groups which are then mobilised by political parties (1986).

13 We would do well to emphasise here that Lipset and Rokkan themselves will not have believed that their macro-sociological model could ever have accounted for all votes. From the electoral perspective, it is simply designed as a basic model that could explain the principal dynamics in voting (and party system array) across systems.

4

Rational Choice Theories of Voting

Summary box

- What is rationality?
- Rationally linking parties and voters
- The role of uncertainty
- Ideology and policy-space
- The rational abstention paradox
- Extending the rational model
- The effect of rational choice on voting research.

Introduction

As individuals we all have beliefs and desires which make up part of who we are. Many if not all of these beliefs and desires will be shared by other people – not necessarily in the same combinations, but for the most part in subsets which correspond to different areas of life. For instance, many of us have religious beliefs which tend to correspond with members of the same religion or denominations within that religion. All Christians, for instance, believe in a monotheistic deity. Not all, however, believe in the Holy Trinity – the Unitarian Church, for instance, rejects this notion. On a more mundane but more relevant level (for this book, at least) we were able to identify different groups of people according to their social group characteristics – religion, class, ethnicity, gender and so on. Similarly for these groups of people, we could identify some tendencies in their attitudes towards politics as demonstrated by their voting behaviour. However, even within these groups there was sufficient variation to be of interest – for instance, French and Italian peasantries with both Catholic and secular-Communist voting.

In this case, the cross-pressures of economic and cultural/ideological influences indicated a priority in voting terms, and this would, in all likelihood, be associated with different attitudes towards cooperatives, hierarchy and so on. In other words, unless we believe an entirely deterministic model of voting behaviour, the differences and attitudes betray not only a concomitant desire for different outcomes, but also the ability to choose between different outcomes – in the electoral arena, outcomes that are represented and promised by political parties competing for government.

In other words, rather than looking at the profile of voters from a social standpoint and then extrapolating to voting as a function of this profile, we can instead focus on individual voters and try to explain by what decision-making process they come to choose the party for which they vote. This does not deny that voters have social contexts which affect the decision-making process, nor that they may have party loyalties which also help them in this process, but it does shift attention from 'social input → vote output' to the actual mechanisms which take place in the black box of a voter's mind when she makes the choice.

A theory looking at this decision-making mechanism needs to encompass all voters, not just a subset. Despite a potentially infinite range of motivations feeding into this mechanism, it also needs to provide an answer which can be channelled into a limited range of responses. In other words, although decision-making in daily life can sometimes provide a very large array of responses (for example, the decision as to where to go on holiday has a very large number of possible outcomes; or what to have for dinner this evening has even more perhaps), the number of choices that are available in an election are often limited to perhaps two parties, abstention and spoiling a ballot. In predictive terms, this might seem like a simpler task than predicting a decision which could have any number of outcomes. However, taking account of the potentially boundless variety of influences that could play a role in helping an individual decide how to vote, the theoretical basis must provide a very clear set of assumptions which can encompass such motivations satisfactorily.

The theoretical basis which has proved overwhelmingly dominant in voting studies to date is the rational choice paradigm. Developed from a combination of theories of social action and economic theories of rationality,[1] rational choice theory essentially ascribes the motivations of individuals on whether to vote and how to vote to a calculation of the likely benefit to be derived from the preferred decision. In other words, voters decide upon their course of electoral action on the basis of what they expect to get from it. Each potential outcome has a benefit or a cost, and the voter will choose the one which benefits them most or costs them least.

The two major works from which most of contemporary rational choice theory derives are Downs' *An Economic Theory of Democracy* (1957) and Olson's *The Logic of Collective Action* (1965). We will concentrate principally on the former and its derivatives in this chapter, as this has the most to say about the voting decisions made by voters. Downs and his followers also have plenty to say on the subject of parties as well – as we shall see, one of the key elements to his economic theory of democracy is that the electoral arena is like a market place, and for this we need supply (parties) and well as demand (voters). We will consider some of the implications of rational choice theory for parties, to the extent that these have an effect on voters' decisions.

In this chapter, we will begin by spending some time on a number of the elements which Downs introduces, not only because we feel it gives a good introduction to the theory itself, but also because he employs concepts relating to voters and their decision-making processes which have wider applicability than rational choice theory itself. Having looked at the Downsian perspective, we will then look at its subsequent development by other authors, in particular in addressing the thorny problem of why people bother to vote at all according to this framework – the 'Paradox Which Ate Rational Choice', as many have termed it. We will then turn to look at the spatial model of voting which represents how voters and parties interact in the electoral arena. The more developed spatial models of issue voting will be considered in Chapter 5.

Indeed, it is worth noting at this point that many of the theoretical elements introduced in this chapter will reappear in subsequent chapters. This is also true of the social variables which we considered in Chapter 3. However, the individual elements to vote decision-making are important because, as we have already noted, they focus in particular on the mechanism itself, rather than the context. For recent explanations of voting, these mechanisms have been extremely helpful in looking at the individual rather than the collective. As Erik Allardt, one of the contributors to Lipset and Rokkan's seminal political sociological account, has summarised: 'The present popularity of the rational choice theory has in my opinion in the social sciences had some positive, perhaps largely unintended, consequences. Rational choice theory brings to the fore people's intentions and motives, and it has given an additional and fruitful push to account for human agency and to apply agential explanations.' (2001: 24).

Downs and rational choice

What is 'rational'?

For social scientists, rational is a much abused word in the English language. Politicians call for 'rational debate' on issues which polarise the electorate, meaning that those who do not agree with them are clearly ignorant and hysterical and would take a different point of view if only they understood the problem. Share dealers ask investors to take a 'measured and rational approach' when markets look unstable, meaning 'Please don't sell all your shares at the first sign of trouble, or the stock market will collapse.' Conversely, people who act without apparent motive are often described as being 'irrational'.

There is nothing wrong with this usage in everyday life, and indeed each of these uses contain elements relevant to the social science context. For a theory of voting, however, we need to have a more formal definition which clearly defines what is rational and what is not in the context of the electoral arena. Downs defines rationality as engaging in the pursuit of goals in the most reasonable way possible. Taking his lead from economic theory, the most reasonable way possible is 'a man [moving] towards his goals in a way which, to the best of his knowledge, uses the least possible input of scarce resources per unit of valued output.' (1957: 5).

In other words, when faced with a decision which affects his interests, the rational individual is interested in the most cost-effective means of maximising his gains. If we can assign a numerical value to both the means and the gains, then the value of the latter should exceed the cost of the former. Obviously, if there is more than one possible decision, then the rational individual will take the decision which should maximise his gain. The individual in this case is said to be *maximising his utility*, the utility being the difference in gain between the chosen option and the rejected option.

Downs then adds five criteria of rationality which must pertain if the above definition can hold (1957: 6):

1. the individual is able to make a decision when presented with a range of alternatives;
2. the individual is able to rank the preferences in order;
3. the preference ranking is transitive (i.e. the individual prefers alternative 1 over alternative 2, alternative 2 over alternative 3, etc., and consequently he must prefer alternative 1 over alternative 3);
4. the individual will always choose the most preferred alternative;
5. if presented with the alternatives at different points in time under the same circumstances, the individual will always make the same decision.

These criteria clearly assume that the individual has a clear notion of what he wants as an outcome, of how the alternatives relate to such an outcome, and additionally has a steady set of criteria by which to assess the different alternatives which ensures a single alternative wins out each time. They all imply that the individual has *information* to hand which can allow him to make these choices. As we shall see, information is a key element in rational choice accounts of voting. However, we can already see that these criteria might not match reality particularly well, either in voting or in other choices. Do individuals always have a clear preference ranking, or do they sometimes/often make decisions on a whim? Consequently will they always choose the highest preference?

Such problems, and the problem of information more generally, are implicit in Downs' view of rationality, however. He also emphasises that such criteria cannot be tested by looking at the outcomes of individuals' choices, but only on the mechanism of how the choice is made. In other words, just because an individual makes a rational decision does not mean that the outcome will always be the expected one. The rational individual will undoubtedly take account of outcomes in future decisions – a point which has often been overlooked in many uses of rational choice theory – and will certainly look at the likelihood of such an outcome, but outcomes *per se* do not indicate the rationality of a decision.

Downs emphasises that, in terms of voting, only political and economic motivations to voting decision should be regarded as rational. His fear is that, if broader motivations such as family pressures, clientelism and the like are introduced, the explanatory framework becomes tautological – in this case, individuals are not voting to maximize their utility, but instead are 'employ[ing] a political device for a nonpolitical purpose.' (1957: 7) He uses the tragic example of a man who votes in a specific way because otherwise his wife will nag him about this. As we shall see, this attitude to rationality is not shared by many of Downs' successors, but for him such explanations devoid the rational framework of any value, reducing it to saying, 'People vote the way they do for a variety of personal reasons many of which aren't related to politics.'

How does the rational voter relate to rational parties?

From the economic supply-and-demand perspective, rational voters can only be said to exist if the parties for which they vote are also rational. Parties too need to maximize their own utility and act in rational ways if voters are to be able to make decisions that are based upon the criteria highlighted above. Parties' utility derives from governmental income, power and the prestige that these give (1957: 28). Parties and politicians are office-seekers, aiming to maximise their vote in order to ensure sole tenure of, or at least participation in, government.[2] Governments want to maximise their support so as to ensure re-election, and opposition wishes to maximise its support in order to displace government. Ideologies, social group appeals and so on are designed, in the Downsian view, only as means of garnering support. Parties have no social designs or philanthropic ends in mind when they are elected – victory is the sole aim.

This might seem a cynical view of what governments and parties are. However, one of Downs' aims was to try to show how a government may discharge its social function – that is, manage society effectively and improve many of its citizens' standard of living – without intending this as one of its own objectives. How can actors act in their own interests and at the same time provide social goods? In order to win power and hold onto it, parties must respond to voters' preferences and provide a measure of the expected utility. This consequently benefits the voters, and if sufficient will ensure the incumbent retains power. Governing parties, and indeed their opposition, thus have an interest in responding to voters' desires and wishes if they are going to win office. But, to emphasise, the social function is a by-product, not an objective.

So, given these motivations for parties and for voters, how does the voter look at parties come election time? The first point that Downs makes is that voters firstly look not at parties *per se* but at the government that was incumbent up until the election. They calculate what that government will provide them with in terms of utility if it stays in power. Subsequently they look at what the opposition would offer them if it were in power – and whichever provides the higher utility wins their vote. *Ceteris paribus*, if there is no utility difference between the two, the voter abstains. Why? We need to remember two things. Firstly, that the basic rational voter has nothing else in mind beyond what she gets out of it – there are no broader considerations, no party-specific biases. Secondly, voting is not a cost-free activity. The mere act of going to the polls costs time and potentially some money. Thus, if she thinks that whichever party wins will make no difference to her expected utility, there is simply no point in incurring the cost to go to vote: either outcome is equally as satisfactory.

To be precise, Downs adds a number of additional steps in the decision-making process between considering the alternatives and deciding to abstain. In particular, there is a different onus on returned incumbents or victorious oppositions in their actions in government. A re-elected incumbent will see victory as a referendum on its time in power to date, and thus will regard its new mandate as 'carry on as before'.[3] An opposition party, *even if it has an identical programme to the previous incumbent*, will change some of the outgoing party's policies in order to differentiate itself from the previous incumbent (1957: 42). This adds an additional parameter to the rational voter's decision to vote or not. We have said that if the party differential is zero, then the voter will abstain. However, this does not imply the parties' programmes are identical. Two radically different programmes can produce identical utilities. For instance, holding other things equal, the incumbent party may levy income tax such that the voter pays 1000 'utiles' tax a year.[4] The opposition may have committed itself to removing income tax completely, but introducing a dog licensing system which costs 1000 utiles a year. For a dog-owning rational voter, the parties' policy platforms are very different, but the cost is the same.[5]

In this case, the voter still abstains, because she can see where the change will occur. However, if the parties have identical platforms, she knows that the opposition will change at least something, even though, on the basis of their platforms, the derived utility is identical but it will not be known what changes will occur if the opposition wins. If the voter can calculate that the probability of change is more likely to raise than lower her utility, then she will vote for the opposition. If it is on balance more likely to lower her utility, she will vote for the incumbent. If the probability is equal, or she cannot calculate it, then she abstains.

Uncertain voters and parties

Theoretically, our model of the interaction between voters and parties is very clear. Parties offer policies, voters look at those policies, decide which maximize their utilities and vote accordingly. But there are problems which this simplicity causes. Firstly, an incumbent is going to look at voters' preferences and adopt the position which satisifies a majority so as to secure re-election. Given that voters have a variety of preferences, the party is unlikely to be able to satisfy the entire electorate, so it must look for the majority position on all salient issues (1957: 55). But this position is not unbeatable. Given that different policies will be salient for different people, an opposition party can put together what Downs calls a 'coalition of minorities'. Whilst in power, a government will appeal to the majority preference on each of the issues which it represents. However, unless the majority on each issue is composed of exactly the same voters – i.e. the government's majority is entirely homogeneous – then on each issue there will be a series of minorities whose position is not represented by the government.

A very simply example suffices. If we take three voters, A, B and C, and three policy issues – higher income tax, abolition of the death penalty and greater environmental protection – we can array their preferences as shown in Table 4.1.

Table 4.1 ***Majority positions for incumbents and the 'coalition of minorities' problem***

	Higher income tax	Abolition of Death penalty	Greater environmental protection
Voter A	+	+	–
Voter B	+	–	+
Voter C	–	+	+

+ = in favour of policy
– = against policy

Voter A wants higher income tax, the abolition of the death penalty but does not want greater environmental protection. Voter B wants higher income tax and greater environmental protection but does not want the death penalty to be abolished. Finally, Voter C wants the death penalty to be abolished, greater environmental protection but does not want higher income tax. A well informed incumbent, wishing to ensure a majority, chooses to promote higher income tax, the abolition of the death penalty and greater environmental protection because these stances reflect the majority desires of our three-person electorate. However, Downs then posits that all an opposition party need do is look at voters' preferences, note the minority positions and then adopt these. Over the course of time, a government will take many decisions, each of which will displease some of the voters (as above, Voter C would be displeased by higher income tax, Voter B by the abolition of the death penalty, and so on). Downs needs the additional assumption that voters will feel more intensely about positions upon which they are in a minority, rather than positions upon which they are in the majority (1957: 68). Consequently, the opposition party takes the opposite position to the incumbent on every issue, forms the so-called 'coalition of minorities' and wins Voters A, B and C upon the basis of their minority positions on the three policies.

But as Downs himself notes, this is patently absurd.[6] No rational incumbent party would ever go to the trouble of taking a majority position as the opposition could simply identify the minority position and win at the next election. The whole theory risks falling apart at this point, not least because parties clearly do look to adopt majority positions and opposition parties do not overthrow incumbents as of right. One of the main reasons parties cannot do this is that elections do not take place in a vacuum: parties have previous policy positions which act as a brake on them drastically redefining their existing position, even if strategically it would be more advantageous (1957: 109). Policy shifts must be gradual if they are to ensure credibility remains.

Also, there is uncertainty on the part of voters and of parties (1957: 80–2). Voters' utilities change between elections, but to what extent is this due to governmental action? Voters may simply be unaware of government's actions and alternatives to it. Finally voters do not vote in a vacuum – they have views on how other voters may vote and can adjust their decision accordingly. From the parties' point of view, they are not necessarily aware of what policies each will adopt, nor can they know what the outcome of their policies will be on voters. Parties are also uncertain as to what exact preferences voters have, or how aware they are of policy alternatives.

Thus uncertainty and information for both parties and voters play roles in ensuring that, whilst each set of actors' decisions may be rational, they do not take place under conditions of perfect information. At the level of voters, Downs distinguishes amongst different types of voter according to their levels of information and view of parties (1957: 84–5). He distinguishes, for instance, between certain voters such as 'agitators' and 'passives', who are well informed about parties and use this to inform their own vote and, in the case of agitators, to persuade others to vote the same way; and uncertain voters such as 'baffleds' who do not have sufficient information to make up their minds. He also notes the loyalist phenomenon, whereby voters who were previously informed in past elections stick with this decision at subsequent elections, as long as their utility does not change markedly for the worse, so as to save on the costs of information gathering.

Thus, for the rational voter, information gathering is an important means of coming to a decision, but the search for information is costly, either in terms of obtaining it or in terms of the time it takes to digest it and integrate it with existing information. Some voters will be willing to invest time and resources in collecting information – others will not. The Downsian view of information is that a voter will stop collecting information once the cost of doing so outweighs the value of possessing it (1957: 215). Once the voter is sure that she has sufficient information to choose which party to vote for, then it makes no sense to keep acquiring information which will confirm that choice.[7]

However, parties are conscious of the uncertainty that voters have over policies, expected outcomes and the like. One of their strategies may be to concentrate resources on voters who may influence others – agitators, for instance. Many voters looking to reduce information costs will rely upon the (forceful) opinions of others to make up their mind. They may also provide a basic signpost, which any voter can use, to indicate their general policy outlook. And in this way, Downs explains why actors whose entire motivation is office-seeking, rather than social planning, possess ideologies.

Ideology, parties and electoral choice

According to Downs, parties only need ideologies because voters are uncertain: 'When voters can expertly judge every detail of every stand taken, and relate it directly to their own views of the good society, they are interested only in issues, not in philosophies.' (1957: 98). The party's ideology consequently provides a convenient information short-cut for voters who cannot judge every detail expertly. In calculating likely utility outcomes, the voter can orient herself according to the general view promoted by the party. It is only rational to do this in the short term, however. If parties' actions in government do not match their words, and obtaining more reliable information can be done relatively cheaply, then the voter should not continue to use ideology as a viable information short-cut. In the same way that a consumer may buy a toothpaste because it promises 'Whitest Teeth Ever!', and then switch to another brand because his teeth remain grey, so a party which does not live up to its billing risks losing its voters. How close to the billing the party needs to come depends on the expectations of the voter – coming close may be enough to keep the voter's loyalty, in the same way that the consumer may make do with Fairly White Teeth, rather than start buying and testing other brands.

If parties are to win voters over time, then, they consequently have an interest in providing a level of consistency in their ideology, and their actions should to some extent reflect their ideological standpoint. Parties are also unlikely to change their ideology and/or actions overnight, if they wish to remain credible with the electorate. Indeed ideologies tend to remain fairly stable. Robertson links this to how parties enter the electoral arena. They first need to provide the ideological signpost, which they do by providing a series of policies which match this ideology. Assuming this is not necessarily the optimum position for maximising their votes, once they are sure that the ideology is secure in the electorate's mind, they then gradually amend their policy programme to approach what the majority want (1976: 44).

Therefore, what parties need to decide is where the majority of the electorate's preferences lie, so that they can position themselves in terms of their policy bundles which constitute their proposed governing programme. Assuming that there are a range of preferences amongst voters, parties will never be able to win all the voters as the competing party or parties will ensure that they position themselves to win another tranche of the electorate. But they make their appeal as broad as possible without losing credibility with contradictory policies designed to win anyone, whatever their preference structure.

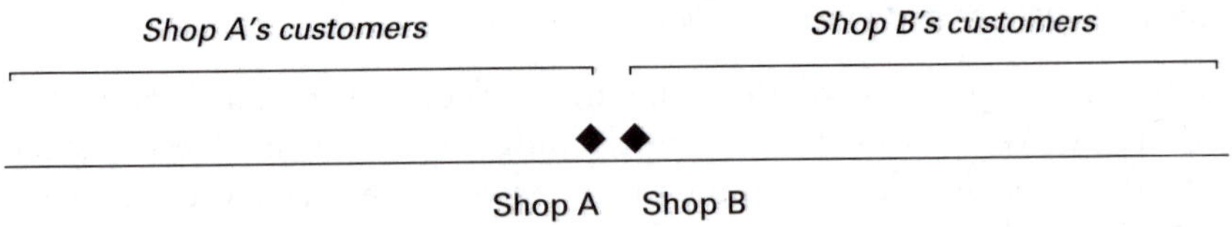

Figure 4.1 *The rational shopping street*

If these ideologies and policy bundles are going to be effective in a decision-making context, however, Downs needs to introduce a formalised notion of how they function. What is the basis of the policy-bundles? How do voters view these, and how do they choose? To do this, Downs borrows a spatial concept from the economics literature (Hotelling, 1929; Smithies, 1941). In this, economists tried to work out where the optimum spot for shops to position themselves on a street would be in order to maximize the number of customers that frequent the store. The basic model assumed that there was only one street, providing a single dimension,[8] that potential customers were distributed along the street evenly, and that they would decide which store to shop in on the basis of price and of the transport costs of getting to the shop. In such a situation, the ideal point to position the shop would be halfway along the street. If prices were identical, no competing shop would be able to find a position which cost less to get to for a majority of customers. Consequently, the best place for a competing shop to position itself (if it has the choice) is right next door to the centrally located shop. Evidently it cannot locate at the identical position, but by placing itself just to the left or right of the first shop, it can 'win' all the customers either to the left or to the right of the first shop, respectively (Figure 4.1).

In adopting this, Downs drew analogies between the economic market and the political market. Firstly, there is a political 'street'. This he took to be a policy dimension based upon the economic perspective of political parties, running from complete state intervention in all economic matters to a completely free-market economy (*laissez-faire*). He assumes that the bulk of important policy matters are related to this dimension – an arguable assumption, but one which, as we shall see, is important for the clarity of the model. Secondly, there are political 'shops' – the parties, which have to choose where to place themselves in order to maximise the number of sales made, i.e. the number of votes they receive. The price of the goods is by definition equal – one vote, which each voter has to 'spend'. The position of the parties and voters on the political 'street' is determined by the content of their policies and ideology for the former, and their preference structure for the latter.

Of course, this being only an abstract street, some of the economic constraints do not apply. Firstly, there is no reason why either parties or voters cannot position themselves at identical positions. However, parties have no incentive to do this because if they look too much like each other in terms of their policies, many voters will be indifferent as to who wins, and will consequently abstain. Parties consequently have an incentive to maintain some distinctiveness. Voters, on the other hand, have no such incentive and indeed the fact that there are many individuals with similar if not identical preferences allows parties to position themselves effectively on the spectrum.

How those preferences are distributed and how many parties represent these varies. According to Downs, two-party systems will allow stable and effective government in systems where there is a degree of consensus amongst its citizens (1957: 114). By this, he assumes that there will be small ideological distance between the bulk of the citizens, with decreasing numbers of voters the more extreme one moves along the axis. If the bulk of voters are to be found at the very centre of ideological space, with a similar distribution of voters spreading away in both directions and decreasing towards the extremes, then the normal distribution shape would be found (Figure 4.2, curve A). However, Downs hypothesizes that due to the distribution of voters in society, the actual ideological position will be skewed somewhat to the left – towards state control as desired by the working class (Figure 4.2, curve B).

The dotted line indicates the position of the 'median' voter for each of these distributions – the voter who is in the middle of the electorate inasmuch as equal proportions of the electorate lie to either side of her position. For the two distributions, the median voter is in a different ideological position, of course. In a two-party system, parties have an incentive to get as close as possible to the position of this voter in policy terms because this will ensure that they maximise the number of votes they can receive. If we look back at Figure 4.1, replacing 'shops' with 'parties' and 'customers' with 'voters', party A will get all voters to the left of its position and party B will get all voters to the right. In this case, we might hypothesise that the only voter lying between them is the median voter herself. Assuming that they are equidistant from the median voter, she will abstain, of course, resulting in a tie, unless she votes for a reason other than ideology or policies. This situation is said to be in *equilibrium*: neither party can find a strategy – in this case a position – which secures a better outcome.

This is an ideal type of model, of course. In practice, parties do not resemble each other to such an extent, even in policy terms. There are a number of reasons why not. First of all, the distribution of preferences in the electorate may not be 'single peaked', that is with the proportion of the electorate

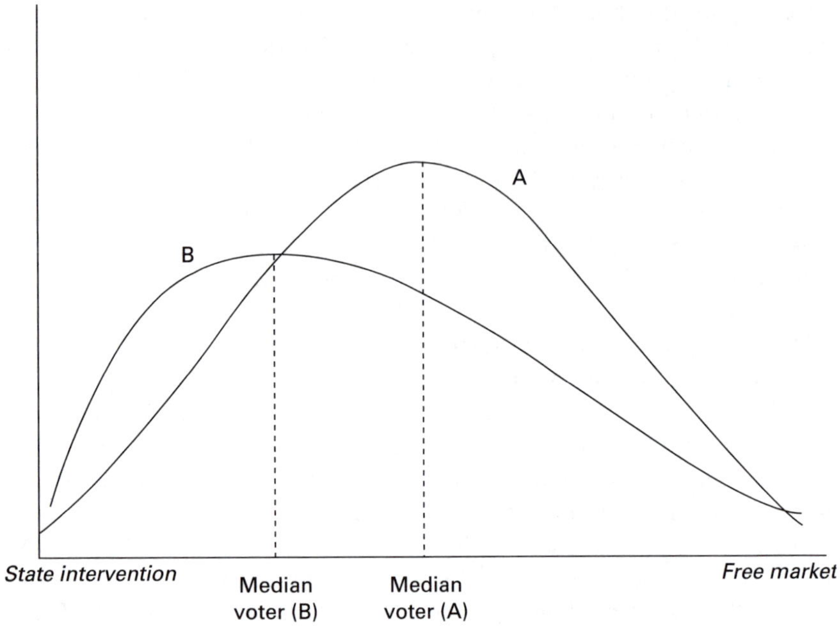

Figure 4.2 *Downsian distributions and median voters in the electorate*

holding divergent positions from the median falling steadily away on both sides. A 'bimodal' distribution, with two peaks as shown in Figure 4.3, will more likely cause the two parties to remain under their respective peaks, and consequently they will not converge on the median voter.

As McLean notes, one must introduce a couple of additional assumptions for this to be the case – that extremists, who are more common in such distributions, may abstain if their party moves closer to the centre; or that new parties may spring up to represent the majority opinion on either side of the spectrum if the existing party does not reflect its preference more closely (McLean, 1982: 80–8). For Downs, this would be particularly prevalent during the extension of the voting franchise to, say, working-class votes (1957: 129). In the British case, the more Left-oriented preferences of these new voters were capitalised upon by the new Labour party, squeezing out the now more centrist Liberal party which had previously represented the left. However, whether a new party can enter the system depends on the institutional structure, and in particular the electoral system. Under proportional systems, according to Downs, one thus tends to find multi-party systems representing polymodal (many-peaked) distributions of preference,

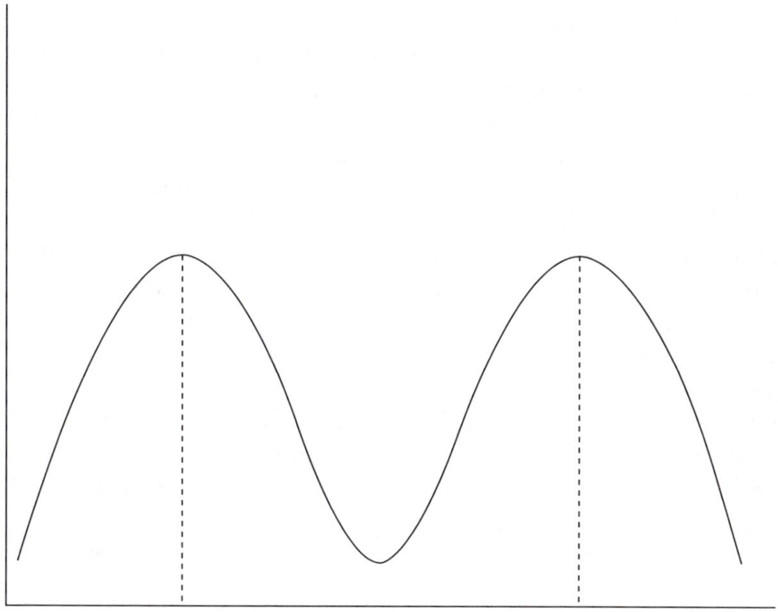

Figure 4.3 *The bimodal distribution*

whereas two-party systems tend to be associated with the unimodal (single-peaked) case.

The extremist abstention argument was also used to argue why parties would not converge on the centre under a unimodal distribution. To try to force parties to stay closer to their desired radical policy position, extremists could threaten to abstain if they moved to too moderate a position.[9] However, parties would never have an incentive to give in to extremist blackmail, as this would still cause them to lose the election (Barry, 1978). A more rational solution would be in fact to move in the opposite direction, to shrink competitive space and render the extremist vote redundant. In some situations, this would clash with Downs' assumption that parties cannot leapfrog each other (1957: 123) because of the loss of credibility this would produce amongst their voters. Thus a party may only move adjacent to its competition. However, one thing is clear – satisfying the extremists' demands is a losing strategy.

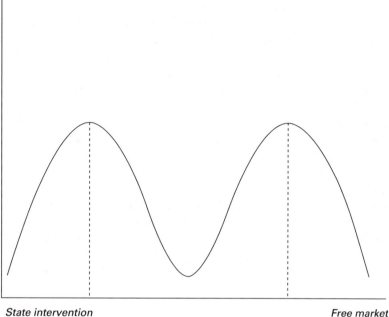

The last element which we need to consider briefly at this stage is Downs' assumption of a single dimension to competition. As we have already seen with the 'coalition of minorities' problem, there may be an array of issues, not all of them economic, which determine a voter's choice. As we shall see in Chapter 5, it is possible to operationalise spatial models so that the single dimension of space is a function of a number of dimensions. However, if we explicitly assume, say, two independent policy dimensions which are relevant to vote, then it is incredibly rare that we can find an equilibrium position for parties looking to maximise their vote. Essentially, as with the coalition of minorities, any position that one party takes to win a majority can virtually always be beaten by another position. We do not have the space to go into this here, but to understand the problems associated with multi-dimensional space, Chapter 7 of Green and Shapiro's critique of rational choice provides an excellent explanation (1994).

One problem, however, which we need to spend some time looking at, because of its fundamental nature and the amount of literature which has been devoted to its resolution, precedes any considerations of party placement strategies and challenges the starting premise of the link between voter preference and party policy-bundles, namely that the voter votes in the first place.

The paradox of voting: do rational voters vote?

Rational choice presents its proponents with what some might consider an ironic task: the explanatory power and parsimony which are its strengths also pose a thorny problem for the very application of rational choice to voting behaviour. Quite simply, if voters are rational, they should rarely if ever vote. If we return to the basic model, voters pick a party on the basis that they expect this party to maximize their utility. In a two-party system, they calculate the expected utility derived from the incumbent and from the opposition, and vote accordingly. If they see no differential – that is, there is no benefit to be had from either party in particular being in power – then they do not vote. However, we also know that voting itself incurs costs, so presumably the expected utility of voting should exceed the cost of voting. In the same way that we would not pay a £10 bank charge to close an account with £5 in it, so it makes no sense to vote if the expected utility is less than the cost of going to the polling station in the first place.

The key word here is *expected*. As is obvious from the entire electoral context, voting for the preferred party does not ensure that the voter gets what she wants. Indeed, the likelihood of casting a vote that is instrumental in ensuring that she gets the party of her choice – in other words, that cast the deciding vote – is very small indeed, at least in legislative elections. In economics and decision-theory, this probability is factored into the equation deciding the utility that the voter expects to gain, and is calculated as the value of the preferred outcome multiplied by the probability of that outcome. Taking a simple example first, if someone offers to toss a coin, and pay you £20 for heads, and nothing for tails, then the expected utility is $(.5 \times £20) = £10$.

But now we have a problem for voters. As we have mentioned, in a national election involving thousands of voters in a constituency or millions of voters at the national level, the probability of influencing the outcome with the deciding vote is tiny. Thus the expected utility of the vote is going to be a tiny fraction of the difference in value between the preferred party and the rejected party winning. Assume the utility of one party winning is £1000. If we estimate the probability of influencing the outcome, this could easily be as low as 1 in 100,000.[10] In this case, then, the expected utility is $£1000 \times .00001 = 1$ penny. So, as long as the costs of going to vote are less than one penny, the voter will vote. Otherwise, she will abstain. Whether voting costs one penny depends upon the voter's view of the value of not having to take time to go and vote, whether that cuts into free time or taking time off work which has to be made up later; the financial cost of getting to the voting booth, perhaps by car or public transport; and, as we have already seen, all the time and energy spent in deciding how to vote. In other words, it probably makes more sense for the rational voter simply to ignore voting, unless the difference between parties is truly enormous.

A number of amendments have been suggested to alter the rational model so that it can account for the inconvenient fact that many millions of people do turn out to vote. Some have been more successful than others.

Voting isn't costly

Downs himself saw the problem of costly voting, and suggested that voting might not be costly, in which case only those indifferent to the outcome for reasons of utility would abstain. Anyone with a preference would vote (1957: 261). Other authors have followed up on this (e.g. Niemi, 1976) by stating that the costs of voting are very small, and indeed one may look upon voting as an activity much like having a beer on the way home from work or reading to the kids (1976: 115). This suggests that people are in fact gaining a net benefit from the vote itself, rather than incurring costs. Presumably, if we perceived a net cost in having a beer on the way home from work, we wouldn't do it. As long as there is a cost to vote, this will always be likely to outweigh the expected utility given the low probability of influencing the vote.

Not voting is costly I – to the voter

A more radical consideration is that the vote itself is more than just an instrument of utility maximization from policy output. Niemi also mentions this, as well as Overbye (1995) and Bufacchi (2001). Voters wish to portray themselves as members of society who contribute to the good of the community, who take an interest in their fellow citizens and who can be trusted. This has nothing to do with altruism or civic-mindedness necessarily, but to do with the longer-term benefits which will accrue if this is how people around her perceive the voter. Not voting, on the other hand, could lead to ostracisation, a feeling that the non-voter is selfish and untrustworthy. People will not want to do business with this person. Reputation can have tangible repercussions. As Laver notes, however, could one not look at this from the opposite perspective – a rational individual will look at the *non*-voter and think, '"There's somebody I can do business with – a sensible person who doesn't waste time on the pointless act of voting."' (Laver, 1997: 97). Bufacchi also mentions that, if this instrumental motivation does pertain, then would it not be likely that fellow citiziens would be suspicious that the reputation-conscious voter was doing it precisely for those reasons, and not for reasons of civic-mindedness? (2001: 717). More generally, there is little evidence that people do think in this way about their fellow citizens.

Not voting is costly II – to democracy

Downs introduced another notion of 'cost' into the voting equation, which could apply if people did not vote. He termed this the 'long-term participation benefit', namely that by voting, voters ensured the continuation of democracy. If no-one voted, democracy would collapse – and the costs of this would far outweigh the cost of voting (1957: 269).[11] However, there is a fundamental problem with this explanation in terms of rational voters: in the same way that their vote is highly unlikely to influence the outcome, so the individual's vote is highly unlikely to save democracy in the long, or indeed short term. If others vote, then democracy is saved and the voter still need not turn out. The expected utility of saving democracy will be discounted by the probability that the voter's participation saves democracy – and in practice this means the expected utility will be nought (Barry, 1978: 20). As Blais also notes, it may well be that people do vote out of a feeling of bolstering democracy as a result, but this cannot be for rational reasons but rather for the good of the democracy itself, i.e. the community (2000: 3).

Voters have selective incentives to vote

The act of voting itself can be seen as providing a broader range of benefits, which have been broadly categorised as 'psychic gratification' (Green and

Shapiro, 1994: 49). In Downs' original formulation, the benefits which an individual would enjoy as a result of the election of his preferred party are not conditional on the individual voting. These are the 'collective goods' referred to in Chapter 1: the abstainer sees his utility maximised if his preferred party is elected despite not voting. Consequently, why subtract the cost of voting from this utility if the vote makes no difference? Similarly, voters will not have their utility maximised if the unfavoured party wins, but if their vote incurs additional costs, why compound the costs by voting needlessly in an election where the outcome will not be influenced by their vote?

However, many researchers have followed Riker and Ordeshook's (1968) lead by introducing selective incentives. In their formulation, they emphasise that many citizens feel that they have a duty to vote. Consequently, voters will reap the gain of satisfaction (a) from having behaved dutifully (and avoid the cost of feeling guilty for not having done so); (b) from demonstrating allegiance to the political system; and (c) of 'standing up to be counted' by supporting a party, *inter alia* (1968: 28). These satisfactions are not collective goods, because they depend on the voter turning out.

Downs excluded such considerations due to his tight definition of rationality, which precluded every motivation that did not have a political or economic motivation – a definition which is too tight according to Riker and Ordeshook (1968: 26). However, critics of the selective incentives explanation contend that to include broader notions of duty and intangible, psychological benefits goes contrary to the fundamental principle of rationality, namely that an individual's future self-interest is the primary motivation. Psychological benefits may well play a role, but they do not fit the rational framework (Barry, 1978: 15; Blais, 2000: 3).

Voters think they count

Because voting is an activity in which individuals participate together, the decision to vote and how to vote is not taken in isolation but with regard to how other people will vote as well. In other words, my decision will be influenced by what I assume other people will do. Consequently, it may be rational for me to vote if I make the assumption that other people will abstain. The argument can be made more nuanced, namely that if I believe that other voters will assess their likelihood of affecting the vote as very small, and consequently abstain, then they will not vote – and my vote has a greater chance of being decisive. As Ferejohn and Fiorina note, this makes for an endless chain of strategy, or as Downs termed it, 'conjectural variation' – 'If a citizen calculates according to the conventional analysis, he will decide to abstain. But all citizens will arrive at the same decision; therefore a smart citizen would vote and singlehandedly decide the election. And yet, other citizens would also follow this strategy, so maybe he should abstain after all. But if other citizens reason similarly, maybe ... and so forth. Clearly we have a highly complex situation.' (Ferejohn and Fiorina, 1974: 527)

Less strategically, voters may simply over-estimate the chance they have of affecting the overall outcome. For instance, campaign coverage and opinion polls may give them the impression that the race is extremely close and that there is everything to play for. Such information may mislead voters into thinking that there is a high chance that their vote will be decisive. In rational terms, however, such an explanation is not helpful – if voters can make such a fundamental error of judgement, is it reasonable that they will be able to engage any calculation of utility maximization? In the words of one author, we move from the paradox of not voting to the paradox of foolish voters (Schwartz, 1987, cited in Green and Shapiro, 1994: 55).

Finally, voters can fool themselves in another manner. Voters are aware that their preferred candidate needs to win votes from large numbers of voters to win, and their contribution to that will be minimal. As we have seen, the costs of voting as an individual are consequently very likely to exceed the benefits, given that the collective benefit will not require the individual's participation. However, the voter may be aware that the preferences they hold will be shared by many among precisely the group of voters who will secure this collective benefit. There is evidence from the psychological literature that such a voter may think, 'If someone like me goes to vote, then people like me will also go to vote.' (Quattrone and Tversky, 1988: 733).

Voters in this case are said to be unconsciously mistaking 'causal' contingencies – where what they do has an effect – with 'diagnostic' contingencies – where there is simply an association between what they do and what happens. As with the examples of the foolish voter and the causal/diagnostic mistake, such modifications do not save rational choice explanations. Instead they posit non-rational explanations as to why voters turn out. Critics of the rational choice paradigm conclude that if the paradigm cannot provide the means for its own survival, then it cannot be a useful explanatory framework.

The cost of regret

The last adaptation of rational choice theory to concern us here rejoices under the name of 'minimax regret' theory (Ferejohn and Fiorina, 1974). In an attempt to avoid the 'highly complex situation' explained above, they distinguish between decisions which are taken under the conditions of risk and those taken under conditions of uncertainty. Under the former, it is possible to assign probabilities to events, and this corresponds to the traditional rational choice approach. However, as Downs made clear, uncertainty is key to the relationship between parties and voters. Under these conditions, the probability of events is not known. Consequently, perhaps voters do not try to assess the probability of their vote being decisive, and so do not overestimate this. And discounting this explanation is useful in getting rid of the problem of the foolish voter – being uncertain of the probability, voters simply ignore this.

Instead, they work on the basis of the voter's reaction to the outcome of the decision (in this case, of the vote), i.e. when the event is knowable with probability of 1, because it has occurred. In essence, they ask what the reaction of the voter would be had she decided not to vote, and as a result her favoured candidate had lost by a single vote, or a draw had occurred when, if she had voted, her candidate would have won. Consequently, the voter's reaction will be one of regret – 'If only I had voted.' So before the election, the voter thinks '"My God, what if I didn't vote and my preferred candidate lost by one vote? I'd feel like killing myself."' (1974: 535) Whether self-destruction follows or not, the regret that would ensue is also calculated as a function of utility, but the theoretical premise is that the voter will decide to engage in the action which minimises the chance of maximum regret – hence minimax regret. Ferejohn and Fiorina derive a function which implies that the election of the candidate need only exceed a multiple of the cost of voting for the voter to turnout, a situation which is far more likely than the traditional model implies (1974: 528). Unfortunately, this last improvement also has problems, most tellingly that, despite being unable to calculate probabilities, voters are still capable of realising that one vote is not going to change anything (Aldrich, 1993: 259).

Conclusion: for what purpose rational choice?

'The function of theory is to explain behaviour and it is certainly no explanation to assign a sizeable part of politics to the mysterious and inexplicable world of the irrational.' (Riker and Ordeshook, 1968: 25)

Given the paradoxes engendered by rational choice, and the criticisms that have been raised against it, it might look like rational choice serves no use in explaining electoral behaviour. And indeed many critics of rational choice have been notoriously brusque in proclaiming the paradigm to be effectively useless. This is no doubt partly due to a certain fear on the part of non-'rational choicers', that this immensely popular paradigm has become (or at least, was becoming) a new orthodoxy in studies of politics, and a *sine qua non* of prestigious publishing and research. It is also true that many of the proponents of rational choice were fairly aggressive in consigning sociological studies in particular to the dustbin of social science history. Even those not claiming the omnipotence of rational choice could present it as objectively 'better' than other approaches and a new future for social science – '[A] rational choice model, if it can be made to work, offers more hope than any work in the Berelson tradition.' (Robertson, 1976: 181)

So, can it be made to work? What do rational choice theories offer as value added? A number of points can be made in the paradigm's favour as concerns voting behaviour. Firstly, the theory places the individual firmly at the centre of the analysis. The theories developed in the previous chapter referred to individuals, but in terms of their location in the social structure, group identity and social norms. Whilst these social elements are obviously pivotal in determining the voters' values and attitudes – after all, if the socialisation process does not perform this function, what does? – and has also formed the basis for mobilisation by political parties, the relationship between the different social aspects and their combined effect on vote has often remained vague, particularly in earlier literature. To boot, many of the assertions made by one political sociologist would turn out to be inaccurate in the empirical testing of another political sociologist. Compare the assertion of Lipset – 'Trade unions, for example, help to integrate their members in the larger body politic and give them a basis for the loyalty to the system' (1959a: 1) – with Butler and Stokes' finding that 'Although a man's Labour allegiance may owe more to prior beliefs than it does to his experience as a union member, his union involvement may heighten his political involvement.' (1971: 203).

Thus, just because we can map the empirical relationship between social structure and vote does not mean that we can understand *why* it occurs. Why specifically should individuals participate in group activity? Which group activity? What are their incentives? (Chong, 1995) Rational choice theory starts from precisely this point by specifying the mechanisms of individual decision-making which should pertain whatever the context. Consequently, if the theory is adequate, then it should help to explain individuals' behaviour within different contexts. Rather than looking for patterns and trends and then providing explanations as to why these might occur (the *inductive* approach) rational choice tries to come up with some first principles of behaviour which can then be tested against empirical reality (the *deductive* approach).

Secondly, many of the elements of rational choice theory have contributed to the development of separate fields and sub-disciplines, three of which we shall look at in the following chapters: issue models, economic models and the study of abstention. For issue models, one can see commonalties with the belief system work of Converse which we shall consider in Chapter 8. However, the explicitly spatial approach derives from Downs, Enelow and Hinich and their conceptualisations and operationalisation of political space. In the economic models, many of the starting assumptions are 'real-world' – political events and the state of the economy can affect the fortunes of those who are responsible for their management – but the way the individual uses these to make voting choices, looking retrospectively at how the incumbent has done, and then looking at the next term's prospects uses rational choice as its starting point (Fiorina, 1981). Finally, abstention may be approached inductively from the social perspective, and the bulk of empirical analyses have done so. However, as Blais has noted, most research into abstention started from the assumption that people did not turn out because they were distant from the political system and hence somehow abnormal (Blais, 2000: 141). Rational choice, on the other hand, shows that there may be perfectly good reasons not to vote – and, as we shall see in Chapter 7, these reasons may be becoming increasingly relevant in contemporary polities.

Overall, then, rational choice cannot necessarily explain everything, but it can give us insight into a process to form the basis for further testing of individual hypotheses. Similarly, however, the rational challenge has also presented a useful foil to the sociological tradition which had to react to criticisms of obsolescence and vague theorising. Some sociological analysis has tested rationality amongst voters for specific parties, for instance Communist parties (Korpi, 1971). Others have shown how the rational premises of individual action do not fully account for voting choice, and that there is still an important independent element of 'social determinism' at work (Weakliem and Heath, 1994). As a spur to development, then, rational choice has certainly been useful.

Summary box

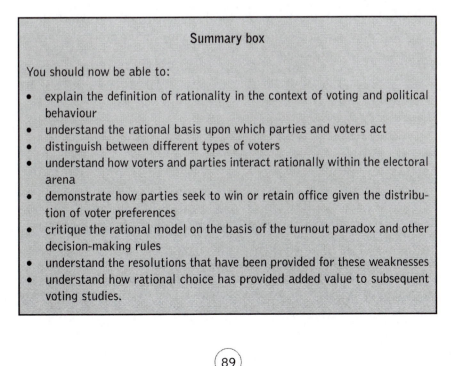

You should now be able to:

- explain the definition of rationality in the context of voting and political behaviour
- understand the rational basis upon which parties and voters act
- distinguish between different types of voters
- understand how voters and parties interact rationally within the electoral arena
- demonstrate how parties seek to win or retain office given the distribution of voter preferences
- critique the rational model on the basis of the turnout paradox and other decision-making rules
- understand the resolutions that have been provided for these weaknesses
- understand how rational choice has provided added value to subsequent voting studies.

Related reading

Aldrich, J. (1993) 'Rational choice and turnout', *American Journal of Political Science*, 37: 246–78.

Barry, B. (1978) *Sociologists, Economists and Democracy*, Chicago: University of Chicago Press.

Bufacchi, V. (2001) 'Voting, rationality and reputation', *Political Studies*, 49: 714–29.

Downs, A. (1957) *An Economic Theory of Democracy*, New York: Harper and Row.

Fiorina, M. (1981) *Retroprospective Voting in American National Elections*, New Haven: Yale University Press.

Friedman, J. (ed.) (1996) *The Rational Choice Controversy. Economic Models of Politics Reconsidered*, New Haven: Yale University Press.

Green, D. and I. Shapiro (1994) *Pathologies of Rational Choice Theory*, New Haven: Yale University Press.

Laver, M. (1997) *Private Desires, Political Action. An Invitation to the Politics of Rational Choice*, London: Sage.

McLean, I. (1982) *Dealing in Votes*, Oxford: Martin Robertson [Chapter 4].

Niemi, R. (1976) 'Costs of voting and nonvoting', *Public Choice*, 27: 115–19.

Olson, M. (1965) *The Logic of Collective Action*, Cambridge: Harvard University Press.

Overbye, E. (1995) 'Making a case for the rational, self-regarding "ethical" voter … and solving the "Paradox of not voting" in the process', *European Journal of Political Research*, 27: 369–96.

Quattrone, G. and A. Tversky (1988) 'Contrasting rational and psychological analyses of political choice', *American Political Science Review*, 82: 719–36.

Notes

1 Rational choice theories are often referred to as 'economic' theories of voting. This can lead to some confusion with regard to the theories which we will look at in Chapter 6, which are also referred to as economic theories. Whilst the latter theories are largely derived from rational choice and employ many similar assumptions, not all rational choice theory looks explicitly at the state of the national economy, for instance. Consequently, we will refer to the theories discussed in this chapter as 'rational choice' and the theories in Chapter 6 as 'economic'.

2 In most tests of rational choice theory and voting, a two-party system is used. Assuming that a grand coalition does not occur, sole tenure of government by a single party is implicit. However, a high-profile branch of rational choice concerns itself

with coalition formation and decision-making in multiparty government. See for instance Laver and Schofield (1990).

3 One could however argue that an incumbent with a much reduced majority might see this as a signal for some sort of change, despite being re-elected.

4 'Utiles' are an economist's common currency. Because rational individuals are always assumed to be calculating what their net gains and losses will be, we need to have a denomination of value. Currency is often too nation-specific and confusing – 'the voter makes a net gain of £48,000 from party A's election' brings all sorts of extra assumptions into the reader's mind – and in addition many of the items of utility that a rational individual may derive may not be quantifiable in real currency. 'Freedom from racial discrimination' is certainly a net gain in utility that one party may offer over another, but it is difficult to give it a price. Consequently, utiles are used as a umbrella unit of value for everything, regardless of real-world price.

5 We assume that the net financial and emotional cost to the rational voter of getting rid of the dog, and thus avoiding the licence fee, exceeds 1000 utiles.

6 Although, as we shall see in Chapter 6, there is evidence that governments do become unpopular over time, *ceteris paribus*. Whether this allows oppositions to identify and mobilise minorities in the way Downs suggests, however, is another matter. Unpopularity may relate to incompetence in enacting desired policies, as well as alienating supporters on their minority positions.

7 This theory epitomises one of the problems of rational choice theory, namely how imperfectly informed voters make such decisions. In this case, as Elster notes, how does a voter know that the information she may collect in future will exceed its value in collection costs? (Elster, 1986).

8 Another popular context is ice-cream sellers on a beach. The author is indebted to Jonathan Simon for this example.

9 The function of distance between party and voter has also been incorporated into probabilistic models of voting, whereby just because the party is the closest one to the voter does not mean that she will definitely vote for it. The greater the distance, the less likely she will be to vote for it. This is introduced in particular in some of the spatial models (e.g. Enelow and Hinich, 1984, 1990) which we will look at in Chapter 5.

10 Calculating the probability of casting the deciding vote depends on the number of voters and their party distribution in the constituency. Evidently, leaving aside draws, the other votes must vote exactly 50/50 for the two candidates or parties. Meehl adds that often the chances of casting the decisive vote in a Presidential election are roughly the same as being killed whilst driving on the way to the polls – 'hardly a profitable venture' (1977: 11).

11 This would not be the case for the indifferent abstainers, because they are aware that some people do have preferences, and so as long as these latter vote, democracy will be safe.

5

Issues and Space: Proximity and Directional Theories of Voting

Summary box

- Issues and the political process
- Collecting and using issues
- Voters and parties in political space
- Distance in space: the proximity function
- The directional challenge to proximity
- Resolving proximity and directional differences
- Issues in context.

Introduction

In contemporary polities, one word is probably given more coverage than any other in the general reasons why and how people vote – 'issues'. It is not difficult to see why. Voters as individuals have a range of concerns, some general, some specific, which influence how they lead their lives – what decisions they make, what behaviour they engage in and, more importantly in the context of politics, the effects that these decisions and behaviour have upon the individuals as they interact with their environment. In modern states, all individuals rely upon a range of actors – other individuals or groups – to supply economic, social and cultural goods and services. Of course, the vast majority of interactions between individuals and other actors are outside the realms of the polity: friends and family, and relationships with these, would all be included under the heading of interaction. But an important minority of these interactions are in areas where the state is responsible for defining the terms of such interaction and the means by which this takes place. Health-care; unemployment benefit; income support; housing; rules of the economic market; policing; justice – all are goods and services whose provision is defined through a framework put in place and amended by the incumbent government under the auspices of the state.

We have already seen in previous chapters how political parties traditionally develop ideologies which, through their views on what an ideal society should look like, suggest how to construct this framework. Given their tight linkage with the social structuration providing their electoral support, the policies of these parties generally represented the interests of their electoral pool as well as offering other groups in society sufficient incentives to ensure nothing more divisive than constructive opposition. More recently, the rational choice theories argued almost a mirror image to this view, as the last chapter showed. Under this framework, parties' principal aim is to divine the distribution of the electorate's views and position themselves accordingly to maximise the number of votes received. As we have discussed, this suggests that parties are driven by pragmatism, not ideology: the latter is important only in that this is derived from the optimum position perceived by the parties. However, in terms of deriving theories of voting, and particularly predictive theories, the two approaches have a commonalty: they suggest that voters' policy preferences will be close to the party for which they have voted.

Only in the case of a voter entirely devoid of any views on policies whatsoever – theoretically possible under a highly determinist account of social structural voting, but unlikely given the cognitive effect of mobilisation – would such an assumption be impossible to make. Of course, those concerns which motivate individuals to vote a certain way are not necessarily related to policies *per se*. They may instead relate to the personality of a candidate; the desire to send a wake-up call to the political class of a country by voting for an extreme candidate whose policies one doesn't really like; overall competence in managing the economy. Those elements relating to policies and ideology from the voter's point of view are what we will refer to as 'issues', and which the so-called issue theories and models of voting generally employ in their operationalisation.[1]

Collecting and using issues

That one can employ these issues empirically presupposes that data on them can be collected, and the expansion of survey research has allowed individuals' views on the health service, law and order, immigration and many other policy areas to be collected, both from the large-scale national election surveys carried out shortly before or after legislative elections and

Table 5.1 ***Issue saliency in vote choice***

Policy issues	% of respondents citing issue
Healthcare	68.2
Unemployment	51.7
Public transport	34.9
Environment	9.2
Defence spending	8.6
Other	7.4

Question: 'Which of the following policy issues had an influence on how you voted in the recent general election?'

also from cross-national comparative surveys, such as Eurobarometer and the World Values Survey. However, we are only interested in formalised notions of issue voting, and the vast majority of research employing voters' issue positions do not adopt any formalised framework.

Look at the following example (Table 5.1): in an imaginary post-election opinion poll carried out after an equally imaginary election, a cross-section of the voting population were given a list of issues and policy areas and asked to indicate which had been important in deciding how to vote.[2]

This table may tell us that healthcare was more important to people than the level of unemployment, which itself was more important than public transport, etc. However, it does not tell us *why* the above issues were important – was it because the respondents felt that greater spending was needed, or less spending? And it does not tell us anything about how the issue related to the party for which the respondents voted. In other words, from the perspective of voting theories, this information on its own is effectively useless. Yet many pieces of research about elections include similar tables. As part of a description of a particular election, this information is perhaps informative. Furthermore, if linked to the additional information that healthcare was important because the previous government had made massive and unpopular cuts in healthcare spending, leading to their defeat in the election, then we can begin to understand the context of this particular election and indeed the way in which healthcare spending was probably important to the majority of voters: they wanted more of it, and so voted for a party offering this.

But it is precisely in adding this supplementary information that we begin to make assumptions that are derived from more fundamental theories of issue voting. If we say that voters voted for a party which promised to spend more on healthcare than its opponent because of this promise, then we can make the assumption, just as the rational choice model did, that the voters were in some way *closer* to the party which they picked on this particular issue than the one they did not.

A second question which is less easily resolved concerns those individuals in the poll for the imaginary election who mentioned more than one issue. Given that there are '180 percent' of responses, a large proportion of the cross-section must have mentioned more than one issue. Perhaps some even mentioned three or four. Now we must ask ourselves, 'Were they all important to the same extent?' (Answer: probably not.) More fundamentally, 'Were some actually that important at all?' (Again, probably not.) These questions relate to so-called 'issue saliency'. In simple terms, some issues matter more than others in how people vote.

Say a voter has a choice between two parties. This voter is in favour of high spending on healthcare by the government and low spending on defence. In the election campaign, Party 1 promises high spending on healthcare by the government and high spending on defence. Party 2 promises low spending on healthcare and low spending on defence. If both issues are equally as important to the voter, then she has a problem choosing: both parties give her an outcome she wants and an outcome she does not. Unless there is some other criterion by which she can make her mind up, she is stuck. However, if we know that she is more concerned about healthcare getting a cash injection than the military seeing their budget cut, then she will vote for Party 1. It might not be the voter's ideal choice, but it is certainly the better of the two on offer.

Precisely this consideration is important in how different spatial theories are operationalised and this will be dealt with in the sections that follow.

Placing voters and parties in political space

The inference that voters are close to the parties for which they vote and distant from those they shun is represented quite explicitly by the methodology of spatial modelling. Such theories assume that there is a metric distance between voters' position on policies and issues and the parties' equivalent positions. As we shall see, the distance between the voters and parties signifies different things according to which theory is being tested. However, there is an underlying assumption common to all the theories, namely that there is variation in distance between a voter and the parties on offer; and that a function of this distance can identify the party which is chosen at an election by each voter.

How, then, are voters and parties placed in this artificial political space? The most effective means of doing this is simply to plot both of these groups according to a number of dimensions which correspond to the policies or issues of interest and which are generally measured using opinion poll or survey data. A simple example provides the best means of

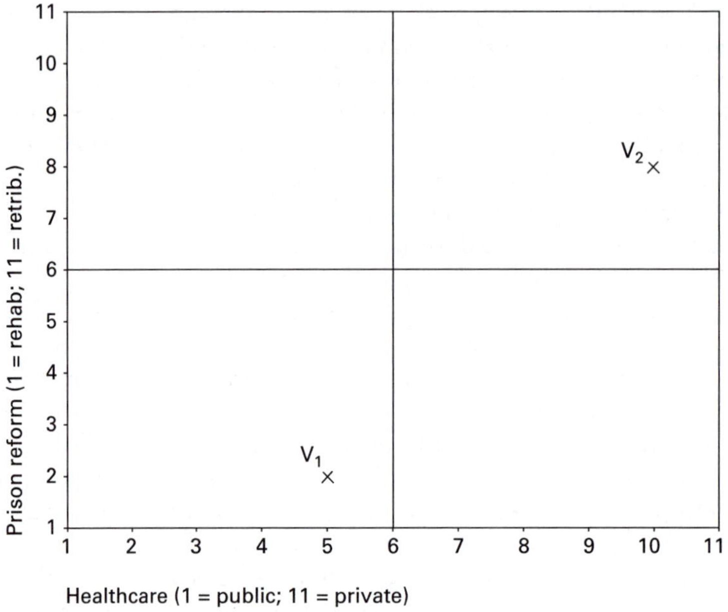

Figure 5.1 *Placing voters in two-dimensional policy space*

explanation. In Figure 5.1, we have located two voters, formally labelled V_1 and V_2, in a two-dimensional space defined by two policy areas, healthcare provision and prison reform.

The two dimensions have been constructed using two questions from an imaginary opinion poll survey. The one corresponding to healthcare provision asked:

'One of the key concerns in this country today is how much healthcare should be provided by the State, and how much should be provided by individuals using private insurance schemes and the like. Below is a scale, with one end representing the view that the State should provide all healthcare; and the other end representing the view that individuals should be responsible for all their own healthcare provision, together with that of their dependents. Where would you place yourself on such a scale?'

1 2 3 4 5 6 7 8 9 10 11

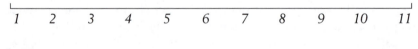

Public healthcare ***Private healthcare***

The one corresponding to prison reform asked,

'There are differing views as to what role prison should play in society. Some people think that prison should serve more as a means of retribution against those who have committed crimes in society. Others think that its principal function is to rehabilitate criminals so that they do not commit crimes again. Below is a scale, with one end representing the view that prison reforms should aim to provide the most effective means of retribution; and the other end representing the view that prison should aim to provide the most effective means of rehabilitation. Where would you place yourself on such a scale?'

1	2	3	4	5	6	7	8	9	10	11

Prison reform = rehabilitation ***Prison reform = retribution***

Each of these scales clearly provides eleven different positions, indicating different policy mixes, including a centre position (6) which is assumed to be a balanced position between the two sides. Fairly obviously the two voters have been placed in a two dimensional space simply by regarding one question as the x axis, another as the y axis and their positions plotted accordingly.[3] Reference lines have been included at position 6 on both scales to indicate where the balanced position between the two extremes is to be found. V_1 is moderately in favour of state healthcare and strongly in favour of prison rehabilitation; V_2 is conversely very strongly in favour of private healthcare provision, and moderately disposed towards prison as a system of retribution.

Of course, we also need to place the parties, and given that parties are not individual respondents in the way that our voters are, we cannot use a similar methodology. One strategy would be to use party policy documents, such as the party programmes as coded by the Comparative Manifesto Project, to scale a party's position on the same items. If the scale is not identical, normalisation could be used, whereby the scales are converted to an identical metric. However, we would still need to find an identical policy item to the one included in the voters' survey and this would not necessarily be available. The alternative, and more common strategy, is to use party positions on the same issue as the voters derived from questions in the survey which say 'Having now placed yourself on this scale, where would you place party P_1, P_2, P_3, … P_n to indicate their position on this policy?'.

A dilemma appears at this point. Quite simply, how do we plot the party according to these items? Granted, we have identical questions and scales to those used to position the voters, but do we use each individual's positioning of the different parties to map them, or do we use the overall population mean? Some researchers maintain that to use the individual voters' score is problematic on two counts (*Journal of Theoretical Politics*, 1997). Firstly, it risks becoming somewhat of a self-fulfilling prophecy to ask individuals to place themselves and parties on different policy scales, simply because the likelihood of an individual placing 'his' party closer to his own position is greater than doing so for a party for which he does not vote. Given what we know of the average voter's political knowledge, it is very likely that many survey respondents know what *they* feel about certain policies and issue, but, as far as their party is concerned, they may simply make the assumption that they follow a similar line.[4] In short, voters will bias their responses. Secondly, as we saw with the rational choice theory from which the original spatial theories derive, proponents of the objective mean position argue that there is a need to assume that parties have a single 'true' position in political space if the assumptions about party vote-maximisation strategies relating to voter distributions are to hold.

Their opponents, who support the use of individual or 'idiosyncratic' positions, maintain that it makes no sense to use the parties' average position across all voters because what matters are the individual's perceptions of where a party lies in policy terms. An individual's perceptions may be completely at odds with the rest of the electorate's perceptions, but the rest of the electorate's perceptions are irrelevant to the individual. To this argument, 'mean position' supporters reply that psychological research demonstrates that in fact voters tend to make up their minds about party's positions before elections using short-term information rather than previous perceptions, and as such all voters are receiving a common picture during the course of a campaign prior to an election. Thus the objective measure is superior on these grounds as well.

To date, there has been no satisfactory resolution of the debate for the disinterested observer. Both methods have their drawbacks – and, for the theories which follow, bias in favour of one or the other, thus prolonging the debate. Given that the aim of this book is to expound the different theories, failure to champion one of the two does not cause problems. We simply need to be aware of the debate. On this basis then, the party placements in Figure 5.2 may be regarded as either the mean or idiosyncratic policy positions of the two parties P_1 and P_2.[5]

A second dilemma is – having placed the parties and voters in a common policy space, what exactly do we want to predict from this? What is our dependent variable? The most obvious answer is 'which party do the

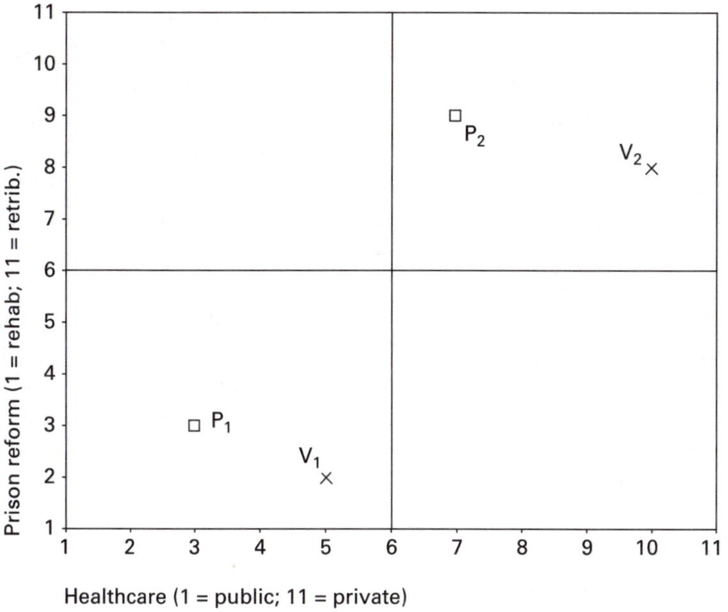

Figure 5.2 *Placing voters and parties in two-dimensional policy space*

individuals vote for?'. In other words, on the basis of a function of the distance between the voter and the different parties, can we predict which party the voter will choose? And indeed, many analyses will use a logit model to look at how many of the voters in their dataset can be correctly predicted using the distance function. However, this restricts researchers to using actual electoral outcomes and their connected surveys. Consequently, the scope of the models has been expanded to include how people *would* vote were there an election tomorrow; party identification; and in particular the 'thermometer scores' for parties and for individual candidates highlighted in Chapter 1. Given the use of this continous scale as the dependent variable, a variant of the linear model is the most common statistical technique employed in such cases.

Distance in space – the proximity function

The last choice to be made, and certainly the most important, comes down to defining exactly what the 'distance function' will be. As we have already seen in the previous chapter on rational choice theory, the Downsian model is based precisely upon perceived political space and distance between parties and voters. The distance function in this case will simply be the unit distance between the policy position of the voter and that of the party. Of course, utility maximisation does not necessarily imply that distance *per se* needs to be measured or that it needs to be represented spatially. However, as we saw in Chapter 4, the political analogy to Hotelling's shop positions does imply distance in terms of party's placing themselves on the 'street'.

Spatially, then, the implication is clear: other things being equal, the voter will choose the party which, in policy terms, is least distant from them. This is commonly known as the 'least distance hypothesis' or proximity theory. There are a number of ways in which this distance can be measured. Perhaps the most intuitively appealing is Euclidean distance using Pythagoras' Theorem. Simply, the distance between two points is the square root of the sum of the squared lengths of a right-angled triangle where the distance to be estimated forms the hypotenuse. Algebraically:

$$z = \sqrt{x^2 + y^2},$$

where z is the length of the hypotenuse, x is the length of the adjacent and y is the length of the opposite.

Figure 5.3 shows the example for V_1 in her choice of whether to vote for P_1 or P_2. The distance z_1 between V_1 and P_1 is calculated as $\sqrt{(1^2 + 2^2)} = \sqrt{(5)}$ = 2.24; and the distance z_2 between V_1 and P_2 is calculated as $\sqrt{(2^2 + 7^2)} = \sqrt{(53)}$ = 7.28. Consequently, other things being equal, she will vote for P_1. This example works in two dimensions, but the same logic applies to more or fewer dimensions. Clearly, in one dimension – along a Left–Right scale, for instance – the distance is calculated simply by subtracting the voter's score from the party's. In three or more dimensions, Pythagoras' Theorem remains valid, although we cannot depict this graphically. To understand this, notice how the two sides of the triangle other than the hypotenuse are each defined by a single dimension. In other words, in Figure 5.3, the horizontal side depicts the healthcare question, the vertical side depicts the prison reform question. The square root of the summed squares equates to the Euclidean distance.

If one wants to add more dimensions – say, a foreign policy issue – then one simply adds another term to the equation, so that

$$z = \sqrt{x^2 + y^2 + a^2 + \ldots + n^2},$$

where n^2 refers to the last dimension which one wishes to include. As we noted above, this is not the only unit of distance which is employed. Some researchers use the squared Euclidean distance, others the 'city-block metric', so called because it sums the absolute differences between parties and voters along the relevant dimensions. These different measurements are

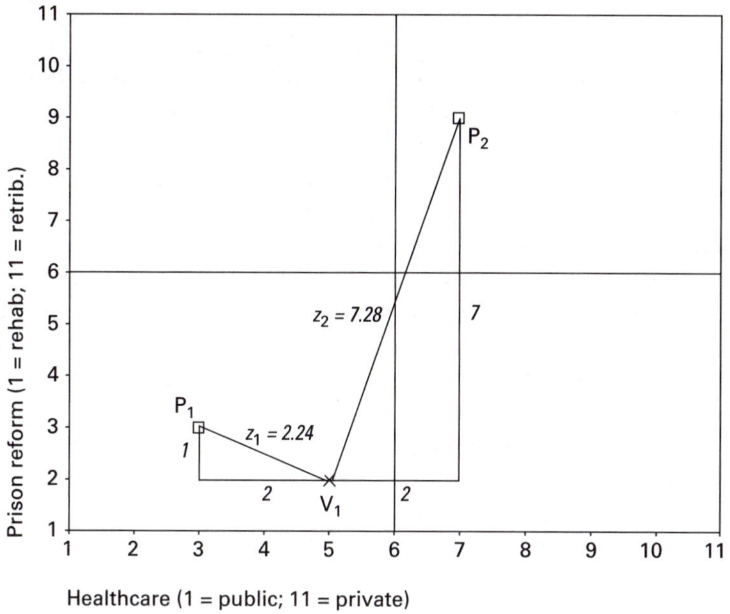

Figure 5.3 *Calculating euclidean distance between a voter and parties in two-dimensional policy space*

used because of their mathematical properties – for instance, the difference between a linear and quadratic function in the case of Euclidean and squared Euclidean distance. Whichever is used, however, the principle is essentially the same: a single index measuring the policy distance between party and voter.

Despite being intuitively appealing because it measures the actual spatial distance between the party and voter in our artificial *n*-dimensional political space, there is a drawback to a single index to which we alluded at the beginning of this chapter. Using such an index combining all issues clearly assumes equal salience amongst all issues dimensions. In other words, we are left with a single score for each party-voter distance, composed of equally weighted dimensions. This implies that the distance between a voter and the parties on offer along, say, an economic dimension will have exactly the same implication for the vote as any other issue: the economic dimension is no more or less important in this respect – and clearly, this is unlikely to correspond to reality.[6] Instead, some authors recommend using independent dimensions which are included in the model separately.[7] Thus, instead of including a single index for all dimensions, we can include a variable based upon the healthcare dimension, another based upon prison reform, a third based upon the environment and so on. This then allows us to test precisely for the differing impacts of the issues.

However, this method is not without its disadvantages either. Principally, the more issues we include the less room for manoeuvre we have in including other variables in our model. Assuming that we have a limited number of cases upon which to test our theory, the more separate variables we throw into the equation, the less confident we can be of our findings. Including a large number of issues in a single index may fall down for being arbitrary and lacking parsimony – we should be selecting our predictors on a theoretical basis, not just including everything we can think of – but at least we only have to include a single score for each respondent, rather than a host of them. As usual with such dilemmas, there is no 'correct' answer: if there is good reason to believe that the dimensions in question are independent and equally salient, then an index is an acceptable choice. If, however, relative saliency is of interest to the researcher and only a small number of dimensions need to be included, then it is more satisfactory to include individual variables.

Directional theory's challenge to proximity

Until recently, the proximity function was the accepted theoretical norm for modelling party and self-placement data. In keeping with its rational choice roots, it was challenged for the reasons discussed in Chapter 4. Many authors offered nuanced proximity models whereby a great element of reality was introduced into the models to correct perceived flaws. For instance, Grofman (1985) produced his 'discounting' model, whereby the expectations of voters as to what parties could actually achieve once in government, given the policy status quo prior to their election, were used to predict *expected* shifts rather than *ideal* shifts. This provided an explanation of why parties did not always converge on the median voter. Similarly, many authors relaxed the rational choice assumptions about parties' vote-maximisation strategies and voters' maximising utility and simply used the idea of proximity to look at more generalised attitudinal dimensions, such as liberalism-conservatism and libertarian-authoritarian scales, and their relationship to vote. We will look at this further in Chapter 8.

However, until the late 1980s, very few had offered a viable alternative framework to challenge the rational choice and proximity assumptions.[8] Thus, the proximity explanation almost enjoyed supremacy by default. In 1989 in an article in the *American Political Science Review*, Rabinowitz and Macdonald threw down the gauntlet to the proximity model by 'presenting and testing an alternative spatial theory of elections that we argue has

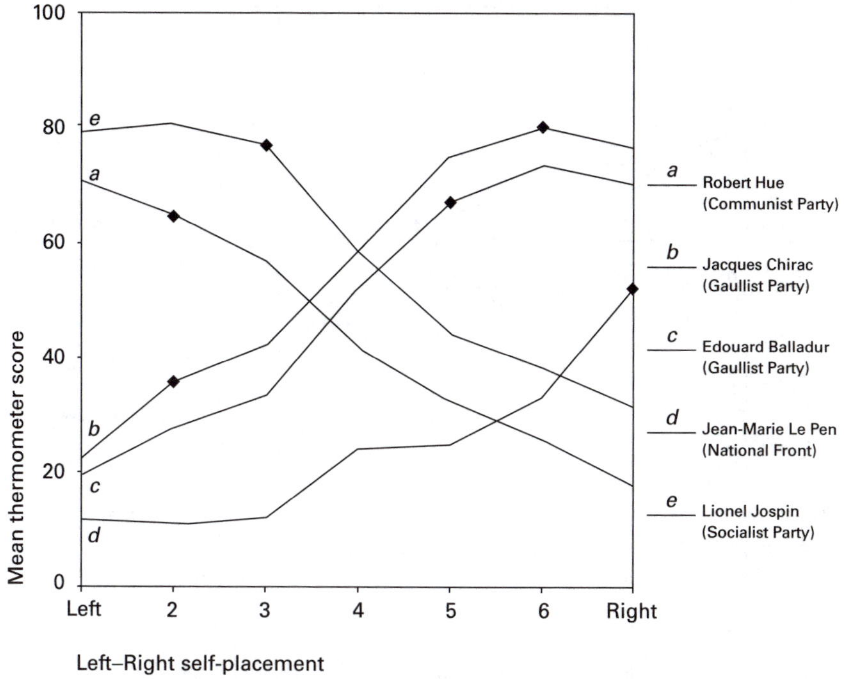

Figure 5.4 *Mean thermometer scores for candidates according to voters' left–right self-placement (France, 1995)*

Source: SOFRES 1995 French presidential election survey data

greater empirical verisimilitude' (Rabinowitz and Macdonald, 1989: 93) – their *directional* theory.

Before considering the bases to and assumptions of this theory, we can gain an insight into why it was needed, and why it may contradict the proximity theory, by considering two very basic depictions of voter preferences for political candidates according to the voters' Left–Right self-placement. Figures 5.4 and 5.5 have been plotted using electoral survey data from 1995 in France and 1993 in Norway, respectively. In the Norwegian case, the x axis represents where Norwegian voters placed themselves on a ten-point Left–Right spectrum. (Those who did not place themselves or refused to answer have been excluded.) The lines use the thermometer scores for the main political parties. The French graph is very similar, except that it uses a seven-point Left–Right spectrum and the thermometer scores for the five main presidential candidates in the 1995 presidential election.[9]

Let us consider how to interpret these lines. Firstly, it is clear that most candidates and parties are more popular (have higher thermometer scores)

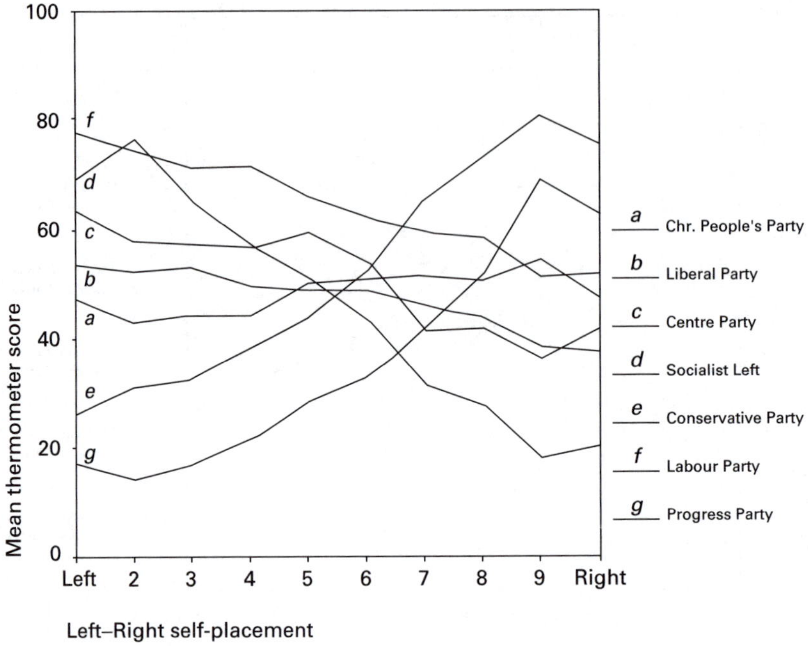

Figure 5.5 *Mean thermometer scores for parties according to voters' left–right self-placement (Norway, 1993)*

Source: NES 1993 Norwegian legislative election survey data

on one side of the spectrum. For instance, Edouard Balladur in Figure 5.4 is more popular on the Right, and the Norwegian Labour Party in Figure 5.5 is more popular on the Left. This is precisely what we would expect, given that the Labour Party is a party of the Left, and Balladur was a Right-wing conservative party candidate. But if the proximity theory is to believed, what we would expect to see more precisely is:

1. The voters whose placement is closest to the candidate's/party's own placement being the most 'warm' towards the candidate/party in question;
2. The voters becoming less warm to the candidate the further they are from the candidate's position.

Using the median Left–Right placement scores for the French presidential candidates (indicated by the black diamond on each candidate's line in Figure 5.4), then, these should be the peak of support for the candidates according to the proximity model. Are they?

In some cases yes, in some cases no. Allowing for the small number of positions on the *x* axis, ideally we would expect to see a smooth inverted-U curve peaking at the candidate's own position. In some cases, this inverted U is visible, but often the peak is *after* the candidate's own position. For instance, Lionel Jospin's greatest support comes from those at position 2, one position to the Left of his own median placement. Furthermore, support may not peak at position 1, but it is still higher than position 3. For an extreme candidate such as Jean-Marie Le Pen, the leader of France's Extreme Right National Front party, it is impossible to tell: as he is on the furthest position to the Right, we do not have any positions further to the Right to see whether or not the thermometer scores drop. But for more moderate candidates, the median-oriented inverted U is somewhat of a leap of faith to make.

Equally as worrying, in the Norwegian case the three parties generally accepted to be centrally located along the Left–Right continuum – the Christian People's Party, the Centre Party and the Liberals – all have very flat scores from Left to Right. The differences as one moves across the spectrum are minimal, and certainly there is no evidence of an inverted U peaking at the centre. Of course, there are many intervening factors which may be responsible for diverting the line – measurement error; the personalities of the candidates which may warm or cool voters' views of them, irrespective of ideological position; familiarity with the candidates may have the same effect. However, in the current context, the question to ask is the following: if I had to pick an 'ideal' shape to match each line on the graph, would I pick an inverted U? Or would I be better off picking a straight line? Looking at Figures 5.6a and 5.6b, which has taken the Labour Party example from the 1993 Norwegian data, which shape would provide the better fit?[10]

Supporters of the directional theory would in all likelihood advise picking the straight line (Figure 5.6a) and reject the inverted U (Figure 5.6b) of the proximity theory. The theoretical reasons for this form the basis for the directional model, and essentially come down to how to interpret the self-placement and candidate placement data taken from the surveys.

As we have seen in Chapter 4, most individuals are not particularly knowledgeable about political issues or indeed about their own candidate or party's exact position on all policy matters. This is why they use information short-cuts or heuristics in their decision on how to vote. As we have also seen in the critique of rational choice theory, it is unlikely that most voters can detail the exact policy positions of the parties and candidates or indeed for themselves, let alone shrink these down to an accurate single position for each actor on the Left–Right continuum. And yet, the rational choice theories and the proximity spatial theories *do* work to a certain extent. If the survey data upon which they are based are riddled with

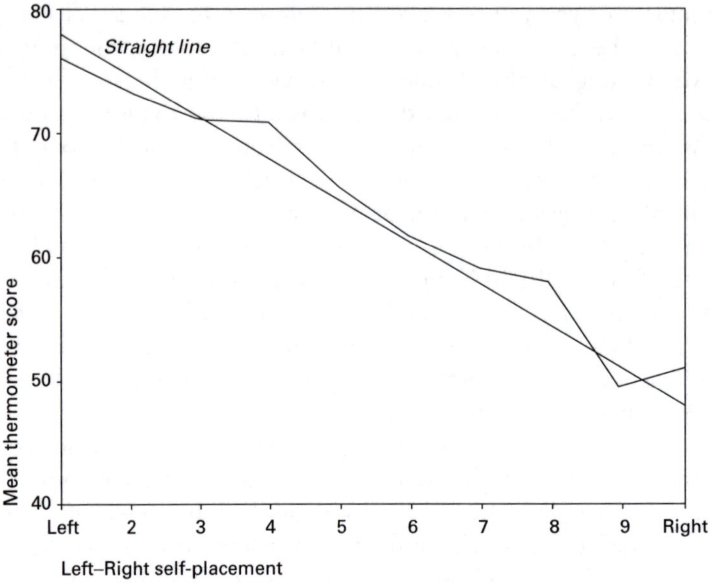

Figures 5.6a *'Curve-fitting' for Norwegian Labour Party thermometer score according to voters' left–right self-placement: the directional 'straight line'*

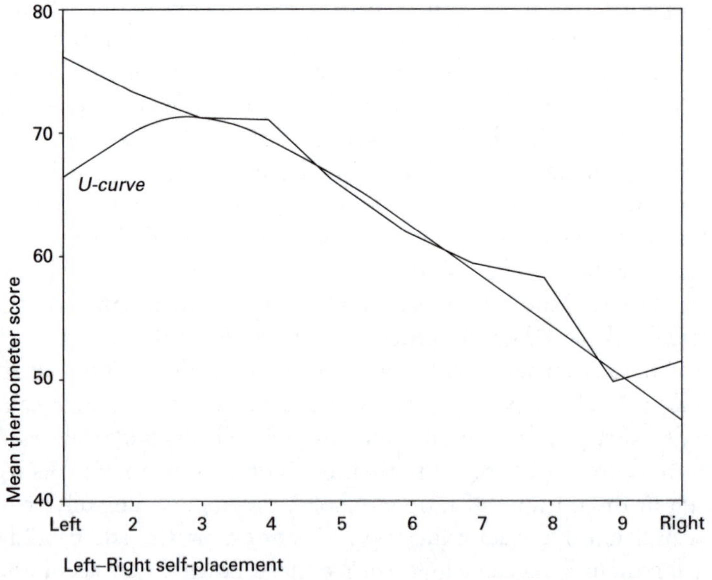

Figure 5.6b *'Curve-fitting' for Norwegian Labour Party thermometer score according to voters' left–right self-placement: the proximity 'inverted U-curve'*

errors, top-of-the-head responses and other arbitrary allocations, we would not expect the data to provide much of a pattern whatsoever. Directional theorists argue that this is because the data is valid, but that it is being interpreted wrongly.

They argue that, when voters place themselves and parties on a scale, whether Left–Right or a more focused policy-dimension, they are not summarising a specific policy-bundle at all, but instead are subconsciously performing a simple two-step psychological 'calculation'. For themselves:

1. On which 'side of the fence' am I situated as regards this dimension?
2. How strongly do I feel about this issue?

They then do much the same calculation for the parties and the candidates, although the strength of feeling element is probably better interpreted in this case as the clarity and vociferousness with which the political actor talks about such an issue. In the terminology of psychology, there is a 'cognitive' element – side of the fence – and an 'affective' or emotional element – strength of feeling.

This interpretation of how voters are responding to issues and politics in general is in many ways more satisfying as an explanation of their consequent placements on a scale. Looking at the two issues we used to illustrate the proximity theory – healthcare and prison reform – both can be seen in dyadic terms, that is, both have two fundamental sides to the argument. In the former, the conflict is essentially public versus private healthcare; in the latter, the conflict is essentially 'prison as reformatory' versus 'prison as punishment block'. And indeed many, if not most, political issues tend to come down to two conflicting views.

This does not mean that there is not a whole range of views in between, and that some people do not hold these views and explain the famous 'policy-bundles' which are associated with each. But for the majority of people, the psychological explanation is more apt. 'On balance, am I someone who favours rehabilitation or retribution as the principal goal of prison? I'm in favour of punishing criminals – I'm "retribution". Now, how strongly do I feel about punishing criminals? Well, I think they should be locked up 24 hours a day in their cells and denied TV and radios. Then they won't be in a hurry to steal cars again.' On that basis, our respondent can probably be placed towards the extreme end of our prison reform scale. Evidently, he has a simplistic view of prison reform compared to political parties and politicians – but that is precisely the point that the directional model and the social psychological research from which it derives make. On most issues, most people have basic tendencies and strength of feeling rather than sophisticated policy-stances.

How does this affect their views of political parties and candidates, and consequently their choice amongst these at an election? The key assumption that the directional theory makes is that, having chosen a side of the political fence and given the strength of affective intensity which they feel on the issue, voters will prefer parties which have clearer positions on the issue to those with more mixed positions. Additionally, the party should preferably have a clearer policy stance than the voter. This is where the interpretation of the centre varies radically between the proximity and directional theories. In the case of proximity theory, the centre has been seen as an equidistant 'midpoint' policy position or policy-bundle. Moreover, under rational choice assumptions and a normal distribution of voter preferences, the centre point as defined by the median vote is the vote-maximising or equilibrium position.

Under the directional theory, the centre has no such policy or indeed competitive value. From a policy perspective, it indicates a 'neither nor' or 'don't know' position – no choice of sides and no affective intensity. For a party it indicates no stance on an issue. Given the assumption that voters want a clear stance, the centre position is the losing position, contrary to the proximity theory. Thus, the directional theory provides a possible explanation as to why parties do *not* converge on the centre – it would be a vote-*minimising* strategy.

Secondly, unlike the proximity theory, the directional theory implies that equal distance – and indeed distance in general – does not equate to equal propensity to support a party or candidate. What matters is the relative position of party and voter on the dimension in question. Take the one-dimensional example presented in Figure 5.7.

Voter V has a choice between three parties, P_1, P_2 and P_3. Under the proximity theory, she would choose P_1, given that the distance is the smallest. However, under the directional theory, P_1 is out of the question as a choice because it is on the other side of the fence from V: P_1 falls at the cognitive hurdle. P_2 and P_3 both clear this hurdle, but according to the affective assumption, V will prefer P_3 to P_2, other things being equal, because P_3 has the clearer or more intense stance on the issue.

Operationalising a directional model

How can one operationalise this dimension, then, in order to take into account both the cognitive side of the fence and the affective intensity? The easiest way is simply to shift the scale so that, instead of being 1 to 10 or 0 to 10 or whatever has been chosen, the values are now a balanced scale around a 0 midpoint – for instance, –5 to +5.[11] This provides a scale

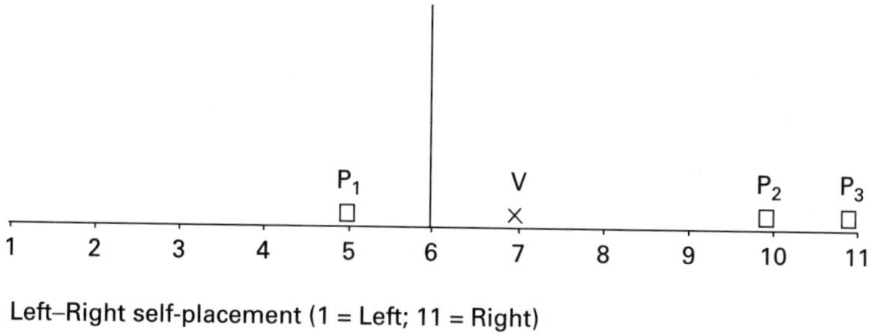

Figure 5.7 *Contradictions in vote prediction between proximity and directional models*

conforming intuitively to the dyadic nature of an issue – negative versus positive and an indifferent or 'null' centre. Subsequently, the *product* of the voter and party scores is used rather than the difference. Thus, rescaling the array from Figure 5.7, as in Figure 5.8, and providing the product scores of V and the respective parties, we can see that P_3 produces the largest score and thus indicates the party winner. In this case, the proximity and directional models predict different outcomes from each other. Of course, situations can easily pertain where they predict similar outcomes: a party which is more extreme than a voter may equally well be the closest party.

This also explains why we offered the reader the possibility of choosing a straight line rather than an inverted U-curve as the ideal shape to fit the Labour Party's curve in Figure 5.6b. If one calculates the product scores for a party against all positions, the highest score will be at one extreme – that on the side of the party itself – and the lowest score will be at the other extreme. The line in between will be straight – that is, there is a monotonic relationship. Furthermore, the highest product score possible will be one where both voter and party are situated at one extreme of the spectrum. Conversely, parties towards the centre will have a small range of scores. If we calculate the possible range of scores on an eleven-point spectrum, ranging from +5 to –5:

Party position:	–5	Range of possible product scores:	–25 to +25
Party position:	+5	Range of possible product scores:	+25 to –25
Party position:	+1	Range of possible product scores:	+5 to –5
Party position:	0	Range of possible product scores:	0

Therefore, if we assume that there is a positive association between product score and thermometer score, then parties towards the centre of the spectrum

Product scores:

$V \cdot P_1 = (1 \times -1) = -1$

$V \cdot P_2 = (1 \times 4) = +4$

$V \cdot P_3 = (1 \times 5) = +5$

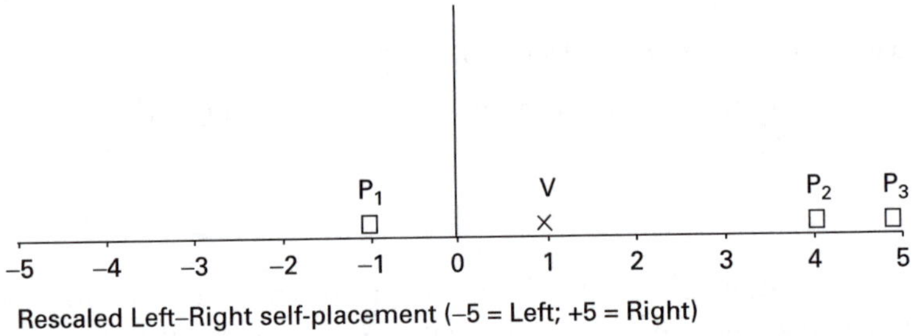

Figure 5.8 *Calculating directional product scores in one-dimensional space*

will only elicit moderate levels of sympathy (and indeed of animosity) from the electorate. Thus, in Figure 5.5, the centre parties' thermometer scores across the spectrum remained fairly moderate and did not shift significantly – the flat line which we noted.

As with the proximity model, a single index can be calculated in *n*-dimensional space, although it is slightly more complicated than the Euclidean distance or its alternatives used in that model. Because of the intensity component which needs to be taken into account for both party and voter, the distance between the two actors cannot be used as a measure. Instead the product scores are calculated using the following formula:

$$\text{Product score} = |P_n| \times |V| \times (\cos P_nV),$$

where P_n is the party vector – that is, the distance from the neutral centre point to the party policy-position – V is the vector from the neutral centre point to the voter position, and cos P_nV is the cosine of the angle between these two vectors. In two dimensions, the relevant elements are depicted in Figure 5.9, although as with Euclidean distance, the same formula holds in any number of dimensions – the party and voter vectors simply need to take into account the other dimensions.[12]

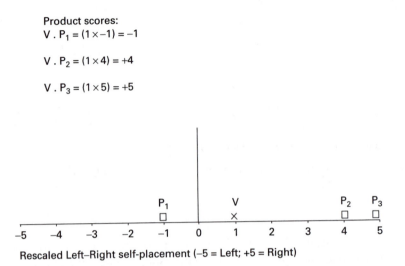

One of the interesting geometric properties of the cosine of an angle is that the cosine of 0 is equal to 1; the cosine of 90 is equal to 0; and the cosine of 180 is equal to –1. Imagine a two-dimensional example, where a party has position 0 on issue A and a position plus some level of intensity

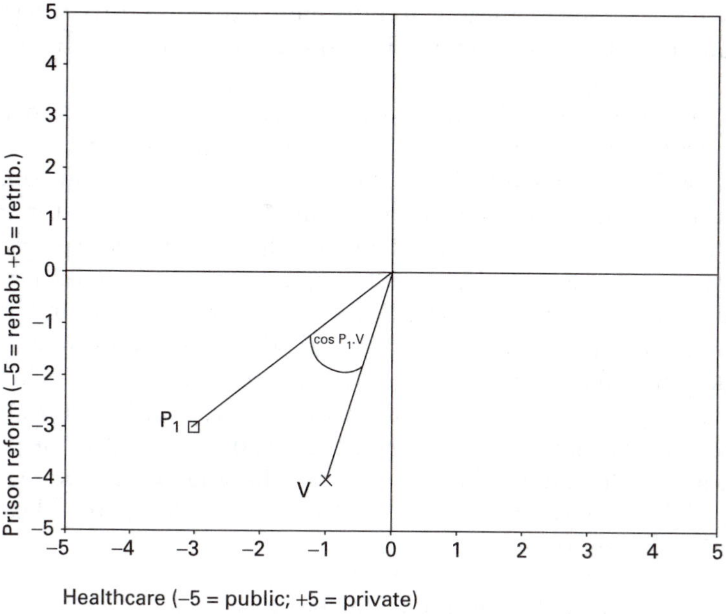

Figure 5.9 *Calculating directional product scores in two-dimensional space*

on issue B; a voter has a position plus some level of intensity on issue A and position 0 on issue B. If we draw this, it becomes clear that, no matter what intensity is allocated to the party on issue B and the voter on issue A, the angle between the two vectors will always be 90 degrees. In real terms, the voter does not care about issue B, but on issue A the party does not have a stance. Thus, the product scores are 0 for both issues – equivalent to the cosine of 90 degrees. Using similar examples for the 180 degree angle would depict a voter and party opposed on both issues – hence a negative product score, but this time dependent on the intensity with which the party and voter are opposed.[13]

These geometric properties have beauty in their simplicity, but alone they fall short of the mark in mirroring reality. There is a final element which needs to be introduced into the directional theory if it is to be satisfactorily operationalised. Looking at Figure 5.8, it becomes clear that the directional theory potentially makes a prediction as erroneous as the proximity theory's 'centre-seeking winners' that it seeks to refute. The largest product scores will derive from parties who are on the extremes of the spectrum. In other words, the clearest position is also the most extreme one. As such, all parties should try to move to the edge of the spectrum, i.e.

become as extreme as possible, and the more extreme a party, the greater its vote share should be. But real life tells us that extremist parties rarely win.

To correct this fault, the directional theorists make the assumption that there exists what they refer to as a 'region of acceptability' beyond which parties will be penalised for going. In simple terms, voters want parties to have a clear line on an issue, but not many want it so clear that it crosses over into extremism. In a directional model, the region of acceptability is a way of introducing a penalty when testing the theory which discounts the actual support, whether measured by a thermometer score or in terms of proportion of the vote, that a party outside this region will win. How one decides where this region starts varies, and is open to criticism. One method is to identify those parties in a system which are regarded as extreme, find their most proximate 'acceptable' neighbour, and then calculate the penalty according to the distance between the two. In other words, the region of acceptability begins after the last moderate party. This method begs two questions, however:

1. Can we assume that what is acceptable to one voter is acceptable to all voters?
2. Can we assume that the last 'moderate' party has stopped just on the bounds of acceptability?

In short, this version of the region of acceptability is an *ad hoc* addition to the theory to allow successful modelling: it prevents the model from making absurd predictions about systems with extremist parties, but without modelling the region of acceptability as a function of the array of parties and voters. An alternative means of defining the region of acceptability and doing so in a way which is idiosyncratic to each voter – i.e. which resolves both of the above questions – also helps to resolve the apparent contradictions of the proximity and directional theories, and instead allows the combination of the two in a single model. Perhaps unsurprisingly, given the prevalence of the proximity model and the lack of viable alternatives for many years, the rivalry between proponents of directional and proximity theory has elicited a number of academic debates in the literature.[14] However, this does not mean that, despite their apparently very different assumptions and consequently predicted outcomes, the two theories are not complementary rather than simply incompatible.

Iversen (1994) and Merrill and Grofman (1999) suggest that implicit in voter choice are elements of both proximity and directional theory. Essentially, they argue that voters do indeed look for parties with stances which are clear and in the same political camp as themselves but that, as the distance between the party and the voter grows, so the voter's support for the party will gradually wane. In terms of the region of acceptability, the implication is that each voter's region will be conditional upon their own position in political space. Using quadratic Euclidean distance (that is the Euclidean distance squared) and the directional product, they show that, in deciding between or evaluating parties or candidates which are relatively close, voters will employ a directional logic to their decision. However, as the parties become more distant, they will increasingly employ a proximity logic.

Finally, they add the Grofman 'discounting' function to the equation to reflect the fact that voters assess parties realistically rather than ideally. Again, the model is open to criticism: the authors favour idiosyncratic party and candidate placements and also employ an index rather than individual issue dimensions. However, to date this provides the most complete formal model of issue voting, encompassing both the rational choice elements of the proximity model and the psychological processes of the directional equivalent.

Conclusion: issues in context

As Macdonald, Rabinowitz and Listhaug note (1998), one can test theories of issue voting simply by including different issues in a model and seeing the relative predictive strength of these regarding vote. However, they emphasise that such models are under-specified. In other words, they do not take into account other influences on vote that may bias the results when issues alone are included.[15] For instance, certain parties or candidates may do consistently better than their competitors not for reasons related to their issue positions *per se* but because of their personality or that of their leader – precisely one of the intervening factors that the Michigan model hypothesised between party identification and vote.

Moreover, by simply including issues directly into a model, we cannot assess the extent to which sociodemographic variables are affecting vote. It may well be, for instance, that people over the age of 65 have a consistently different view of certain candidates or have a greater propensity to vote for a certain party than people under that age. Similarly, it may be that those over the age of 65 are significantly more likely to support public healthcare provision, irrespective of their other views. Thus, if we do not include these variables in our issue model of voting, we cannot discern what is the effect of issues and what is the effect of sociodemographics or other non-issue effects. We consequently need to include these as control variables so that we can be confident that the effects we see are the independent effects of the issues themselves and nothing more.

This should remind us of an important broader consideration when looking at such individual-level predictors. As we noted in Chapter 2, a number of contextual reasons led to the use of individual-level data, such as the advent of survey research, the improvements in technological capacity and concomitant refinements in social science statistical techniques which allowed the use of such data. Over the past thirty years, the combination of these advances with the undoubted socioeconomic and politics shifts in post-war democratic societies has led to increasing emphasis being given to the individual predictors such as issue positions, economic models (Chapter 6), protest voting and the like, and – perhaps pre-emptively – less time devoted to social structural models.

This should in no way be taken as an indication that issue theories and their individual-level counterparts have somehow disproved social structural theories, or shown that they are wrong. Firstly, an issue model without sociodemographic controls tells us absolutely nothing about the role sociodemographics may be playing 'behind the scenes' and consequently distorts our view of the role issues are really playing. Secondly, we should not forget that no matter how strong the relationship between an independent, explanatory variable (an issue position) and a dependent, effect variable (vote), no statistical model can prove causality. Our only proof is the solidity of our theory, and a continual testing and retesting of this theory to show that the relationship we have hypothesised still pertains. Consequently, when we look at an issue model and see a high level of significance in the relationship between vote and a certain issue, are we sure that the issue *per se* is important, or is this issue acting as a proxy for something else – a more general political attitude or proclivity, for instance? The more generalised attitudinal models we refer to in Chapter 8 make such an assumption, rather than referring specifically to concrete policies and issues.

Thirdly, and most importantly from our perspective, 'issues matter, so social structure doesn't' is a fallacious leap (albeit one made all too often). As the sociological theories made explicitly clear to us, our positions on issues, on policies, our interaction with the outside world, all decisions we make – they are all heavily influenced if not entirely determined by our context and by our socialisation, particularly in the early years of our life. As such, why would someone's position on healthcare *not* be related to their social context – occupation, income, class background, and so on?

To reiterate our conclusions from Chapter 3, one would be very ill advised to assert that nothing had changed in terms of social structure. Obviously the old Marxist dichotomy of working/middle class is no longer applicable. Such fundamental cleavages as class and religion may no longer play as strong and independent a role in mobilising broad sections of society. But this does not mean that social structure is now entirely absent or entirely without effect. The new social structures within which younger cohorts have grown up and will continue to grow up will surely influence their views and beliefs. In brief, voters' positions on issues clearly matter in terms of how they vote, but we must not forget to ask ourselves where those positions stem from.

As we shall see in the following chapters, the same logic must be applied to such matters as economic voting and abstention – areas of voting which might not initially seem to be linked directly to social structure. Otherwise, in employing individual level data, we risk hypothesising a world of entirely isolated individuals locked into their own unique decision-making procedures – a hypothesis which is chaotic, devoid of pattern and, fortunately, wrong.

Summary box

You should now be able to:

- explain how issues relate to the political process
- understand how to measure issues using survey data
- place parties and voters in *n*-dimensional space and calculate the distance between them
- explain the basic assumptions of proximity theory [remember to review the rational choice theory in Chapter 4]
- critique the proximity theory and explain the added value provided by the directional alternative
- calculate the product scores and vectors needed to operationalise the directional theory
- explain how the two theories are complementary rather than contradictory
- comment on the place of issues in a broader theoretical context.

Related reading

Enelow, J. and M. Hinich (eds) (1984) *The Spatial Theory of Voting: An Introduction*, New York: Cambridge University Press.

Grofman, B. (1985) 'The neglected role of the status quo in models of issue voting', *Journal of Politics*, 47: 230–7.

Iversen, T. (1994) 'Political leadership and representation in Western democracies: a test of three models of voting', *American Journal of Political Science*, 38: 45–74.

Journal of Theoretical Politics (1997), special edition – 'Symposium: the directional theory of issue voting', 9: 1.

Listhaug, O., S. Macdonald and G. Rabinowitz (1994) 'Ideology and party support in comparative perspective', *European Journal of Political Research*, 25: 111–49.

Macdonald, S., G. Rabinowitz and O. Listhaug (1998) 'On attempting to rehabilitate the proximity model: sometimes the patient just can't be helped', *Journal of Politics*, 60: 653–90.

Matthews, S. (1979) 'A simple direction model of electoral competition', *Public Choice*, 34: 141–56.

Merrill, S. and B. Grofman (1999) *A Unified Theory of Voting: Directional and Proximity Spatial Models*, Cambridge: Cambridge University Press.

Middendorp, C., J. Luyten and R. Dooms (1993) 'Issue-voting in the Netherlands: two-dimensional issue-distances between own position and perceived party position as determinants of the vote', *Acta Politica*, 1: 39–59.

Pierce, R. (1995) *Choosing the Chief. Presidential Elections in France and the United States*, Michigan: University of Michigan Press [esp. Chapters 5 and 7].

Rabinowitz, G. and S. Macdonald (1989) 'A directional theory of voting', *American Political Science Review*, 83: 93–121.

Westholm, A. (1997) 'The illusory defeat of the proximity theory of electoral choice', *American Political Science Review*, 13: 277–90.

Notes

1 In this chapter, we refer mainly to the proximity and directional theories, i.e. the spatial theories of issue voting, because these are the principal frameworks which have been used in the voter-oriented literature.

2 The respondents were allowed to give more than one choice, and so the percentages in the table add up to more than 100.

3 By plotting the positions on *x* and *y* axes, the so-called 'orthogonality' of the axes – that is, the fact that they meet at 90 degrees – means that the two policies are regarded as independent: whatever position someone has on one policy has no bearing on the position they have on the other policy. If one were to visualise a situation where one axis met the other at a slanted angle, then moving along one axis would also change one's position on the other. Such a situation would mean that the dimensions, and thus the policies, were not independent, i.e. they were correlated with each other.

4 Another common complaint by the 'individualists' is that unsophisticated voters may not know party positions on policies, but will provide essentially random responses anyway. To eliminate this, one may use only the responses of sophisticated voters – selected using a threshold score on a short political quiz included in the

survey – to place the parties. This will not eliminate response bias due to voters' own political tendencies, but it will eliminate the random responses.

5 Those interested in following the debate should refer to Appendix 4.3 in Merrill and Grofman (1999) which, although coming down firmly on the side of idiosyncratic positioning of parties, provides an excellent overview of the literature beforehand.

6 Clearly, the more dimensions which are subsumed in a single index, the more information is lost. Indices subsuming two dimensions are fairly common and have generally been considered robust, however. See for instance Middendorp, Luyten and Dooms (1993).

7 For examples of such models, see Pierce (1995: 125–9) and Macdonald, Rabinowitz and Listhaug for a justification of their use (1998: 660).

8 Some early work on the directional model began in the 1970s by Rabinowitz (1978) and by Matthews (1979) but it was only later that this work became salient enough to challenge the rational choice-based work.

9 In both countries, we have excluded smaller parties and less successful parties for the sake of visual clarity. The same analysis could be performed on these parties as well, of course.

10 The example used is merely illustrative – we are not saying either is *necessarily* the correct interpretation for this party.

11 This is clearly easier if the original scale is made up of an odd number of scale positions, as on an even-numbered scale there is no centre position. It is possible, however, to rescale even-numbered scales to produce an artificial centre point, even though by definition no-one can have chosen this as an actual position.

12 The vectors themselves can be calculated using the Euclidean distance formula.

13 This logic applies to one-dimensional analyses, although the simple product score is evidently sufficient. Applying the cosine function, the angle can either equal 0 degrees (party and voter on the same side) and thus the score will (redundantly) be multiplied by 1; or 180 degrees (party and voter on opposite sides) and thus the score will be multiplied by –1, thereby indicating the opposite sides of the fence with a negative product score.

14 See in particular the opening papers in the special edition of the *Journal of Theoretical Politics* (1997), as well as the exchange between Westholm (1997) and Macdonald, Rabinowitz and Listhaug (1998).

15 Under-specification turns out to be crucial when comparing proximity and directional models empirically. If a fully specified model is used, the two theories turn out to be indistinguishable as vote predictors. The reasons for this relate to the mathematical properties of the two functions when used to predict choice (which implies *relative* distances). Such a problem does not occur when using the models to predict candidate or party evaluations (which imply *absolute* scores). For a full explanation of this, see Macdonald, Rabinowitz and Listhaug (1998: 661–5).

6

VOTING AND THE ECONOMY

Summary box

- Economics and elections
- Defining the VP-function
- Aggregate models and their developments
- Introducing individual perceptions
- Retrospective and prospective models
- Pocketbook and sociotropic models
- Further refinements and future developments

Introduction

'If I were told I could only have one variable to determine the outcome of the [2000 US presidential] election it would be economic growth. Then I would take presidential popularity.' *Prof. Michael Lewis-Beck, ENN, 17 May 2000*

The fact that advanced industrial and post-industrial societies generally also enjoy the highest levels of democracy has been an association that has been taken largely as read in political science and its sub-disciplines. It has motivated much of policy-making and agenda-setting in democracies as well. It has also driven much of the policy of Western governments and NGOs such as the World Bank towards the democratisation of Central and Eastern Europe – and, economic growth being an attractive proposition, this policy was, initially at least, embraced by these countries. That such an association is also simplistic to say the least does not reduce the potency of the myth, nor does it reduce the importance of economic matters in democratic life. Governments are required as part of their democratic mandate to manage the nation's economy competently. An economy which goes contrary to citizen's expectations in this respect can result in more than simply governmental turnover, engendering extremist challenges and even regime collapse.

Traditionally, governments have been seen as the principal manipulators and controllers of the economy, and different ideologies reflect different approaches to this. Left-wing supply side economics evidently involves the state and governments more deeply in the day-to-day running of an economy, but even more *laissez-faire* approaches see government responsible for the levels of reduction of state intervention, and management of what remains, leading to better or worse economic performance. The Thatcher government of the early 1980s or the Chirac and Juppé governments in France in the late 1980s and early 1990s would both be judged to varying degrees on their respective privatisation programmes and ostensible withdrawal of the state and its effect on national economies. As such, one of the main roles, if not *the* main role, of governments of whatever political colour is to manage economies as a means of implementing their policies. After a very short 'honeymoon' period in power, citizens will begin to look at what the governing parties promised before their election and see whether they have lived up to that promise. Moreover, they will look at the unspoken promise of all parties contesting elections with a view to winning power, namely that they are capable of doing the job of government, and in particular of ensuring the financial well-being of the country, however they choose to do this ideologically.

Although the level of involvement of other social actors, such as trades unions, employers' groups and pressure groups, in economic planning and decision-making varies from country to country, the vast bulk of economic decisions are in the last instance down to government. Social Democrat Chancellor Gerhard Schroeder in Germany, a country traditionally renowned for its corporatist approach to economic policy, could still see a plunge in his popularity mere weeks after his party's re-election to office in September 2002 for the economic downturn that followed. Similarly, the roles of the civil service and state bureaucracies in economic management vary markedly, as does their level of politicisation, but officially they are there to implement and at most advise on government policy, not to define it. Moreover, governments have traditionally been the sole benefactor of tax revenues: they decide where and how these taxes are spent. They have also largely determined the rules of the economic game with regards to domestic and foreign trade, imposing customs duties, tariff barriers and the like. Overall, then, when the economy goes wrong, voters should blame government – and, conversely, when it goes right, they should reward government. Government popularity ratings should fluctuate with the ups and downs of economic performance, and the litmus test of popularity – the vote – should provide a similar demonstration of their current success in economic management.

It is of little surprise, then, that economic theories of voting have become a major feature of the psephological literature. In this chapter, we will look firstly at the original aggregate models which link government, elections and economic conditions together in a basic 'vote calculus'. We then turn to the principal revisions of such models. Are all governments judged in the same way on the economy? Is there variation in which economies are judged? More fundamentally, we then ask whether the causal relationship is as simple as these models assume, or whether we can refine it further using individual data. Specifically, are all economic decisions driven by the state of the economy, or are they also influenced by expectations and perceptions? Do voters attribute concerns about their own financial situation to governmental action, for instance? If so, is this more or less important than the general state of the economy overall? And to what extent are these concerns related to the social and ideological position of voters?

Election results and the economy

The basic model

Let us begin with two very basic examples of how a proposed economic model might work. Below, we present two graphs, one relating to Austria, the other to Italy. Both plot the electoral scores of the largest incumbent party, the Austrian Socialist Party (SPÖ) between 1971 and 1999, and the Italian Christian Democrats (DC) between 1963 and 1992, against the absolute level of unemployment in the year preceding the election. The assumption is that the major – or in the first three Austrian governments, the only – governing party will fare decreasingly well as unemployment rises.

Looking at the Austrian situation, there appears to be a very close relationship between the Socialist vote and the unemployment rate. Across almost three decades, the higher levels of unemployment are accompanied by concomitantly lower levels of Socialist vote – only 1975 bucks the trend slightly. The 'best fit line', which we have superimposed on the graph, illustrates just how closely the pattern fits a linear relationship. What about Italy? We can still superimpose a 'best fit line' but frankly it is a lot less convincing than the Austrian situation. For the first three elections for which we have unemployment data, there is no relationship

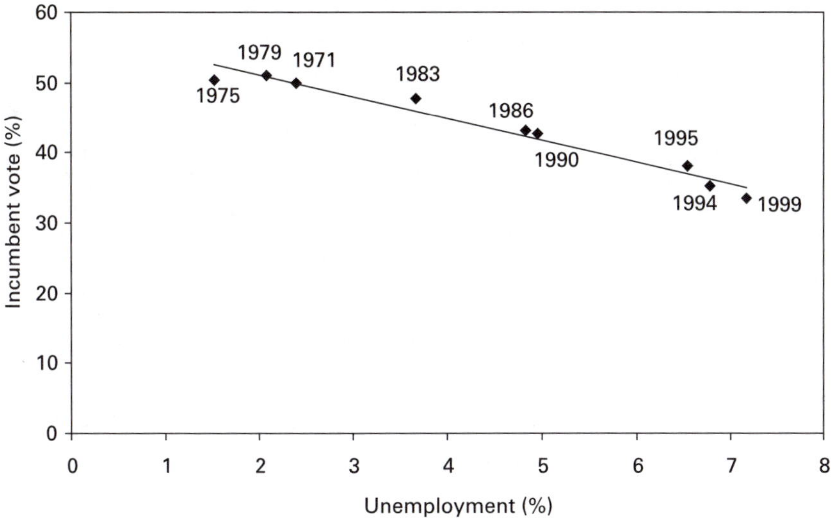

Figure 6.1a *Incumbent party (SPÖ) vote and unemployment rate in Austria, 1971–1999*

Source: electoral figures taken from Siaroff (2000: 182 & 313), Bartolini and Mair (1990), Istituto Cattaneo database, EREPS database, unemployment rates taken from OECD Main Economic Indicators dataset. Missing years due to unavailability of unemployment figures.

between unemployment and DC vote. Unemployment is higher and vote lower in 1987 – but then the lowest level of vote, which is found in 1992, has a lower rate of unemployment. In terms of change from 1987 to 1992, the relationship between unemployment and DC vote is the opposite to what we might expect – lower unemployment seems to produce a *drop* in the DC vote.

In the Austrian case, then, the bivariate association seems remarkably effective. The Italian model is less obliging. But does this mean that economic voting does not occur in Italy, or is it rather that a more complex model is necessary, including such elements as we mentioned at the end of the introduction? Would the improved model account even more satisfactorily for the Austrian case[1] – or indeed show that the relationship is to some extent spurious?

To establish such a tight argument for the influence of the economy on voting, we would expect to find a formal statement of the relationship between the two indicators, controlling for other possible effects. And indeed, in much of the literature on economic voting, we find this statement in the shape of the so-called 'VP-function'.

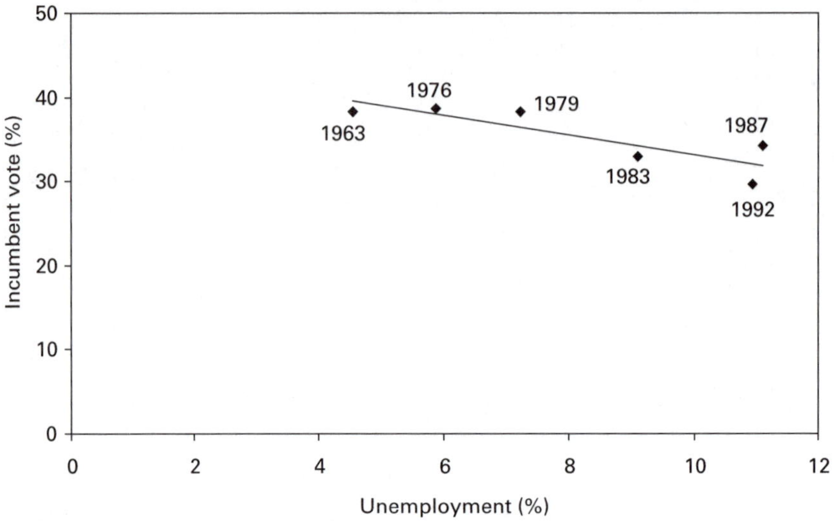

Figure 6.1b *Incumbent party (DC) vote and unemployment rate in Italy, 1963–1992*

Source: electoral figures taken from Siaroff (2000: 18–2 & 313), Bartolini and Mair (1990), Istituto Cattaneo database, EREPS database, unemployment rates taken from OECD Main Economic Indicators dataset. Missing years due to unavailability of unemployment figures.

Governmental responsibility and the VP-function

The VP-function stands for 'vote/popularity function' and refers to the assumption that the vote for a government in an election, or the popularity of a government in an opinion poll, is determined by ('is a function of') a series of conditions, economic as well as political, and events which have occurred during the government's incumbency. Generally, the relationship between these conditions and either vote or governmental popularity is hypothesised to be the same at a conceptual level. The reason that popularity ratings are often used is that, for modelling purposes, opinion poll data provide far more cases than vote: opinion polls may be carried out once a month, whereas votes normally occur only once every few years. Similarly, the economic data, which are used to look at macroeconomic conditions, are also available on a more frequent basis. Models using opinion poll popularity often provide a better fit than those using vote. This is not only for statistical reasons concerning the number of observations that the model includes, but also because responses to polls are a 'gut' response, and hence a simple expression of a voter's reaction to a government, whereas vote is a more convoluted decision determined by more than just the perceived economic conditions of the time (Paldam, 1991: 16). However, for our purposes, we should regard vote and government popularity variables as essentially interchangeable.

This function is often expressed algebraically. For instance, Paldam (1991: 13) uses the following expression:

$$\Delta C_t = \{a_1\ \Delta u_t + a_2\ \Delta p_t + \ldots\} + [c_1\ D^1{}_t + c_2\ D^2{}_t + \ldots] + \varepsilon_t$$

What at first sight may be an off-putting array of symbols is in fact a very clear expression of the basic expected relationship between vote or governmental popularity and economic and political factors. Firstly, ΔC_t – the dependent variable – means the change in vote or in governmental popularity at time *t* – the election or the date on which the opinion poll to measure popularity is held.[2] As we have already discussed in Chapter 4, voters can be seen as holding government responsible for enacting policies and exercising power subsequent to an election: voters have expectations which will to a greater or lesser extent have been met. As we just mentioned, one of the key expectations is that the government can run the economy. If so, how voters feel about the government (their popularity function tapped by opinion polls) or their result in the next elections (their vote function) will depend on how well the economy is running. If voters hold the government responsible for the state of the economy, then C should fall or rise proportionate to the improvement or decline in the economy.

Before turning to u, p and D, the independent variables in the calculus of support, it is worth considering the element of change in C. In Figures 6.1a and 6.1b, for instance, we used an absolute measure of vote. However, in the equation above, Paldam explicitly specifies change in the vote. At this stage, we should simply be aware that in the economic voting literature, both change and absolute levels of vote or governmental popularity are used in analyses as dependent variables. It is beyond the scope of this chapter to look at the differences between the two, but the choice is largely determined by the statistical method and type of data used by the authors. Usually, however, both variables will provide similar findings.[3]

What, then, is C composed of? Firstly, the elements included in the winged brackets are the economic elements, u (unemployment) and p (rate of price rise, or inflation). These are both measured at time *t* as well. a_1 and a_2 are the coefficients which indicate the strength of the relationship between the vote and unemployment and inflation, respectively. The '+ …' indicates that these are not the only economic variables which we might include. We could also put in an indicator of economic growth, such as change in GDP, or of public debt, interest rates, and so on. However, the general consensus is that unemployment and inflation are the 'big two', i.e. the two main economic factors in the VP-function (Lewis-Beck and Paldam, 2000: 114). Over time, they are the two macroeconomic indicators which give the best 'snapshot' of the state of the economy. They are also the principal areas which party policies try to influence favourably. Consequently, they are the indicators to which voters are most likely to react.

Despite employing simplifying theories which detractors would perhaps see as simplistic, those investigating the effects of economic indicators on vote and governmental popularity are not so blinkered as to think that *only* economics has an effect. Consequently, it is important to consider the economic theories in the VP-function context as a subset of wide-ranging political factors which may consistently affect vote. In Paldam's equation, these are the D variables. In the following section we will see some of the variables which have traditionally been used. As with the economic variables, these have their own coefficients, c_1 and c_2 in this case, which indicates the strength of the indicator in accounting for variation in the dependent variable C. And again, the '+...' has been included to show that one may include as many political indicators as one desires, within the bounds of parsimony and the capacity of the statistical model due to sample size.

This leaves us with the term ε_t. This is known as the 'error' or 'disturbance' term. Effectively, in our equation this term encompasses all the variation in vote which is not accounted for by the independent variables explicitly included in the model. The larger this error term is, the less vote change is accounted for by our independent variables. We will never be able to eliminate it entirely, but generally, if the error term is large, this implies that our model is under-specified, i.e. that there are other important variables which we should include to account for variation in the vote. We will not make any further reference to the error term *per se* as it is usually not reported in analyses, although we have encountered a related term, the R^2 coefficient, which we discussed in Chapter 1, and which is reported in most models.

To show briefly how the equation works, let us include the unemployment rate and exclude the other variables for the moment. Our very basic equation would look like this:

$$\Delta C_t = a_1 \, \Delta u_t$$

Now let us include some notional values for the sake of illustration. Say that in an election at time *t*, the incumbent party loses 5 percent of its vote as compared with the previous election (which might be given the notation

t–1).[4] If we assume that all of this loss was due to the changes in the economic climate, and specifically of unemployment (which is unrealistic, but serves the purposes of illustration), then we can work out how this economic variable is related to vote. We look at the change in unemployment between time t and, say, one year prior to time t and find that it has increased from 5 percent to 15 percent, i.e. a 10 percentage point increase (this economy is clearly in dire straits). Putting these values in the equation, we therefore have:

$$\text{5 percent incumbent vote loss} = a_1 \text{ (10 percent increase in unemployment)}$$

or:

$$-5 = a_1 \, (+10)$$

Consequently, the value of a_1 must be –.5. This indicates that there is a negative relationship between change in unemployment and change in governmental vote and, because we are assuming that the relationship between the two is linear, that the change in vote will always be half the change in unemployment.

If we include both economic variables, the situation is more complicated – we suddenly have two variables which we need to calculate, one for unemployment and one for inflation. Say the change in inflation has been an increase of 5 percentage points, from 2 percent to 7 percent (the economy is in meltdown ...). Our 'filled in' equation would now look like this:

$$\text{5 percent incumbent vote loss} = a_1 \text{ (10 percent increase in unemployment)} + a_2 \text{ (5 percent increase in inflation)}$$

or:

$$-5 = a_1 \, (+10) + a_2 \, (+5)$$

Looking at this, a_1 could be –.25 and a_2 –.5 (which would imply that the change in inflation rate has twice as strong an effect as the change in unemployment). However, $a_1 = -.5$ and $a_2 = 0$ would also work in producing –5 percent (meaning that the relationship between unemployment and vote remains the same as in our first example, and the change in inflation has no independent effect whatsoever). Indeed a potentially limitless range of different values would provide the correct answer. With the evidence we have of the single election at time t, we cannot say which is true. With a second observation of vote, unemployment and inflation, we could use a simultaneous equation to work out the exact values.

However, when we take into account that the relationship between the economy and vote is very unlikely to be as simple as our illustrative example suggests, and that we will wish to test our more complex hypotheses using a large number of cases, it becomes impossible to find a relationship that fits as exactly as the above relationships do. Consequently, researchers employ multivariate models, usually based on a linear model, to test the range of possible economic and political variables which contribute to the VP-function, and estimate as accurately as possible what the coefficients associated with each variable are. At the very least, researchers wish to be able to say with some certainty what the sign in front of each coefficient is – in other words, is there a consistently positive or negative relationship between vote and certain economic indicators? – even if they will not always be able to give a precise value of the coefficient for all countries at every point in time.[5] The progress in the field of economic voting has come from researchers precisely trying to make their findings as robust and precise as possible, by testing their theories on as wide a range of data as is possible, refining their assumptions as to which economic factors matter, and analysing which social and political conditions may mediate the effect of economic conditions on vote and governmental popularity. After considering the initial research that employed the VP-function, we then move to considering these refinements.

Early economic models

Three analyses are generally cited as the beginning of economic models within the VP-function paradigm – Goodhart and Bhansali's analysis of British governmental popularity since 1947 (1970); Mueller's analysis of US presidential popularity from the beginning of the Truman administration in 1945 to the end of the Johnson administration in 1969 (1970); and Kramer's analysis of national vote in US House of Representative elections between 1896 and 1964 (1971).[6] All three assume that governments and, in the case of Mueller, presidents are held responsible for the state of the economy and will be judged accordingly. To test this, all three rely on aggregate time series data, consisting of national-level vote/popularity levels and economic indicators across the time period in question.

The political indicators column in Table 6.1 provides the D variables which we saw in our original equation. These are important to include, because they are likely to have an independent effect on vote and popularity, and hence we need to control for them before we can accurately measure the effect of economic indicators. For instance, under Mueller's specification, the downward effect on Harry Truman's presidential popularity engendered by the Korean War might lead us to mis-estimate the effect of unemployment if the war variable were not included.[7]

Table 6.1 ***Summary of the principal indicators in early economic models***

Model	Dependent variable	Economic indicators (u, p, ...)	Political indicators (D_1, D_2, ... D_n)	Principal economic findings
Goodhart and Bhansali (1970)	Governmental popularity	Unemployment Inflation	Electoral cycle effects	Unemployment and inflation both significant in predicting popularity
Mueller (1970)	Presidential popularity	Unemployment	Incumbency cost 'Rally-Around-the Flag' War	Asymmetrical effect (higher unemployment = president punished; lower unemployment = no reward)
Kramer (1971)	Congressional vote	Monetary income Prices (consumer cost-of-living index) Real personal income Unemployment	Incumbency effect Presidential 'coat-tails' effect	Real personal income significant in predicting vote Unemployment and price inflation not significant

Notes

- Electoral cycle = the shifts in the governmental popularity according to the time during the incumbency this is measured.
- Rally-Around-the-Flag = hypothesis that there will be an increase in presidential support during his participation in international 'events' (in this case, e.g. Bay of Pigs, Cuban missile crisis, Truman Doctrine, etc.).
- War = hypothesis that there will be a decrease in presidential support when the country is at war.
- Presidential 'coat-tails' effect = hypothesis that vote of candidate from victorious presidential party benefits from this latter's popularity.

What is immediately obvious is that the authors choose different economic variables to include in their models, and that the economic conditions have different effects in different contexts. The effects across countries and even within countries, according to electoral context, look remarkably unstable. For instance, as regards unemployment, a linear 'reward-punishment' relationship exists for Goodhart and Bhansali, whereas Mueller finds only an asymmetrical relationship whereby higher unemployment is bad for incumbent popularity, but lower unemployment provides no gains.[8] Kramer finds no relationship at all. Similarly, for inflation, Goodhart and

Bhansali find a similar situation as with unemployment; Mueller does not test it; and Kramer finds it has an effect, but only when monetary income is used. His preferred model is one including real personal income (which is monetary income deflated by the cost-of-living index) but here inflation itself is not significant. Why such large differences between the models' findings?

The first pessimistic answer could be that the relationship between the economy and vote is simply unstable and varies widely for many different reasons, including time and place. Consequently, we can never hope to find a clear link between the two. But if we believe this argument, then there would be no point in testing such theories any further. Furthermore, it would be foolish to believe this on the basis of three models which include different measures of the economy. A more hopeful possibility, but not one that the researcher always has control over, is that there are errors in the measurement of the data which are biasing the results. For instance, polling data of popularity may be subject to all sorts of biases deriving from who is asked the questions and under what circumstances. Thus, the researcher has incentive to use the best possible data source which reflects the 'true' situation and uses identical sampling techniques across time to promote consistency.

What about differences in national political context? If we can find data which include similar economic measures, we can include a number of countries in a pooled cross-sectional or cross-national comparative analysis. Evidently, if one is only interested in a single country, which may be useful for testing hypotheses relating to nationally specific contexts, then cross-national data provides no advantage – and indeed, one is generally more likely to find richer data for the country in question amongst national sources. However, if the researcher's aim is to come up with a generalised theory of economic voting which works regardless of context, then it is crucial that the theory be tested in all of these contexts, and thus comparative testing becomes indispensable.

A final possibility, and the one that has led to the developments in economic models just as it contributes to all developments in scientific research, is simply that the models are mis-specified. That is, the theory of which economic conditions have an effect and in what contexts may not have been accurate. Once we have good quality comparative data containing comparable economic measures, we need to decide exactly which other measures to include. For instance, there may be institutional conditions which dampen economic effects. If we fail to control for these, then we may consistently underestimate the effect the economy has, *ceteris paribus*. If our theory is lacking, our findings will never be robust, even though they may be stable. Thus, the search for better theory has been the incentive behind the main developments which we consider below.

Developments in aggregate economic models

Developments in aggregate models I: holding government responsible

One of the major theoretical developments in aggregate model testing has been that economic voting may differ between nations because of the institutional framework and political context within which it takes place. The VP-function assumes that people hold the government, and by extension the governing party/parties, responsible for the state of the economy. Thus, when an election arrives, the voters are assumed to look at the state of the economy, then reward or punish the party/parties which form(s) this government. This implies the notion of 'clarity of responsibility'. If voters are going to punish the government, they first of all need to be sure that the government *is* responsible for the changes in the economy and then they need to identify the party responsible.

Taking ideal-type institutional arrangements for the sake of example, this allocation of responsibility would be clearest in a system with a one-party majority government in a unicameral system where the opposition has no influence over policy and where party cohesion is strong. In this case, a single party in government is running the economy with no outside interference from opposition parties or another legislative chamber, and with a strongly cohesive view emanating from its party corpus – if responsibility is allocated, it will be overwhelmingly focused on this party. At the other extreme, a multiparty government in a bicameral framework, where opposition parties have policy-changing powers in the legislature and where party cohesion is weak, makes the allocation of responsibility much more difficult.

First of all, who within the government should be blamed for economic policy? There is a range of parties within the government all or some of whom may have had responsibility for government. Additionally, even if voters do ascribe responsibility and hence shift their vote, in multiparty coalition governments the likelihood of switching to one of the other incumbent parties is high. Government support will thus not actually drop. Secondly, where a second chamber exists, and particularly where it is controlled by the opposition, it may amend economic policy and thus be more or less responsible for economic changes, deflecting some of the government's responsibility. Similarly, if opposition parties chair some of the legislative committees, their amendments may deflect responsibility from the government. Lastly, if parties are weakly cohesive, policy compromises have to be made within parties and in coalition governments, across parties, and, consequently responsibility will be obscured.

When researchers have tested these differences in effect of economic variables on governmental vote according to political context, they have found that those countries which display high levels of clarity of responsibility manifest higher levels of economic voting than those with more confused lines of responsibility (Powell and Whitten, 1993; Whitten and Palmer, 1999). In addition, Anderson suggests that the 'clarity of available alternatives' will also exercise an effect in punishing economically unsuccessful governments (2000: 156).[9] That is, when there is a clear opposition to replace the government, voters will be more willing to punish the incumbents. If, however, there are a number of possible replacements, and consequently it is unclear who the replacement might be, voters will tend to reserve judgement. Again, this proves to be the case (2000: 166). These reasons help explain why countries such as Italy, with its former predominant centre-based Christian Democrat coalition, have traditionally been seen as less sensitive to economic conditions in voting behaviour, and one of the reasons our basic model in Figure 6.1b left much to be desired. Generally, though, we should take the clarity of responsibility and alternative governments into account when looking at the overall effect of economics on elections.

Developments in aggregate models II: holding which governments responsible for what?

Even at the aggregate level, the relationship between indicators can also be made more subtly. For instance, Figure 6.1a showed that there seemed to be a relationship between unemployment and incumbent vote in the case of the Austrian Left. But would Right-wing governments (which are traditionally more concerned with inflation) be as prone to punishment due to unemployment as Left-wing governments (who explicitly set out to lower this)? Conversely, inflation, being the traditional bugbear of Right-wing parties, should cause greater incumbent rejection. Indeed, following the 'Phillips curve' economic argument (Figure 6.2), there is a trade-off between inflation and unemployment and so it should be impossible to keep both low.[10]

Parties must therefore decide which they will emphasise in their policies, and 'Left – unemployment/Right – inflation' is the overriding pattern, with Left-wing supporters usually belonging to social strata more threatened by unemployment, and Right-wing supporters being more concerned by price increases.

Consequently different parties have different policy 'ownership'. According to policy responsibility, then, voters should reward and punish Left-wing governments on the level of unemployment, whilst ignoring the inflation rate. However, a Right-wing government will be judged upon price

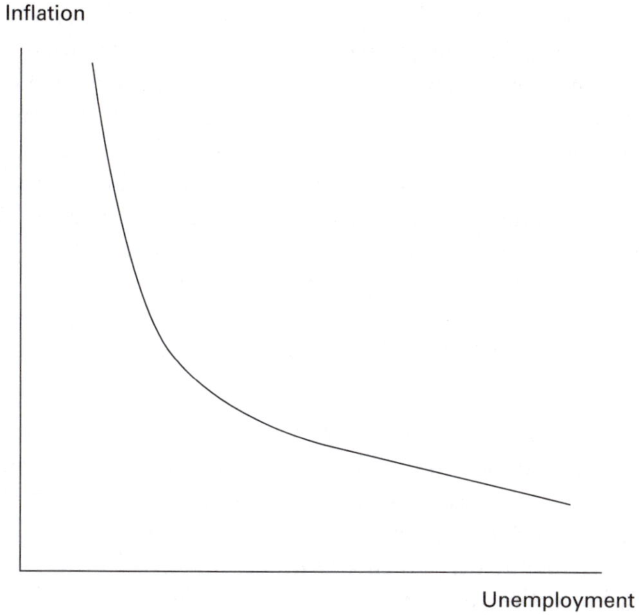

Figure 6.2 *The Phillips curve*

rises, rather than on unemployment. In the same articles in which they tested the 'clarity of responsibility' hypothesis, Powell and Whitten (1993: 408) and Whitten and Palmer (1999: 59) test this hypothesis and find it to be accurate. Moreover, they also find that parties which perform well on the indicator other than the one they officially 'own' can be penalised for this: for example, Left-wing incumbents can be punished for improving inflation. Additionally, from these findings they posit a fascinating corollary which they demonstrate using the case of France in its 1986 elections (1999: 60–1). Using very much the same process of calculating vote losses and gains that we demonstrated earlier in this chapter, they calculate that the French Socialist Party, which was the incumbent government before the 1986 elections, lost around 4.7 percent of the vote because of macro-economic performance. However, this was because it was a Left-wing government. Had it been a Right-wing government, its good performance on inflation but not on unemployment would have seen its vote *rise* by 0.7 percent, implying that under identical circumstances, a Right-wing party would not necessarily have lost the election as the Socialists in fact did!

Such findings are thrilling for researchers, because they allow us to engage in the counter-factual fantasy of which historians are very fond:

'What if …?' But we should be careful in predicting such anti-mondes on the basis of statistical findings, especially given that under a Right-wing government the macroeconomic circumstances of the country might well have differed from those that pertained under the Left. However, such models illustrate the important distinction that needs to be made when we are looking at how a country's economic performance will affect an election outcome. A commentator predicting the demise of a governing party because of rising unemployment would do well to look at what political colour the party is before making such predictions.

Developments in aggregate models III: disaggregating the national patterns

Our focus of attention so far has been the nation. However, it is evident that national economies do not always enjoy consistent economic fortunes throughout their territories. In the UK in the post-war period, the service and tech-industry South has traditionally enjoyed much stronger levels of growth and economic performance than the former industrial heartlands of the North-West, the North-East and South Wales. In Italy, the economic wealth has been generated in the North and Centre, whereas the South has remained economically stagnant. Accordingly unemployment may hit different areas of a nation, and hence will effect voting and governmental popularity to differing degrees according to region.

Rattinger, for instance, finds in his analysis of German counties that political response to higher levels of unemployment are stronger than at lower levels (1991: 60). Thus in regions where unemployment is high, the effect on vote is stronger than in regions with lower unemployment.[11] More in-depth studies at the regional level have been performed by Pattie and Johnston using individual level data to analyse differing economic perceptions according to region in the UK (1995). As with all aggregate models, then, the disaggregated region models can indicate differences in relationship between economic and macroeconomic political variables. Basic controls for regional socioeconomic profiles using census data can also be introduced. From the clarity of responsibility angle, one might also test for the effects of federal systems, where regional executives often compete with national governments over policy-competence.

'Developments' in aggregate models IV: what do voters know and how long do they know it?

The final aspect to look at with regard to the aggregate models is the voter herself. The responsibility hypothesis assumes that voters hold the government responsible for the state of the economy, but this in turn assumes that the voters have views on the economy. The use of the aggregate time series economic data to measure unemployment and inflation implies that voters have a view of the economy which matches reality. Not only that, but the changes which occur in the state of the economy should be followed quite closely by the changes in voters' support for the government, especially when using popularity data which is collected on a monthly basis.

Looking first at the time element, most studies suggest that voters are myopic or short-sighted. In other words, they assess economic performance and judge the government's responsibility on a short-term basis. Mueller's 1970 study of the VP-function relating to presidential popularity assumed that the effect of political events started to die away very soon after their occurrence (1970: 22). And so similarly with the effects of economic evaluations, for instance in Britain, where the impact of economic evaluations on vote intention are relatively immediate: as voters change their economic evaluations, so their past evaluations are rapidly discounted (Pattie et al., 1999: 921). Nannestad and Paldam are even more explicit on this point: 'In VP-functions, all effects decay very fast – often within one year.' (1994: 217). Indeed, the very nature of aggregate data means that, if economic evaluations and opinion poll data are measured at monthly intervals and then tested without lagging – that is, without hypothesising that the economic conditions take, say, six months to come to bear on voters' perceptions and thus governmental assessment – the hypothesised causal relationship is almost instantaneous. This relationship seems to be the case: there is no strong evidence that a theoretically sound lagged fit between economic conditions and vote or governmental popularity provides a better fit.[12]

In this sense, there has been no development in aggregate models (hence our use of inverted commas for this section). But there is evidence to suggest that voters' economic perceptions need at least to be considered as more complex than simply 'economy now = governmental support now'. Firstly, to take the UK example again, 'the economy' can work on different levels. The fact that the pick-up in the economy in 1992 after the 1990–1991 recession corresponded with majority support for the Conservative incumbents can be seen in aggregate terms as myopic – abandon the assessments of 1990 and 1991, and judge on the upturn of 1992. Yet, as some commentators noted, this support for the Conservatives was due to the fact that 'Labour, quite simply, was not trusted to provide competent macroeconomic management.' (Sanders et al., 2001: 789). In terms of macroeconomic management, for some the memories of the infamous Winter of Discontent of the 1970s, where unions and strike action led to a grinding to a halt of public services and even basic utilities such as electricity and rubbish disposal, after the collapse of its pay policy, may have endured as evidence of Labour's incompetence in running the economy. Perhaps fittingly for older voters who remembered these events, this suggests an element of long-sightedness for some voters.

For some voters – in other words, views of the economy and which elements of the economy voters look at may vary. The aggregate model implies this in its own findings. Other things being equal, we see a relationship between the economic conditions and governmental popularity. But if everybody interpreted the economy identically, and punished incumbents for economic downturns, then at opinion polls or at elections, incumbent parties would score zero. This is obviously not the case – some people punish the government, others do not. The question is – who falls into which category? Aggregate models generally lack the tools to discern this, and so we have to find some other means of doing so. This does not mean aggregate models are useless: on the contrary, they can provide an extremely parsimonious and effective predictive model of election outcomes. As the opening quotation emphasises, economic indicators have proved their worth across time in helping account for election results.[13] But simply they are not functionally able to explore variation at the individual level.

In addition, there are two theoretical paradoxes which the aggregate VP-function model presents and which individual models can explore. Firstly, given its Downsian roots, the VP-function is expectations based: voters should be making rational future-oriented decisions to maximise their utility. But aggregate data makes the decision-making process retrospective, which can be considered irrational. Voters should make vote decisions on the basis of what is going to happen, not what has happened. Similarly, rational voters should be voting on the basis of *their* utilities, not the utility of the economy and everyone therein. Again, not to decide on the basis of the 'personal economy', i.e. the state of their own finances, would seem irrational (Lewis-Beck and Paldam, 2000: 118).

Secondly, given that popularity and economic conditions track each other quite closely from month to month, this suggests that voters are very well informed about the economy. And yet this does not stand up to empirical testing. Looking at Denmark, a country with traditionally a politically savvy population, one study of early 1990s' data found that voters were quite informed about the level of unemployment (about 50 percent could give the approximate level) but that on any other indicators such as inflation or balance-of-payments, they effectively had no idea and even posited surpluses where deficits existed (Paldam and Nannestad, 2000). Similarly, in a study of Britain between 1974 and 1997, Sanders finds evidence to support 'the possibility that economic *perceptions* are more central to voters' electoral preferences than raw macro-economic realities.' (2000: 283).

In other words, we introduce an intervening variable into the VP-function, so that the causal chain becomes:

Economic conditions → voters' perceptions of economic conditions → vote/popularity

But to test whether perceptions matter – and indeed, which perceptions of the economy matter – we need to use survey data to give us access to individuals' views and motivations. We consequently move now to the second major development in economic models of voting, the introduction of micro- or individual-level theories.

Perceptions: the individual and the economy

Let us consider these two paradoxes first before moving on to differences between voters. Given that these – retrospective evaluation and assessment of the national economy – derive from the VP-function's rational roots, what would the rational alternatives be?

Prospective rather than retrospective: do voters look forwards or backwards?

In the first paradox, rational voters would look at how they expect things to turn out in the near future – assuming that voters are still myopic – and make their decision accordingly. Why look at how things have gone economically? Surely what matters is how things will go – and if voters are confident that things will go well, then rationally they should stick with the incumbent. Conversely, if things look dismal, they should switch votes to someone who can provide a brighter future.[14] Thus, come election time, the purely *prospective* economic voter looks at the different policies on offer, works out which is likely to provide a better outcome and votes accordingly. The purely *retrospective* voter looks only at the incumbent's balance sheet and the opposition's most recent balance sheet if it is available (i.e. if they can remember) or what they imagine the opposition would have done in power, and decides accordingly.

Because the prospective model depends entirely upon perceptions – usually tapped by a survey question asking 'How do you think the economy will go in the next year?' – whereas the retrospective model is at least partly based on economic reality, survey data has offered the possibility of examining the causal relationships between future perceptions and vote, and comparing the prospective and retrospective models for individual voters. This does not mean that aggregate models cannot include prospective measures. Indeed, the Essex model which has been used to good effect to predict election outcomes in the UK precisely includes aggregate measures of voters' personal economic expectations (Sanders, 1991). The traditional aggregate model mentioned above only tested retrospective theories simply because prospective time series data were generally not available. However, given that survey data allows the researcher to look at the economic voting equation in more depth and to control for other individual-level effects, the causal chain mechanisms which are unclear in the aggregate model can be explored more fully (Feldman and Conley, 1991: 185).

Since the introduction of the prospective hypothesis and its testing in both individual and aggregate models, there is a general consensus that both prospective and retrospective elements play a role in vote choice. Voters look back on the recent economic situation and make a judgement on this, which will affect their view of the incumbent. However, in keeping with the rational expectations model, they also look at what the different parties running for government are offering, and then calculate the likely effect of these policies.

But we should be careful in our interpretation of the prospective element to the equation being the 'rational' element. For why should it be irrational to include the retrospective assessment in one's vote choice? Voters have limited sources of information upon which to make their decisions and, as we saw in Chapter 4, they are unlikely to take party programmes entirely on face value and assume that this is exactly what will happen should its author be elected. So, what better way to assess future performance than to look at how parties have done in the past? And, as the myopic as well as retrospective voter, what more immediate benchmark to use in general than the current incumbent's competence? Thus, expectations are rational – but as Fiorina (1981) showed, in the absence of any contrary evidence that the future will be different, it is equally as rational to base those expectations partly on what past experience has taught you.

Of course, if voters only judged governments on their past economic performances and voted accordingly, then opposition parties would never need to campaign and could simply wait for the incumbents to come unstuck at some point. Interestingly, there is consistent evidence from the VP-function that incumbents generally come unstuck whatever they do whilst in power – Paldam finds that, averaging over 197 elections across 17 nations, incumbent parties lose 1.6 percent of the vote per incumbency (Paldam, 1991: 19). The 'coalition-of-minorities' explanation posited by Downs and cited by Kramer in his early VP-function model (1971: 20) works on this score. Similarly, but more subtly, Powell and Whitten find that incumbents in one-party or pre-election coalitions tend to lose some of the swing votes – the centre-ground floating voters held by politicians in particular to be crucial to winning elections – at the following election (1993: 397).

But, despite these inertial effects, opposition parties still go to great pains to demonstrate either that they would not have made the mistakes that the incumbents have – if the economy has declined – or would have provided even better returns to the populations and businesses – if the economy has improved. Similarly, incumbents will strongly emphasise their future economic plans, especially if their past record has not been especially impressive. In other words, voters assessing parties and governments need to employ forward-thinking as well as looking at the incumbents' balance-sheet. Voters will therefore consider the claims of all parties before making their choice on the basis of the economic promises which look the most attractive.

The national economy or my economy? 'Sociotropic' versus 'pocketbook' explanations

In the traditional aggregate time series model, the key indicators were macroeconomic, namely unemployment and inflation. These indicated the state of the national economy. However, as Kinder and Kiewiet postulated (1979), if voters are rational would they not be more likely to judge the government on the state of their own finances (their 'pocketbook economy') than the nation's economy (the 'sociotropic perspective')? For instance, in the British case, some people were held to have been put off voting Labour in the 1980s and 1990s because of promised/threatened tax rises. Taxation levels affect the individual rather than the national economy, at least in terms of voters' perceptions. Consequently, in prospective terms these voters could be seen as acting egocentrically and obeying the 'pocketbook theory' of economic voting. This rule could work equally well retrospectively as well. If I have seen my level of income decline over the past year, either due to tax rises or due to changes in my work contract due to government changes in labour law, for example, I may punish the government for my own financial decline, even though the national economic situation may be very rosy.

To take a more involved example: Mr Smith is made redundant from his job at the small hardware store six months before the election, and does not manage to find a new job before then. Over the same period, the national economy thrives. But, looking at Mr Smith's personal finances, they have experienced a serious downturn because of the loss of his job. If the small hardware store closed because of the opening of a large out-of-town DIY superstore, and the former could not compete with the latter despite new tax incentives provided by the government for small businesses, then

Mr Smith may not hold the government responsible for the state of his pocketbook and thus this will be irrelevant to his voting behaviour. To boot, the national economy's upturn is held by Mr Smith to be due to the government's policies – for instance, tax incentives for small businesses – and hence he rewards them with his vote. However, if the closure is indirectly due to tax incentives to large retailers such as the DIY superstore to stimulate consumption and competition, then Mr Smith may hold the government responsible for his redundancy and vote against them at the next election. The fact that the national economy is picking up may not be of sufficient solace.

In most comparative tests of pocketbook and sociotropic voting, voters are seen as oriented primarily by the national economy rather than by their own finances, although there are country exceptions (see below). Following the responsibility hypothesis, this makes sense: governments try to run the national economy and make policies to achieve this; they do not make policies to affect individuals' personal 'economies'. For instance, in European elections, even when voters do think that their personal finances have been adversely affected by government policy, this has a very small effect on voting (Lewis-Beck, 1988: 57). To address the rational point of view, this does not mean that voters are necessarily more concerned about the standards of their fellow citizens in a fit of philanthropy. Rather, voters are aware that the state of the economy is more likely to have longer term and potentially deleterious or beneficial effects than their own finances at a certain point in time.

Kramer (1983) argued that this finding of sociotropic assumptions performing better than pocketbook assumptions could be due to model misspecification, i.e. an erroneous or at least insufficient array of causally relevant variables. In the survey items used to measure the state of personal economic well-being, the question asks, 'Have your personal finances improved, remained the same or got worse over the past year?' However, this would include all effects on personal economy, and not just those which are politically relevant (in our first scenario for Mr Smith, the DIY superstore has no political relevance). Some researchers have tested this hypothesis, but have either found that additional questions specifying government effect on personal finances make little difference (Lewis-Beck, 1988) or that the effect is weaker than sociotropic considerations (Markus, 1988).

However, there are exceptions. As above, Markus (1988) precisely shows that US presidential elections have shown evidence of a pocketbook element to the vote equation, even if Congressional elections do not (Kinder and Kiewiet, 1979). The UK also manifests significant levels of pocketbook voting (Sanders, 1991). The two extreme cases seem to be US congressional and Danish legislative elections. In the former case, pocketbook concerns have consistently been found to have no effect. However, in Denmark, the pocketbook variable turns out to be a much stronger explanatory variable than its sociotropic counterpart (Nannestad and Paldam, 1997a). At first sight, this seems paradoxical: the US is perhaps the country with the most individualistic values, whereas Denmark is the archetypal collectively inclined social welfare state. So why do the individualists ignore their own finances, whereas the state-oriented Danes focus on their wallets?

The speculative though ostensibly convincing answer that these authors give is that this response misinterprets how these cultural values work. Instead, precisely because the US is so individually oriented, voters are not going to blame the government for their own misfortunes (or indeed reward them for their good fortune). Individuals look after themselves, the government looks after the economy. However, in Denmark where individuals look to the state for a high degree of organisation and control in economic matters, individuals do not look after themselves – the government does. So if a Dane's personal finances are in decline, she/he feels that she/he has good reason to punish the government at the next election.

Is the economy everybody's economy?

So far, we have been working on the assumption that the effects of the economy have a stable effect on vote, *ceteris paribus*. In other words, when we hypothesise that individuals look at the government's economic record over the past year, for example, and subsequently cast their vote for or against the incumbent on the basis of their perceived positive or negative record, we are implicitly assuming that the perception of the incumbent's record, or the likely effect of the government on the economy in the future has its own, identifiable effect. We should note that we are *not* implying that everybody sees the economic record identically – that is, some will see the record as positive, some will see it as negative and some will have no opinion. Again, this brings perceptions into the equation that the aggregate model based upon objective economic criteria did not. However, are there other variables which may intervene between the economy and the vote and moderate the former's effect on the latter?

We have already referred to the regional effect by which the local economy is of greater importance than the national situation (Pattie and Johnston, 1995). Thus a question asking whether the national economy has improved may not distinguish between voters according to their region. Another possible effect is a class effect, suggested by Weatherford (1978, cited in Lewis-Beck, 1988: 75). In times of economic decline, working-class voters may well be worse hit than middle-class voters because they belong to an economically more precarious social stratum and may not have the financial reserves to offset hardship that the middle class have. As a result, these voters would be more likely to vote against the incumbent. However appealing this may seem, however, there seems to be little evidence to date to back this up in Europe, although Weatherford's own findings in the US in the late 1950s confirmed it.

Similarly, we need to consider the relationship that the voter perceives with the economy and with government, and these are aspects which may vary significantly from country to country. In the case of Italy, where three types of voters were traditionally identified – issue or opinion voters (*voto d'opinione*), exchange voters (*voto di scambio)* and attachment voters (*voto di appartenenza*) (Parisi and Pasquino, 1977) – the exchange voter stood by the incumbent even when economic performance was low, because she relied on the patronage of this party. The more 'sophisticated' opinion voter followed the standard economic model more closely – and the attachment voter, determined principally by subcultural allegiance connected with region, was unaffected by the economy (Bellucci, 1991).

Lastly, one of the elements missing from the theories so far is emotion or affect. In our consideration of the directional theory of voting in Chapter 5, the affective element to the voter positioning herself in space can at one level be seen as a 'strength of feeling' on a certain issue, suggesting an intensity element to the position. Similarly, the state of the economy and how the government is managing it is something which might give rise to strength of feeling. Two people could look at a government's economic management – and, to quote the classic article on the subject, one could be 'mad as hell' about it (Conover and Feldman, 1986), the other less emotionally involved. The former's relation to the economy, at that particular moment at least, is qualitatively different to the latter's. And indeed, the findings to date in the European case as well suggest that those who display anger over the government's handling of the economy will be more likely to vote against them as a result (Lewis-Beck, 1988: 56).

These are all areas which, beyond the principal works cited above, have received remarkably little coverage, however. Affect features in the psychological literature (e.g. Sniderman, Brody and Tetlock, 1991) but in the economic voting literature one must search hard for models retesting these hypotheses. Indeed, aggregate models more generally still dominate the literature, doubtless because of the attractiveness of their parsimony and predictive potential. The one area where individual assessments of the economy are generally now included is in 'full' models of voting where economic perceptions are now an accepted control together with the traditional indicators of sociodemographics, partisanship and ideology. Moreover, even when testing for economic effects alone, standard social, partisan and ideological controls should be included. For example, perceptions of how the economy will go in the coming year will very probably be affected by which party one supports and whether it is in government or not. Similarly, ideological position of a voter may exercise indirect effects on vote via economic evaluations.

The literature list in this respect is potentially endless – and we will return to the notion of the full voting model in the concluding chapter of this book. However, as basic examples, studies of the relationship between partisanship and ideology in vote choice will control for independent economic effects (Evans, 2003). Similarly, any work testing the Michigan School's funnel of causality will generally also include economic perceptions in the equation (Miller and Merill Shanks, 1996). Lastly, the role of economics in voting for particular parties, for instance the Extreme Right, has also engendered both aggregate and multi-level models (Jackman and Volpert, 1996; Lubbers and Scheepers, 2000). It is a measure of success of both individual and aggregate models, then, that they have passed into the mainstream of quantitative tests of electoral behaviour, as well as remaining a sub-discipline in their own right.

Conclusion: the changing relationship of government and the economy

From the early worries that economic models of voting were inherently unstable and produced conflicting results across time and countries, and often within countries as well, the more recent studies have addressed many of these instabilities so that we can say with some certainty how different economic factors affect the electoral process, and also which areas are in need of further research. For instance, as we have mentioned there is still room for more testing and replication of individual-level hypotheses using pooled cross-sectional data, particularly as concerns the relationship between individual voters and the economy. Again, this is not to say that country-studies do not still have a role, as the Bellucci example in the previous section demonstrated. Similarly, looking at effects in rare or unique institutional settings, for instance France's 'bicephalous' executive, can lend insight into how people assign responsibility (Lewis-Beck, 1997).

Moreover, as societies and the economy change, so our existing models need retesting. One of the more recent analyses of Danish voting – as we noted, traditionally an exception in the strength of its pocketbook voting – saw changes in as short a period as 1986–1992 (Nannestad and Paldam, 1997a: 135). Consequently, changes in country-context will certainly merit retesting of economic models, either to test that the bases upon which voters are making electoral decisions or rating governmental performance have changed or to see if hypothesised intervening effects such as institutional arrangement satisfactorily account for changes. More generally, we should look at the global economic context as a possible challenge to accepted economic explanations. First of all, as Lewis-Beck and Paldam note, inflation in the 1990s in the West largely dropped to consistently low levels, and as a result its explanatory power in the VP-function was much reduced – the 'big two' has become the 'big one', unemployment (Lewis-Beck and Paldam, 2000: 117). How will the 'clientele' and 'salient issue' hypotheses cope with just a single economic variable? Will both be judged on unemployment alone? Or will economics become irrelevant to Right-wing incumbents? That is not to say that inflation will not return in the future, and consequently well-specified aggregate times series models incorporating 'high inflation – low inflation – high inflation' periods would be useful to track its fluctuating effect.

Even more 'globally', the clarity of responsibility argument is becoming perhaps even more relevant, though in terms beyond those set out by Powell, Whitten, Palmer and Anderson. Given the largely accepted growth of economic influence amongst multinational corporations, NGOs and independent internal economic actors, notably central banks, governmental control over the economy is certainly being reduced in its breadth, if not in the areas in which it retains control. The effects of this can be seen in any newspaper on an almost daily basis. For example, in late 2002 Tony Blair's 'Iron Chancellor', Gordon Brown, admitted to a shortfall in government revenues of 30 billion pounds on projected public spending. He blamed this on the British economy growing less quickly than anticipated, but blamed this in turn on the slowdown in the global economy. Global slowdowns affecting domestic economies is not a new phenomenon – a similar downturn hamstrung the French Socialists' reforms in the early 1980s. Critics would argue that, in both cases, whilst governments cannot necessarily protect the national economy from global forces or the business cycle, they *can* still anticipate these and plan ahead for periods of economic weakness.

Such a criticism is increasingly a moot point, however. The extent to which voters understand this and see the economy as outside governmental control will determine the extent to which the economic portion of the VP-function should fall. If voters do not understand this – and still expect governments to 'produce the goods', in economic management terms – then we might expect the VP-function to remain. Once again, individual-level analyses of who understands and who does not, and individual or aggregate-level analyses of which areas of the economy disappear from the function, would help our knowledge in this respect.

Summary box

You should now be able to:

- explain the basis of the VP-function
- calculate a basic bivariate relationship between economics and vote
- understand the advantages of using cross-national data
- understand the effects of institutional and political context on economic indicators
- explain why voter perceptions help refine the basic economic model
- explain the different bases to retrospective/prospective and pocket-book/sociotropic models
- understand how economic effects may differ at the individual level.

Related reading

Electoral Studies (2000), special edition – 'Economics and elections', 19: 2/3.

Evans, G. (1999) 'Economics and politics revisited: exploring the decline in Conservative support, 1992–1995', *Political Studies*, 47: 139–51

Pattie, C., R. Johnston and D. Sanders (1999) 'On babies and bathwater: a comment on Evans' 'Economics and politics revisited'', *Political Studies*, 47: 918–32.

Evans G. (1999) 'Economics, politics and the pursuit of exogeneity: why Pattie, Johnston and Sanders are wrong', *Political Studies*, 47: 933–8.

Fiorina, M. (1981) *Retrospective Voting in American National Elections*, New Haven: Yale University Press.

Goodhart, C. and R. Bhansali (1970) 'Political economy', *Political Studies*, 18: 43–106.

Kramer, G. (1971) 'Short-term fluctuations in US voting behaviour, 1896–1964', *American Political Science Review*, 65: 131–143.

Lewis-Beck, M. (1988) *Economic and Elections*, Ann Arbor: University of Michigan Press.

Mueller, J. (1970) 'Presidential popularity from Truman to Johnson', *American Political Science Review*, 64: 18–34.

Nannestad, P. and M. Paldam (1994) 'The VP-function: a survey of the literature on vote and popularity functions after 25 years', *Public Choice*, 79: 213–245.

Nannestad, P. and M. Paldam (1997a) 'From the pocketbook of the welfare man: a pooled cross-section study of economic voting in Denmark, 1990–93', *British Journal of Political Science*, 27: 119–36.

Nannestad, P. and M. Paldam (1997b) 'It's the government's fault! A cross-section study of economic voting in Denmark, 1990–93', *European Journal of Political Research*, 28: 33–62.

Norpoth, H., M. Lewis-Beck and J.-D. Lafay (eds) (1991) *Economics and Politics: the Calculus of Support*, Ann Arbor: University of Michigan Press.

Sanders, D. (1991) 'Government popularity and the next General Election', *Political Studies*, 62: 235–61.

Whitten, G. and H. Palmer (1999) 'Cross-national analyses of economic voting', *Electoral Studies*, 18: 49–67.

Notes

1 Sadly we are unaware of any work on economic models in Austria and so this case must remain a mystery for the moment. In the Italian case, as we shall see, more nuanced views of economic effects on vote do save the economic model.

2 Δ (the Greek letter delta) is the standard mathematical symbol for 'change in'.

3 To note that in a well specified time series model, the use of absolute levels will still look at change in the level across time.

4 We are not interested whether the vote loss is sufficient for the party to lose power – this will depend on a host of other institutional and contextual factors.

5 It is a measure of the complexity of the area and the vagaries of social science research that, in the state-of-the-discipline review in *Electoral Studies*, the editors contented themselves with presenting a summary table of authors' findings in the principal controversies still unresolved in economic voting, (Lewis-Beck and Paldam, 2000). That said, readers will find that the so-called 'e-fraction' – that is, how much of the variation in vote is explained by economics – is often estimated as being around one-third of total variation.

6 Kramer provides a brief overview of those previous studies that looked at the effect of economic conditions on electoral outcomes, but notes that these either rely upon very basic statistical techniques which give no indication of significance or stability of the findings or are essentially anecdotal in their evidence (1971: 133).

7 For the sake of clarity and relevance, we do not look in detail at the political effects here. Interested readers should consult the original articles.

8 Part of this effect derives from a very devious coding of unemployment, whereby increases in unemployment are retained, but decreases in unemployment are all coded 0. This gives the suspicion of the author trying to fit the data to what he wants to find, rather than simply testing a hypothesis. The author himself admits, 'This alteration is a substantive one and is executed as the only way the data can be made to come out "right"' (Mueller, 1970: 23). Perhaps as a consequence, many authors have looked at the asymmetry hypothesis. Although earlier studies found scant evidence for this, more sophisticated testing does suggest that voters punish governments for a bad economy more than they reward them for a good one (Nannestad and Paldam, 1997b).

9 Anderson's analysis in fact uses individual-level data. However, in this instance the theoretical improvement could be equally implemented in aggregate models, and so we have included it here.

10 The Phillips curve has frequently been challenged and modified by economists, particularly since the 1970s and the onset of the stagflation nightmare of contracting economies (implying rising unemployment) and high inflation to boot. However, this has not prevented political parties from emphasising one or other of the 'big two' economic variables. Consequently it does not directly challenge the VP-function hypotheses concerning policy 'ownership'.

11 In contrast to the 'salient issue' hypothesis that we looked at in the previous section, he finds that Left-wing governments in Germany *profit* from higher unemployment: because they will attempt to address this economic ill, their clientele remain faithful to the party. This 'clientele' hypothesis is a competing theory to the salient issue hypothesis in that it predicts a positive relationship between inflation and the Right/unemployment and the Left, rather than a negative one.

12 On the other hand, statisticians can engage in the dubious activity of data-mining whereby data can be transformed using devices like lags, but with very little or no *a priori* theoretical reason for their inclusion other than to make the data fit the initial theory better (Nannestad and Paldam, 1994: 234).

13 Cynics might indicate that the ensuing prediction of the 2000 election by Professor Lewis-Beck using economic variables and presidential popularity indicated a clear victory for the Democrat Al Gore over Republican George Bush. In fact, this does not write off the economic effects in the vote calculus, but simply indicates that other, perhaps election-specific variables such as the personality of the Democrat candidate, the existence of Ralph Nader, the electoral system and the distribution of the vote offset the effects of a buoyant economy and 'Clintonmania'. Gore did also win a 500,000 vote surplus over Bush.

14 The relationship should also work in relative terms: if things look bright under one party, but significantly brighter under another party, then the latter party should be the one which is chosen.

7

Non-Voting and Abstention

Summary box

- Voting and not voting
- Voter registration
- Micro-explanations of turnout: sociodemographics
- Macro-explanations of turnout: country and institutional context
- The micro-macro interaction
- Raising turnout and solutions to abstention.

Introduction

The previous chapters in this book have all asked 'Why do people vote the way they do?' A number of competing theories have offered social and attitudinal reasons to explain the vote outcome. However, in asking this question, we have already implied a separate question, namely, 'Why do people vote?' That is, a social structural or an issue-based theory helps to explain in which box a voter places their tick on the ballot sheet, but neither of them necessarily explains why the voter turned up in the first place. Both assume that the motivations of how someone votes will also be sufficient to make them vote. Indeed, the one theory which does look at this – rational choice theory – seems to posit that the rational voter will generally not bother going to the polls in the first place because her vote will not be worth casting. As we have seen, rational choice theorists have tried to explain the paradox of voting by looking for incentives to vote that may shift the vote cost/benefit analysis in favour of turning out.

If we think of reasons why someone might not vote, it becomes clear that the list is long and varied and goes beyond political motivations. Some people are ill on the day of the election and are unable to get to the voting booth. Others go on holiday and forget to order a proxy vote before they leave. Some people simply forget to go to the polling station before it closes. Yet we must abandon any attempt to try to introduce these apolitical events into a model of abstention for reasons of parsimony and relevance. Firstly, and most importantly, we need to remember that any explanation which takes into account every single possible cause is pretty much useless in scientific terms. Even if we could obtain every single abstainer's reason for not voting in a certain election, it would leave us with nothing more than a very detailed but not very insightful description of events for that election. Who falls ill; who goes on holiday; who forgets to go to the polling station; or who gets struck by lightning on the way – all of these people abstain in practice, but these are essentially random events which do not give us insight into the voting process. Looked at from the predictive point of view, there are variables – attributes or characteristics of voters which we will look at below – which do allow us to predict the likelihood of abstention occurring. However, the kind of random event alluded to above is not something which can reasonably be predicted.[1]

This chapter has three principal aims. Firstly, we want to examine the range of possible reasons that people may have in turning out and not turning out for elections. There are a number of factors which are traditionally said to motivate voting and we would expect these to help account for those who do not vote. As with voting itself, the literature cites a number of social characteristics which increase the likelihood of abstention. Again, it is worth remembering that none of these will necessarily predict abstention with 100 percent certainty, but rather indicate those individuals who are more likely to abstain. For instance, we will see that individuals with lower levels of education are more likely to abstain than those with higher qualifications. However, this does not mean that all individuals with low education abstain. It is only when we combine the effects of a number of characteristics which make people more likely to abstain that we may find that some individuals are more likely to abstain than to vote – but again, this will never be an absolute certainty.

However, as with the economic models we considered in the previous chapter, there are aggregate as well as individual indicators which predict higher levels of abstention at the macro-level, i.e. within different countries and electoral contexts. Thus, the individual level factors needs to be seen as functioning within a stable institutional environment which will have its own overall predicted turnout. But, within that system, individuals will interact with their environment differently. For instance, we will consider the role of the electoral system and the extent to which it allows voters to express their preferences on the ballot paper, rather than just a single choice. We might think that this would incentivise turnout, giving people a greater freedom of political expression. But, as we shall see, whether this is the case or not depends very much on who is ticking the boxes on the ballot paper.

Lastly this chapter will examine the normative implications of abstention. In recent years, much attention has been given to the rise in abstention in most democracies, and the reasons for this. Because of the perception of voting as the symbol of democratic legitimacy and the citizens' principal means of political input (selecting the government of the day and then ousting this government if it does not exercise power satisfactorily) many commentators – but not all – see the decline in vote as highly pernicious. Those abstaining due to their comfortable *status quo* are branded indolent or apathetic; those who abstain due to disenchantment with the system are seen as an indication that something is wrong with the actors or with the system itself. In an attempt to reverse this trend in turnout, a number of possibilities have been suggested that would result in more people voting, either through making the voting process easier or by providing greater incentives to vote. Whilst these strategies are not theories of voting *per se*, they are related to the reasons for abstention and, in their suggested solutions to this democratic 'decline', they illustrate these reasons very well. As such, the chapter will conclude by summarising these strategies and considering whether they are realistic or beneficial in their aims.

Lastly, though it is largely an artificial omission, we will make few references to the rational choice take on turnout in this chapter. Some of the abstention literature refers to rational choice but we have dealt with this theory adequately in its own chapter. For a reminder of its view of abstention, readers should turn back to Chapter 4. However, much of the literature adopts a more empirical perspective on turnout, using social, attitudinal and institutional explanations. Whilst some if not all of these elements can certainly be linked to the rational framework, we will only do so when we believe it adds to the understanding of abstention as a concrete phenomenon (rather than as a by-product of a theoretical decision-making framework).

Before you vote: voter registration

As we have already noted, voting is seen as symbolic of our belonging to democratic society which allows each competent citizen input into the political process and as equal a choice in who governs as any other citizen. Like many symbols, however, the reality is somewhat distant from the truth. Whilst this right to vote is equal, the practice of voting renders remarkably large inequalities amongst citizens both in their desire to vote and indeed in their capacity to vote. The latter of these is perhaps the more worrying from a democratic perspective because the capacity to cast one's ballot is a necessary condition that needs to be fulfilled before the desire to vote can even be considered.

Although this is sometimes overlooked, the key requisite of being able to vote is being registered to vote, and historically the registration process has often been a major obstacle to participation. For reasons of legitimacy and scrutiny, all democratic elections need to have a list of registered voters according to constituency or voting district. How a citizen's name comes to be on this list, however, varies from country to country and often within countries. Some countries require eligible citizens to notify their local administration of their existence so that they can be included on the electoral register, either by post or by going to the administrative office to register. For instance, every year in Britain the head of the household must register all adults resident in his/her household, together with children turning 18 before a specified date. Consequently, voting is linked to the legal list (the so-called 'register of electors') of adult inhabitants in the constituency. In so doing, presence on the electoral register is linked to a host of other civic elements which may influence whether individuals wish to appear on the list or not, despite the illegality of not doing so.

Conversely, the electoral register may simply apply to elections and not be a legal obligation, for instance in the United States. But registration procedures vary from state to state. For instance, in Florida the electoral registration form can be downloaded from the internet and then needs to be filled out, signed and returned to the Supervisor of Elections for anyone who wants to be registered to vote in general (Congressional), primary and presidential elections. In addition, voters must specify a party affiliation to be eligible to vote in party primaries.[2] Philadelphia, on the other hand, requires that a citizen obtain the registration application form in person from a designated outlet.[3] According to state, information on registration and the time limits for registering may or may not be available in other languages, and the ease of access to these varies between states.

Already, we can imagine a number of obstacles to voters registering to vote:

- Non-registration to avoid official recording of residence – my reasons may be fraudulent, to avoid taxes for instance, but this can certainly be sufficient incentive.

- Misunderstanding the rules and regulations due to complexity – I may misunderstand an instruction such as 'The registration books will be closed on the 29th day before each election' and try to register on 29 May for an election held on 1 June.
- Misunderstanding the rules and regulations due to language – in multi-ethnic societies such as US, provision must be made for citizens whose first language is not English.
- Obtaining and returning requisite registration forms due to incapacity – if I am elderly and live on my own, is there alternative provision for me to obtain my registration form?
- Obtaining and returning requisite registration forms due to inconvenience – if I am a working single parent, can I afford the time to go and fill out the registration form?

More generally, however, many voters who would be willing to fill out a form and then turn up to vote may be turned off voting by having to follow complex registration procedures *before* even turning up to vote. Most democracies now have systems which allow relatively simple or effectively automatic registration. Indeed, France and the US are the only two countries where registration requires initiative on the part of the voter, rather than being initiated by the administration. Even registering in the US, whose registration laws even in the 1970s were a disparate array of legal checks and hindrances (Milbrath, 1965; Wolfinger and Rosenstone, 1980: 62–4), has been improved significantly.[4]

Two other important elements to voter registration are also worth noting briefly. Firstly, voter registration can be used – and historically, has been – to disenfranchise voters. Most notoriously, black voters in many Southern states in the US were often prevented from voting by the infamous 'literacy tests' and other often insuperable bureaucratic obstacles attached to voter registration until protest by the civil rights movement forced President Johnson to abolish these in 1965 (Teixeira, 1993: 11).

Secondly, although voter registration is designed to eliminate fraudulent voting, it does not always do so. Despite greater prominence to the phenomenon in new and developing democracies, where much electoral irregularity can be ascribed to learning the rules of the game and imperfect democratic procedure, established democracies are still not free from it. For example, 130,000 voters had to be removed from the Northern Ireland electoral register at the beginning of 2003 subsequent to a governmental White Paper on the topic in March 2001. Similarly, the 2000 US elections were wracked by allegations of fraud, especially in the key state of Florida. This problem threatens to return to saliency with worries about the new voting technologies, designed in part to raise turnout, enabling voting fraud.

Because of the discrepancies which can result between registered voters and the total population of voting age, it is now usually the norm to measure turnout on the basis of registered voters, and most studies and records of turnout do this (Mackie and Rose, 1991). However, due to non-registration, we should bear in mind that the real turnout in terms of citizens who *should* be eligible to vote will always be smaller, though the extent to which this is the case will vary from country to country.[5]

Individual/micro-indicators of turnout: sociodemographics

Why sociodemographics and not attitudes?

The modern view of abstention is as a negative activity commenting on problems within the system. Voters who do not vote are generally viewed as being 'disenfranchised'. Disenfranchisement can mean the removal of the right to vote or more of the rights of a citizen. However, in the abstention sense, it suggests a situation where voters feel that they are removed from a political process which they cannot engage with or which they feel does not represent them. Key ascribed this to socially and economically disadvantaged groups in society lacking organisation to make themselves heard, and hence becoming disenfranchised (cited in Lipset, 1959a: 227). More recent studies of low turnout in the US have also used this argument (Rosenstone and Hansen, 1993).

In this case, the system does not consider their interests: they do not feel part of the political process which becomes distant from them. However, they may also actively shun the system as undemocratic, corrupt or somehow ineffectual and from which they wish to withhold the legitimation which voting represents or, at the extreme, delegitimise by not voting.

Yet this has not always been the interpretation of abstention. For instance, in an attempt to explain why levels of turnout in the US were so much lower than in Europe, Gosnell posited that European polities were socially and ideologically more divided and hence political conflict was stronger (1930). On the other hand, in the US, such conflicts had disappeared, economic development was high and thus 'aggressive' mobilisation was less widespread. Other analysts in the 1930s saw high turnout as inherently destabilising, leading to an intensification of social conflict (e.g. Tingsten, 1937).

More recent studies of abstention have tended to emphasise the first type of abstainer, looking at the individual-level characteristics associated with perceptions of disenfranchisement, although one study at least has found a significant minority of contented, knowledgeable but apathetic non-voters (Doppelt and Shearer, 2000). Generally, 'disenfranchised' abstention is linked either to social group belonging, and consequently belongs firmly in the sociological tradition of group interests which we considered in Chapter 3; or it is linked directly to a series of attitudinal and psychological indicators such as political interest, trust, efficacy, satisfaction and involvement. In the former case, turnout largely becomes implicit: the group belonging indicators which are used to predict who a voter will vote for will naturally imply that such a voter turns out. However, a large number of sociodemographic indicators do additionally affect the probability of turning out, and we shall look at these shortly. The attitudinal indicators can be measured using survey data, and look at questions such as 'How well do you think democracy is functioning in our country?' or ask respondents to agree with statements such as 'Politicians do not care what people like me think'. Those individuals with low scores on these scales tend to be the ones not to turn out. The politically effective, satisfied, interested and trusting vote, as well as participating in political activity more generally (Dalton, 2002: 47–54).

So why we do we not simply use these scales to predict turnout? Because, as Perea notes, they do not really get to the root of voter participation. If voting is an indicator of political implantation and/or efficacy, what we want to know is *why* certain individuals feel effective, not the simple fact that they do – and consequently vote (2002: 647). The fact that those people who are interested in politics and feel politically effective are also more likely to vote is hardly powerful as an explanatory relationship, and more a self-fulfilling prophecy. Citing party membership as a strong indicator of turnout is akin to remarking that people wearing dresses tend to be women.

Does this mean that such attitudinal scales are redundant? Not necessarily: first of all, they can be used as a dependent variable themselves, going beyond the voting/abstaining dyad (and suffering less explicitly from the response errors associated with reported voting in surveys). Secondly, if we wish to calculate a parsimonious index of individual incentives to vote – as Perea does in her own study of abstention – the inclusion of such variables can allow for individuals who do not fit the above profile, but who nonetheless are interested in politics or feel politically effective, and consequently will be more likely to vote.

Now that we have established that we are primarily interested in finding theoretically informative explanatory variables, rather than excellent predictive proxies, which indicators can be used to this end?

Age

The relationship between age and vote has been hypothesised to work in two ways. Some commentators see the relationship as being essentially linear: as age increases, so the likelihood of turnout increases, at least until the 'age of infirmity' (Topf, 1995: 43). Others believe that the age of infirmity has greater weight, and hence have hypothesised a U-shaped relationship, with likelihood of turnout increasing throughout middle-age, and then declining amongst the elderly (Lipset, 1959a: 187). The reason for lower turnout amongst the very elderly is clearly related to the ability to go to the polling station. The lower turnout amongst the young is not a physical restriction, but rather their relationship with the political system and thus motivational. Firstly, they are less implanted in the electoral aspect of the political system because they have not voted before and hence may not have developed the habit of voting. Secondly, they are less integrated into society. More recent testing finds that there is indeed a monotonic relationship between age and turnout: older voters are more likely to vote (Blais, 2000: 53).

Gender

Women have often been cited as turning out to vote less than men. For some, this has been an historical phenomenon indicating the shorter enfranchisement of women and hence their lesser habit of political participation. Lipset also hypothesised that women were more subject to cross-pressures on the matter of vote – in particular wives in working-class households would have been influenced leftwards by their husbands, but may traditionally have been pushed rightwards by church involvement and status concerns (1959a: 217). Given the length of time of enfranchisement, however, and the redressing of the domestic gender balance, these explanations seem decreasingly relevant. Other explanations concentrate on women in some social strata not seeing voting as a female activity, but again these assume a very traditional conservative view of women's social position and status which does not match contemporary society. Most contemporary testings of turnout between men and women fail to find consistent evidence of significant differences (Wolfinger and Rosenstone, 1980: 41; Topf, 1995).

Ethnic groups

Research in the US has particularly focused on ethnic group turnout. Because of the discriminatory registration laws mentioned earlier, black turnout was particularly low until the 1960s. However, since the 1960s much research has found that, *ceteris paribus*, black voter turnout equalled or exceeded white voter turnout in its likelihood (Leighley and Nagler, 1992: 726–7). There is also evidence that amongst the younger strata of black voters, turnout is in decline due to a decline in contact with mobilisatory groups via church attendance, for instance. However, the evidence here is often contradictory (Burnside, 1999: 5–6). Lower education levels amongst young black voters certainly decreases turnout. Research into Latino turnout in the US has consistently found it to be a significant predictor of low turnout (Highton and Burris, 2002).

Education

Higher education is linked to increased turnout for two reasons. Firstly, voters with higher levels of education are more likely to be cognitively mobilised and capable of engaging with political discourse. Secondly, educated voters are more likely to have been socialised into the mentality that voting is a civic duty. Clearly one would expect this to be stronger in education systems which include civics classes at some point (although if these are provided at an early age, then this would not appear as an effect of higher education). However, there is also the implication that, as with attitudes such as tolerance and open-mindedness, education itself is a means to civic-mindedness, whatever its content. Overall, education has generally been found to be the major individual predictor of turnout (Wolfinger and Rosenstone, 1980: 53; Blais, 2000: 52).

Income

Citizens with low levels of income will be less likely to vote because they have more immediate concerns than the political, namely their own standard of living. Of course, this goes directly against the view that voting provides members of low socioeconomic status access to politics which may allow them to offset their lower status, if it still pertains when elections are functioning optimally. Admittedly, it is difficult to say whether the representative democratic process is functioning. However, if low income groups are disproportionately abstaining, this is perhaps a good indicator that it is not. We should also remember that the effects of education and income are likely to be closely related – and where we control for both in a multivariate model, education as the paramount factor usually turns out to be a better predictor of individual turnout. This in turn implies that the political effectiveness and cognitive mobilisation arguments are stronger than material wealth.

Union membership and other organisations

Members of unions are by definition involved in politically active organisations and hence these individuals are more likely to be politically active themselves. Given that voting is the lowest level of political activity, union members are more likely to vote. This is likely to be a stronger effect if the union in question has strong links with a political party, as, for instance, trades unions in the UK traditionally did with the Labour party or the Communist CGU union in France. Moreover, where political organisations beyond the union mould exist, these may also have an effect. Probably the best example of this would be the Catholic Action organisation in Italy, which could be regarded as a political intermediary organisation between the Vatican and Christian Democrat voters. As we saw in Chapter 3, such membership can be regarded as part of 'social encapsulation'. The existence of such organisations should always be borne in mind, although in comparative studies in particular, unions are usually the main organisation tested as they exist in most if not all democracies. We should also remember, however, that the group benefits explanation could also incentivise turnout for members of any organisation, because these have a socially integrating function.

Marital status

Why should married people be more likely to vote than singletons? From the authors of *The American Voter*'s perspective, the family influence engendered by a spouse or partner will help mobilise the borderline reluctant voter (Campbell et al., 1960: 109). From the civic perspective, married individuals are seen as more 'settled' and more implanted in society. Apparently, they have more at stake in a society and are more likely to be affected by government policy. Therefore they have greater incentive to support the party which itself supports their situation. One might argue that couples having children have a greater stake in a stable, well governed society and so will be likely to participate in the political process. In many modern societies, however, marriage is decreasingly correlated with childbirth and hence one could not necessarily assume that this hypothesised relationship works. Instead, individuals would have to be sub-divided into those with and those without children. Whilst data generally confirm the role of marital status, we are not aware of a comparative study of parental status and turnout.

These are a selection of the variables which have been seen to exercise an effect on turnout. However, others have also been looked at – religious practice, unemployment, urban-rural residence (which follows the same argument as the macro-indicator but at the level of individuals). Indeed, in a wry look at the turnout literature 20 years ago, Grofman remarked that those employing social factors as predictors of turnout usually did so with a model 'based on some subset of the variable list in the ICPSR codebook (i.e. every variable known to political science).' (1983: 55) In other words, there has been a tendency to plug in a vast number of potentially relevant variables without much discernment. How can we summarise the key properties of all these variables which are causally related to turnout? Four elements cover these properties:

- Socioeconomic variables which suggest individuals are stably implanted within the social system (marital status, employment, income) and consequently have resources to dedicate to political activity, including voting. Those individuals having to commit their resources to other pursuits – searching for financial income, a job or a partner – commit their resources to these 'socioeconomic thresholds' and hence may not have sufficient resources left to vote.
- Those variables which suggest that individuals are imbued with the feeling that voting is a civic duty (education, religiosity) will be more likely to vote than to abstain.
- Similarly, those variables which bring individuals closer to the political process (unions, political organisations, certain occupations) may reinforce interest in participation, and consequently encourage voting.[6]
- Subsuming these three factors, the feeling of social integration itself, whether due to stability, group belonging or political involvement will be more likely to engender a feeling of belonging and consequently 'wanting to participate'.

We thus have a range of individual indicators linked to turnout. However, in thinking about motivations to vote earlier, we mentioned that some people do not vote because they feel the system does not represent them in some way: the parties competing in the electoral arena do not offer policies they want, for example, or they feel that whoever they vote for will not make any difference, either for positive or negative reasons. Others may feel that the system is simply 'undemocratic'. This suggests that there may be systemic features which contribute to the decision to vote or abstain. That different constitutional and institutional frameworks have implications for the functioning of democracy and representation is the subject of a high profile literature (Sartori, 1994; Lijphart, 1999). How might these macro-level indicators determine turnout at the systemic level? Additionally, are there other country characteristics which play a role?

Aggregate/macro-indicators of turnout

Many of the more popular theories used to explain turnout are based upon general characteristics of the political system, and the electoral context and country-specific contexts more generally (Jackman, 1987; Blais and Carty, 1990; Blais and Dobrzynska, 1998). As the rules of the game under which the election is played out, the electoral system may have an influence on whether or not people want to take part. Similarly, the actual game that is in progress – that is, the perception of the election itself – may also motivate people to turn out more than previous elections had done, or conversely may demotivate them and push them to stay at home. Lastly, the socioeconomic environment of the country can have an effect. We look at these in turn.

Type of electoral system[7]

One of the earliest hypotheses concerning the electoral system and turnout states that one would expect to see higher turnout in systems which are run under proportional representation than those run under a plurality or majoritarian system. Simply, systems based on proportionality are seen as fairer: proportional representation systems are widely held to be more 'egalitarian' than majoritarian systems in the value they accord to the vote. In a proportional system, every voter's vote counts in the final allocation of seats to the different parties and consequently in the choice of governmental winner(s). In a majoritarian or plurality system, however, the influence of individual votes is perceived to be much less. Firstly, all votes cast for a losing candidate are effectively lost or valueless: only those voting for a winning candidate influence the outcome.

Secondly, in a majoritarian system voters are put off voting for parties which have little or no chance of winning a constituency seat. In a proportional system, however, voters can vote for a small or locally less successful party in the confident expectation that, unless it is truly marginal and falls below the threshold which most PR systems impose upon parties to achieve representation, it will have some level of representation relative to its size, and that their vote will count towards it. Thus, voters are more able to vote expressively, and choose the party they really support, as opposed to voters in majoritarian systems who often choose a party with a more realistic chance of winning the seat, or indeed the election overall – sometimes in a 'tactical' vote, whereby, to keep a disliked party from winning, one chooses a lower-preference party instead of the first preference, because this former stands a better chance of winning. The most recent high-profile example of this would be the 2000 US Presidential elections where Democrats called on supporters of the third candidate, Ralph Nader, to vote for them instead because Nader stood no chance of winning, whereas the Democrats needed every vote they could muster to try to beat the Republican George Bush.

Thirdly, this higher level of representativeness is also encouraged by the presence of multi-member districts in PR systems. Where multi-member districts exist, such that more than one representative is elected for each district, it is distinctly less likely that a single party will win all of these seats, even if a very popular party fields candidates for all seats in that district. Thus, if at least one of the seats is available, the level of competitivity in the system will be higher across all districts, with two resultant effects. Firstly, from the demand side, a broader section of the electorate will see their vote supporting an elected representative, thus potentially promoting turnout. Secondly, and from the supply side, parties are more likely to campaign strongly in all constituencies because of the possibility of winning seats and hence increased campaigning and mobilisation might bring out more voters than in a majoritarian system where, for example, a safe seat will be regarded as uncompetitive – a foregone electoral conclusion – by voters and parties alike.

This variable can be measured in two ways: either to separate electoral systems into different categories (such as PR versus majoritarian, or PR versus plurality versus majoritarian versus 'mixed' systems); or alternatively an index of disproportionality can be calculated, whereby the difference between share of seats and share of votes is calculated. Evidently, in PR systems, the share of the vote will usually be closer to the share of the vote than in majoritarian systems.

Party system format

In much previous research on institutional effects, there has been some confusion as to direct and indirect effects of the electoral system (Blais and Carty, 1990). One of the indirect effects has been that mediated by the party system: electoral systems influence party system format, and, as we see below, party system may then affect turnout.

As Duverger's law and its successors tell us in varying ways, proportional systems have more parties than majoritarian ones (Duverger, 1954; Sartori, 1976). Voters are therefore more likely to be able to vote for their 'true' party in a proportional system quite simply because this party is more likely to exist. Majoritarian systems impose high barriers to small parties gaining representation and hence they are less likely to compete in the first place. Conversely, because proportional systems grant a better chance of securing some level of representation, so smaller parties will appear and compete, and consequently voters will have a broader array of parties to choose from, rather than having to make do with the 'least distant' party. Thus, where voters can vote expressively for their 'true' party, where their vote is more likely to be valuable and instrumental in electing a representative rather than being thrown away in a majoritarian system, voters are seen as more likely to turn out.

Unfortunately, a counter-hypothesis seems as convincing theoretically as the above argument. Because a larger number of parties makes coalition government more likely as an outcome than a single party winning government alone, the outcome of an election for voters may be less clear, particularly if coalitions are not announced before the election. Thus, an election where a small number of parties stand and there is a strong likelihood of one overall winner – i.e. majoritarian systems – may be more attractive to voters who prefer a clear outcome. More generally, a large number of parties in the system may simply prove confusing to a potential voter who consequently decides to abstain. The competition between these two hypotheses is resolved in the subsequent section on interactions between micro- and macro-indicators.

Electoral context

Often placed under the party system format, how competitive the election is may affect turnout. If the race is a close one, then the importance of one's vote can be seen as greater than if the election is a landslide. Again, this is a debatable assumption. Firstly, the usual indicator for this variable is the difference in vote share between the first and second placed parties. However, this is not known until *after* the election. We are thus perhaps on shaky ground in causal terms: the effect (turnout) seems to be coming before the cause (closeness of race). However, it can be argued that because of opinion polls, media reports and analysis of the campaign, predictions of likely outcome, and the intensity of the campaign itself, the actual competitiveness of the election itself functions as a proxy for these preceding elements. There is also evidence that competitiveness at the constituency level as indicated by the marginality of the seat, that is, the majority of the first-placed candidate over the second, at the *previous* election will affect turnout – the more marginal the seat, the higher the turnout (Denver and Hands, 1974).

Indeed, the broader election context may well be important regardless of the actual electoral outcome. Interest of the campaign, the particular issues and personalities involved, and the stakes of the election may well stimulate or depress turnout. However, it may be difficult to measure these aspects across time and countries, or indeed within a single country, and hence there has been little or no robust testing of these hypotheses. The one which has been tested in a particular way is that of the stakes of the election. Elections should matter more where they elect a strong executive government, rather than one which shares executive power with a president, or indeed is subservient to a strong presidency. If who governs matters, then turnout should be higher.

Lastly, but perhaps most importantly and obviously, compulsory voting is likely to raise turnout. If it is a legal obligation to vote, with possible fines or the removal of certain civic rights, then people are more likely to make the effort to vote, even if they do not want to. The value of such a vote, and the worry that enforced voting simply encourages those who would have abstained to tick any box almost at random or spoil the ballot, does not impinge upon the argument that legal obligation is a strong incentive, particular in countries like Belgium and Luxembourg where it is strongly enforced.

Socioeconomic context

In studies of Western democracies, the socioeconomic context has usually been overlooked because there simply is not sufficient variation in modern societies' contexts to be able to test the differences in turnout on this basis. However, if one extends the analysis to all democracies rather than simply advanced post-industrial democracies, then the variations are much more substantial. The key variables to consider are literacy, GNP or GDP per capita, growth of GNP or GDP and both the size and density of population (Powell, 1980; Blais and Dobrzynska, 1998).[8]

A low literacy rate suggests that many potential voters will be unable to engage with political discourse due to this major obstacle to their cognitive mobilisation and hence will not become politically mobilised either. The wealth of the country, represented by GNP or GDP, is seen as functioning in a similar manner: a country with a high degree of wealth is likely to have higher proportions of integrated, cognitively mobilised individuals who engage with politics and hence vote. Change in wealth, on the other hand, refers to the disruptive effects that economic decline has on political engagement (Rosenstone, 1982). Conversely, if the economy thrives, individuals should be more willing to spend time on politics than on their personal economic well-being. That said, a counter-hypothesis could be that participation will increase under economic crisis, because individuals will be anxious to have their say in who attempts to drag them out of the crisis. And to return to Lipset (1959a), stable society (which could certainly include economic affluence) would in its turn make people more disinterested in political matters.

Finally, smaller populations are held to be more likely to turn out because there is likely to be greater social cohesion and sense of community, and hence civic duty amongst them than amongst large heterogeneous populations. But in terms of population density, those countries whose populations are more spread out are less likely to have this feeling than those who are densely packed together. In other words, a country with a small population but a large territorial expanse will have two opposing dynamics determining its turnout, if these hypotheses are accurate.

These macro-level indicators are normally tested at the national level and comparing across countries, to look either at the absolute levels of turnout or change in turnout. Given that the dependent variable is a continuous variable, variants on the basic linear model are usually employed. Conversely, the micro-level indicators, such as the sociodemographics and the attitudinal scales, are normally tested using survey data. Given that the dependent variable is usually dichotomous (vote/abstain), a logit model is the most common statistical technique used here.[9]

Interactions between micro- and macro-level indicators

Lastly, we should consider the slightly more complex but essential relationship between micro- and macro-level indicators which should inform our analysis. Thinking about the macro-level indicators, they rely upon individuals' perceptions of and relationship with the variable for their effect. For instance, take electoral system effect and the view that proportional systems encourage turnout more than majoritarian systems, which in turn may discourage turnout because of its mediating effect via the number of parties found in a party system. But we saw that a counter-argument hypothesised that some people might prefer the majoritarian system with fewer parties because the electoral supply is easier to interpret and the outcome – in all likelihood a one-party majority government – is clearer. Given that both hypotheses seem convincing, even if we find that one hypothesis 'wins' if we test just macro effects, might we not find that differences in voter profiles at the individual level still indicate that both hypotheses may be valid, but for different voters?

Similar interactions might be found with other indicators. Do all voters have a similar reaction to compulsory voting? Does the closeness of the race have an effect on everyone in the system, or are some people more likely to perceive the closeness of the race? Despite the obvious importance of these possibilities, very little work has been done on interaction effects. The most recent and complete analysis is that by Perea (2002).[10] Consequently, we will use her analysis to look at the empirical findings for the interaction effects.[11]

Individual incentives in the presence of national context

Although not an interaction *per se*, Perea finds that, looking at the index of individual incentives in different countries, there is an inverse relationship between individual incentives and the level of abstention (2002: 650). Where turnout is high – and thus, by implication, where the macro-context encourages turnout – the effect of individual incentives is lower than in countries where turnout is low and individual incentives tend to have a greater effect. Looking at the difference between citizens with low incentives to vote and those with high incentives to vote, the national context has a greater effect on the low-incentive group, whereas for the high-incentive group, the different national contexts seem to have little effect. This is understandable: the high-incentive voters are simply overwhelmingly likely to vote, and so the system which they find themselves in makes little difference.

Compulsory voting

Under compulsory voting, individual incentives seem to be stronger, and similarly the effects of compulsory voting are stronger when individual incentives are high (2002: 657–8). In other words, the difference between those who are politically effective and those who are socially dislocated is greater when there is a compulsory voting system than when there is not. The other effect indicates that those who are socially implanted take more notice of the compulsory voting rule than their dislocated counterparts. This would either indicate simple awareness that these rules exist, or more subtly a greater feeling of civic duty compared with low-incentive voters who feel less compulsion to follow the electoral law.

Electoral thresholds

Interestingly, given the emphasis placed on the attractiveness of a proportional system over majoritarian systems in increasing turnout, particularly in the debate over electoral reform in the UK, electoral thresholds have no effect for individuals with low incentives to vote: those who are socially dislocated are no more likely to vote, whatever the electoral system (2002: 661–2). It is only for those individuals with high incentives that electoral thresholds matter: 'fairer' proportional systems are more likely to engender turnout than majoritarian systems. Similarly to compulsory voting, this indicates that citizens who understand how the electoral system works, and the extent to which it values their vote, are put off by systems which place a high barrier on entry, whereas less informed or excluded voters are not influenced by this.

Preference expression

Also worryingly for proponents of voting systems which allow greater subtley amongst the electoral system's interpretation of voters preferences, those systems which allow voters to list hierarchical lists of party preferences or to choose specific candidates, do incentivise turnout amongst the socially implanted electorate, but amongst the socially dislocated, the system puts them off voting, presumably because of the complexity of the system (2002: 663–4). This also lends support to the counter-hypothesis discussed in the macro-indicators and effect of proportional systems section: if we assume that systems characterised by preference expression are more likely to be run under PR systems, where the likely outcome is less clear to the participants, some people may be put off voting. We should emphasise that this is not the effect of any PR system, but of that subset run under preference systems, which intensify the disincentives of the system.

Given the paucity of the literature, the area of interactions is evidently one where much more research can be carried out. Although the above interactions are undoubtedly some of the most important ones – especially in informing the views of those proposing electoral system reform – other interactions are still to be tested. For instance, what relationship holds between party system type and individual's profile? Do voters with lower incentives get put off by systems containing larger numbers of parties? Socioeconomic context would also seem a viable area for interaction effects. For instance, is there any difference in participation rate by individual incentives according to GNP or GDP, and indeed does this level of income matter more for individuals with low or high incentives? These are areas for fruitful future analysis.

Normative solutions to abstention

Whatever the reasons for individuals' abstention, and whether or not their decision not to turn out is conceptualised as positive or negative, rising abstention is generally regarded as a bad thing for democracy and for society. Most commentators regard the decline in the active electorate, particularly over the last decade, as symptomatic of modern society's disengagement with the political process and a manifestation of an array of negative views of politicians and political parties ranging from disinterest to outright hostility. Even those individuals happy to let politicians get on with it are seen as problematic: without the participation of a healthy majority of the electorate, how can politicians claim to be legitimised, particularly when they make unpopular decisions?

In the long run, if an increasing proportion of the electorate becomes too acclimatised to doing nothing, two major risks are run:

(1) politicians become increasingly indifferent to and contemptuous of public opinion and end up by becoming an unresponsive oligarchy rather than responsive representatives;
(2) undemocratic forces can win power with the support of just a small minority of the electorate, and the apathetic majority are too dislocated from the political process to react in time.

From the institutional perspective, how should we assess some of the more common suggested solutions?

Institutional change

In majoritarian systems (notably France and the UK), critics propose reform of the electoral system, not simply to increase turnout but to ensure greater representativeness more generally. Because of the wasted votes characteristic of the majoritarian system, however, the shift to proportional representation is seen as a way of making every vote count and hence of giving voters, who have previously been denied a voice, greater electoral worth. However, as we have seen in the previous section, the change in the electoral system may not have the expected effects. In aggregate terms, proportional representation does have a direct positive effect on turnout (Jackman, 1987; Blais and Carty, 1990). But in systems where preference expression is higher, those individuals with low individual incentives to vote will be *less* likely to turn out (Perea, 2002).

More generally, electoral system reform, as with other aspects of institutional change, is a strategy which has much broader implications than simply the electoral system itself. As the Italian system has shown in the three elections since the institutional reforms of 1993, changing the electoral rules of the game will change more than just the balance of power and representativeness within a system: it also changes the very nature of representation in society, not least in the array of parties competing within the system. Whether or not this is a good thing normatively is very much in the eye of the beholder. But proponents of institutional change need to be aware that the effects of the change may go well beyond what was intended in terms of simple representativeness. Nor is this something that analysis of existing and historical systems can necessarily predict. The vast majority of systems across time are characterised more by stability than change, and thus the shift from a majoritarian to a proportional system may not mean that the system takes on the 'normal' characteristics of a proportional system.

Compulsory voting

Many critics of non-voters emphasise that the *right* to vote is accompanied by a *responsibility* to vote. If people are not willing to take this responsibility seriously, then the state has a duty to oblige them. Again, as we have seen, compulsory voting systems unsurprisingly manifest higher levels of turnout than systems where voting is a choice. Thus, to impose compulsory voting would seem a good way of increasing turnout. However, again, we should be careful of the effects of such a change. Firstly, we have seen that the compulsory voting effect is stronger amongst citizens with high individual incentives. In other words, those who are socially implanted in society, interested in politics and identifying with a party are more likely to 'obey' the voting law than those who are more marginalised and turned off by politics. Admittedly, amongst those who hover on the border of abstaining or voting, the compulsory vote could tip the balance. But for those who are most marginalised, the system may not necessarily have any effect.

Additionally, from a normative point of view, we must ask whether simply making voting compulsory addresses the real problem. Forcing people to vote does nothing to address the problem of marginalisation (unless one believes that voting somehow gives individuals a greater sense of social integration by itself) or political apathy. Just because we have to vote for a politician or party does not mean that we have any more faith in them. Moreover, in systems where the democratic norm has historically been the choice to vote, imposing a compulsory system may have precisely the reverse effect, namely incentivising non-voting as a protest at the state's intervention in a previously private choice. Some people could gain something precisely from *not* voting under such circumstances.

Voter facilities

Rather than impose voting on individuals, a more tempered proposal is to make access to voting easier for citizens. People with disabilities; the elderly; those with long distances to travel to the polling station; parents of young children; even people with heavy work commitments – all are hindered to a greater or lesser extent from voting, or indeed from registering to vote. Consequently a wider range of means of voting should be opened up. For instance, computerised voting would allow people to vote from their own homes or from a public access terminal if they do not own a computer. Similar suggestions have been made for the use of interactive television or text-message voting.

Pilot schemes have generally proved very successful – or at least have been heralded as successes[12] – where implemented. Many states in the US, such as Utah and California, now have online voter registration forms, and many other have registration forms which can be downloaded, printed and sent by mail. More radically, voting online using the internet has been tested in a number of elections. For instance, in the Arizona Democratic primaries of 2000, nearly 40,000 people cast their vote via the internet. However, this was less than half of those who voted – and indeed only just over 10 percent of those registered to vote did so.[13] In other words, even though this was an increase on the number of people who voted in the 1996 primary (when Bill Clinton stood unopposed), the people voting by internet are likely simply to have switched means of voting, rather than voted by internet instead of abstaining had the option not been available.

Indeed, this is one of the major 'problems' with the technological solution to abstention: those who use the technology are likely to be the people who would have voted anyhow. Many of the people it is designed to help vote are ones with lower levels of IT usage – the elderly, ethnic minorities, the lower educational strata, those living in rural areas are usually the groups with lowest internet usage. Middle options whereby computer voting is available at polling stations which can be used by anyone regardless of electoral district might resolve some cases of voters living close to electoral boundaries but traditionally forced to travel to more distant polling stations, but this is a minority of cases. The main disenfranchised groups are not helped by this.

The electronic voting media more generally are seen as inherently more attractive to younger voters as well, who, in the British case for example, may be put off by the old-fashioned pencil and paper. Because many youngsters are increasingly using computers and other electronic media as their primary interface with the real world, so voting via these media may seem 'more natural'. Unfortunately, to date there are still technological obstacles and issues of internet confidentiality which are preventing such strategies being tested on a more widespread basis. Although it seems unlikely, the possibility of internet fraud is also one which rules out the exclusive use of the internet in the near future. Similarly, the more-than-likely technical failures mean that large number of voters could effectively be disenfranchised and unable to vote. One advantage of pencil and paper, or even an electronic voting machine in a polling station, is that not much can go wrong in the former, and a replacement can be found in the latter.

More generally, however, we must ask ourselves whether the overall drive to make voting easier is really a positive step. Similarly to the introduction of compulsory voting, just because more people are voting does not necessarily mean that representation or enfranchisement has improved. In some senses, making voting easier devalues the vote. Strident critics of apathetic Western voters point to lesser developed democracies where people travel vast distances and queue for hours in order to vote. Why should money and effort be spent on pandering to lowest common denominator voters, they ask. For those truly unable to make it to the polling station, other possibilities such as postal votes and proxies already exist. Finally, for groups disenfranchised from politics, making it easier to vote does nothing whatsoever to solve the problem of social dislocation – indeed it is somewhat patronising to think that one can solve the problem of individuals who feel alienated from politics by simply making voting easier. We have to ask ourselves – does making voting easy enough for the indolent voter to click on a ballot paper at a whim devalue voting?

New technologies and new democracy

Perhaps the most radical suggestion for preventing the decline in turnout is simply to make turnout irrelevant. The new technology that could allow internet voting is held by some to offer the answer to a new direct democracy utopia whereby the organisations and institutions which dominate the contemporary political arena – media, corporate interests, pressure groups – can be by-passed to a greater or lesser extent using these interactive electronic media to engage in online debate and voting (Morris, 1999). In the most radical view, all political decisions in a society could be subjected to such a process, rendering elected representatives effectively redundant. In this sense, turnout would be irrelevant because whichever government was elected would be at the behest of these referenda, and hence their professed political ideology would make no difference.

Indeed, the very nature of government would converge on that of a bureaucracy – and we might ask whether a government would even be necessary. From a Downsian perspective, voters would have no incentive to turn out in elections – their preferences can be represented in virtual referenda – and parties would have no incentive to stand for election – their own utility income of power and prestige would not exist. Of course, we then need to ask 'Who decides what to vote on in these "virtual referenda"?'. A representative sample of the electorate perhaps. 'How would these be chosen?'. By election … and then we realise we will rapidly come full circle and head back to the *status quo*. The radical view of direct democracy consequently has little going for it.

The more sober view of new technology heralding a new age of democracy – for instance, that put forward by Budge (1996) – states that we will always need politicians and representatives, and these would still need electing as usual, but that their actions can be scrutinised and influenced on a more regular basis by the use of virtual referenda on the most important issues, either determined by the government themselves – akin to issues of confidence upon which governments have traditionally placed the future of their governing incumbency or have submitted to referendum – or automatically submitted to a referendum if such a policy did not feature in the government's programme at the previous election (1996: 183–5).

That in the presence of higher levels of direct democracy, government *per se* becomes less important seems to be borne out by the Swiss case, where referenda and popular initiatives are more frequent and turnout is generally

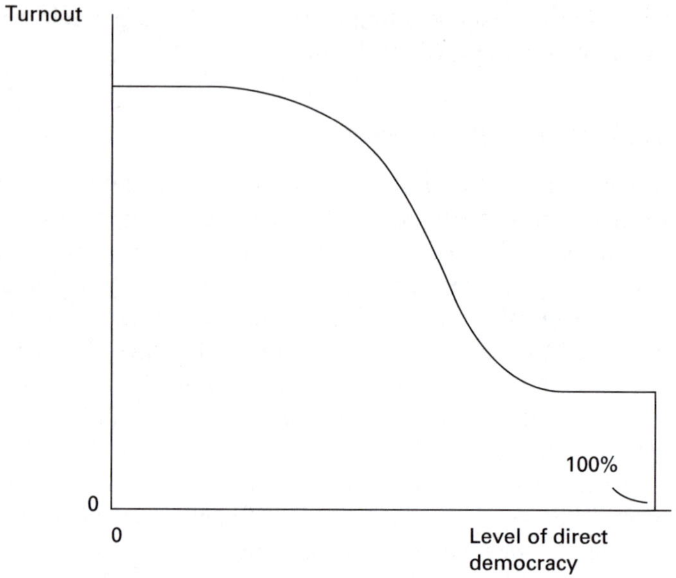

Figure 7.1 *Hypothesised relationship between level of direct democracy and turnout*

lower than in other European states. In the new technology democracy, *ceteris paribus*, we might therefore hypothesise the relationship between turnout and the extent of direct democracy as shown in Figure 7.1

At lower levels of direct democracy, turnout remains relatively unaffected as the bulk of government decision-making is still free from mass intervention. As direct democratic influence increases, so the possibility of influencing policy after the election increases, and thus the importance of picking the government at the election decreases for larger proportions of the electorate. However, turnout will not decline to zero as there will always be a residual electorate, who are either so extreme that no level of direct democracy will allow them to correct the initial government's policies sufficiently, or who have non-ideological or irrational reasons for voting. Only when direct democracy reaches 100 percent – in other words, all policy is decided by the electorate – would turnout drop immediately to zero, as mentioned above.

Of course, this dynamic could be countered by additional incentives for turnout produced by direct democracy: voters becoming more politically involved and hence turning out more due to a feeling of greater enfranchisement. In this sense, medium levels of direct democracy may well be a good thing for reinvigorating political systems.

Conclusion: today, why vote?

In concluding our look at abstention and voter turnout, we present a final interpretation of the apparent phenomenon of falling electoral participation in democracies. Is it not in fact *rational* that people are not turning out in the numbers that they used to? If we recall from Chapter 6 the dynamics of change that challenge the traditional governmental control in the modern political arena are as follows:

(1) an increasing proportion of policies and issues are being decided or determined by actors other than national governments sovereign over their territorially defined nation-states;
(2) even the policies and issues which are under the national governmental remit are constrained in the alternatives available.

To follow Downs' logic, then, the range of ideologies and policy actions that governments and oppositions can credibly promote and take is reduced, and hence there should be less to choose between parties. Of course, parties continue to protest that this is not true, and that they can make a difference that their competitors cannot, even if they accept that many policy-areas are increasingly out of their grasp. Whether or not this annoys voters (who abstain out of dissatisfaction that government is emasculated), or is accepted by voters (who abstain because government is evidently impotent), the rational response must be simply not to vote.

Consequently, both the macro and micro determinants of abstention highlighted above should lose their predictive and explanatory potential over time. At the macro level, institutional frameworks and party systems matter little if the end result of a vote is a powerless actor. Similarly, at the micro level, we should expect the disenfranchised, politically apathetic sections of the community to be joined by those who realise the futility of voting for powerless governments.

This situation has certainly not yet come to pass. Governments still have a role to play and influence our daily lives, and even if they do not always have free rein in choosing their policy positions, they still do have to carry out their representative function competently. Where they do not, citizens are vociferous in their protest – for instance, in the strength of demonstrations against the war in Iraq in February 2003, where such numbers engaged in direct protest had never been seen before in many European nations. Additionally, increasing numbers of policies may be matters of competence rather than ideology, but at the very least these policies still need to be formulated and passed, and most of these still have variations in how they might be achieved. To this extent, voters do still have good reason to turn out. But the fact that the micro predictors *do* still work suggest that one of the primary functions of the vote – to allow otherwise disempowered citizens to influence governments to affect their standard of living positively – is still somewhat dysfunctional.

Summary box

You should now be able to:

- explain why abstention poses different explanatory tasks from voting
- explain how voter registration can hinder people from voting
- distinguish between the uses of associated attitudinal and explanatory sociodemographic variables
- identify the key underlying elements in sociodemographic explanations of abstention
- understand the role of institutions in attracting and repelling voters
- understand how institutions have differing effects on different groups of voters
- explain and critique proposed institutional changes to increase turnout
- discuss the potential future effects of technological advances in voting.

Related reading

Almond, G. and S. Verba (1963) *The Civic Culture*, Princeton: Princeton University Press.

Blais, A. (2000) *To Vote or Not To Vote. The Merits and Limits of Rational Choice Theory*, Pittsburgh: University of Pittsburgh.

Blais, A. and A. Dobrzynska (1998) 'Turnout in electoral democracies', *European Journal of Political Research*, 33: 239–61.

Budge, I. (1996) *The New Challenge of Direct Democracy*, Cambridge: Polity Press.

Franklin, M. (1996) 'Electoral participation' in L. LeDuc, R. Niemi and P. Norris (eds) *Comparing Democracies: Elections and Voting in Global Perspective*, Beverly Hills: Sage.

Gosnell, H. (1930) *Why Europe Votes*, Chicago: Chicago University Press.

Lane, J.-E. and S. Ersson (1990) 'Macro and micro understanding in political science: what explains electoral participation?', *European Journal of Political Research*, 18: 457–65.

Perea, E.A. (2002) 'Individual characteristics, institutional incentives and electoral abstention in Western Europe', *European Journal of Political Research*, 41: 643–73.

Powell, G.B. (1980) 'Voting turnout in thirty democracies' in R. Rose (ed.), *Electoral Participation*, London: Sage.

Teixeira, R. (1993) *The Disappearing American Voter*, Washington DC: Brookings Institution.

Tingsten, H. (1937) *Political Behaviour: Studies in Election Statistics*, London: P.S. King.

Wolfinger, R. and S. Rosenstone (1980) *Who Votes?*, New Haven: Yale University Press.

Notes

1 The random events which do have significance in turnout, and on the results of an election, are those which affect a large proportion of the electorate. For instance, weather conditions were traditionally held to be able to change electoral outcomes. In the UK, for instance, Conservative supporters would have access to cars, and consequently could ferry their supporters and, as importantly, 'undecideds' still open to persuasion, to and from the polling station. The Labour Party was of humbler means and had to rely more on its supporters being willing to get wet on the way to vote. Such explanations tend to be anecdotal, with the exception of Knack (1994). His findings in the US case refute these views.

2 Moreover, if the primary for a general election in Florida only has candidates from a single party (meaning that the primary winner will stand unopposed), then *all* voters are eligible to vote in this primary, whether or not they have registered a party affiliation. This in itself may exclude a large number of potential voters who do not realise they are eligible in such a situation.

3 http://www.phillyelection.com/voteeng.htm

4 The US 1993 Motor Voter Act, mandating states to provide for registration and the possibility of registering when applying for or renewing one's driving licence, has increased registration. However, abstention has subsequently risen.

5 To see the differences, refer to the Institute for Electoral Democracy and Assistance (IDEA) website – http://www.idea.int/vt/index.cfm

6 We should remember Butler and Stokes' finding in Chapter 3 that such interest may be responsible both for group membership and vote, however.

7 For a comprehensive review of types of electoral system, see Farrell (2001).

8 Some authors also consider average life expectancy on the grounds that political involvement assumes that basic needs are being met. We have not included it in our list because we think that economic development is a far more convincing indicator of this aspect.

9 Contrasts between abstainers, Left-wing voters and Right-wing voters is also common (see, e.g. Andersen and Evans, 2003). In this case a logit model is still employed, but one which allows a dependent variable with more than two response categories – a 'multinomial' or 'polytomous' model.

10 Another study acknowledging the explanatory value of interactions is Lane and Ersson (1990).

11 We should note that the macro-level indicators in Perea's analysis are operationalised slightly differently to the way we presented them in the previous section for the sake of a parsimonious analysis. She uses four institutional incentives – compulsory voting; voting facilities (presence of alternative voting facilities such as proxy and postal votes); electoral threshold (to test proportionality); and preference expression (the possibility of choosing more than one party, or choosing specific candidates).

12 Unsurprisingly, the biggest champions of internet voting are usually the companies that manufacture the technology that allows it.

13 Figures taken from Parliamentary Office of Science and Technology *Postnote*, no. 155, May 2001, p. 3.

8

Thinking about voting change

Summary box

- Conceptualising voting change
- Predicting stability and change
- Belief systems in the voting literature
- Belief system heterogeneity
- Voter availability
- Linking psychological traits to vote.

Introduction

The theories which we have considered so far have one thing in common: they try to explain and/or predict vote. This is an obvious focus for voting theories, of course. The logic of the electoral process means that in practical terms the only result which matters is the result of the election in hand. However, as many of the analyses have shown, we can also think of elections as a series of political events, the trends in which can reveal dynamics within these systems. For instance, those concerned with the relevance of class in relation to Left-voting have perceived across-time declines in absolute class voting, but less clear trends in terms of relative class voting. As we have seen, these two competing perspectives provide different insights into class voting, but they both rely upon the element of time.

Similarly, the aggregate times series analysis of economic changes and voting demonstrated that quite recent changes in the state of the economy can influence how well an incumbent does. Across time, then, economic trends should help chart the shifts in electoral performance of the main governing parties, once political context has been controlled for. In both of these cases, however, the changes across time focus more on groups – shifts in the electorate for the economic models and changes in class-affiliation in the sociological models. To the extent that individual dynamics can be implied, these approaches usually need to make a number of assumptions. To look explicitly at the individual level, either panel data needs to be employed, which will allow the study of individual trends over a period of time, or a more explicit focus on theorising change in individual voting behaviour needs to be brought to bear.

When sociological and social psychological accounts mention that individuals subject to cross-pressures are less likely to follow social voting patterns or to develop strong party attachments, for instance, the implication is that such voters will be more influenced by short-term factors and hence more open to changing their vote. Similarly, looking at Robertson's (1976) account of predisposition and policy-preferences in his emendation of the rational choice approach, those in the centre who are more likely to be affected by parties shifting their policy platforms and consequently who are unable to rely upon predisposition, are also assumed to be more likely to shift their vote than those who can and do count on predisposition. But again, this does not formalise the notion of party changers *vis-à-vis* stable voters. This is not a criticism of these theories, simply an observation of what they are attempting to do and what they are leaving aside.

There is surprisingly little literature which attempts to formalise the notion of vote-switching or defection. In particular, one very useful concept which we feel deserves attention is that of voter *availability* (van der Eijk and Oppenhuis, 1991; Bartolini, 1999). This focuses on individuals who have a predisposition to change their vote, in contrast with voters who are 'unavailable'. This concept shifts the argument a stage back: we do not look for voters who change their vote between elections, but for those who are more predisposed to change their vote than others. Though this concept has rarely been developed, we feel that it is a useful theoretical approach which lets us think about voters from a fresh point of view. At the same time, we present some reasons why some voters may be more 'available' than others – that is, more open to more than one party's appeal. The motivations we put forward are merely suggestions and speculative in their nature: they should not be regarded as 'facts' about voters. However, we do think there is merit in these ideas in broadening how we think about voting.

Predictors of voting stability and change

Before looking at availability, what pointers to voters' stability or lack thereof can we summarise from the existing theories we have studied?

Party identification

The most obvious indicator of voting stability is party identification. If the voter has a psychological attachment to a particular party, this will function as a predisposition to voting for that party and hence will make it less likely that she will change to vote for another party. In addition, as became apparent from Miller and Harrop's Michigan diagram (Figure 2.1), party identification also plays a significant role in shaping the political attitudes that in some cases may act as short-term determinants of vote. Of course, attitudes to candidates, policies and groups benefits will not be entirely determined by party identification, otherwise they would be redundant in the voting equation. However, for someone who identifies strongly with a party, the chances of such short-term factors varying the vote will be significantly reduced.

In Chapter 3 we discussed the extent to which party identification could be assumed to exist as an intervening variable between social determinants and vote. The US case in many ways looked to be propitious for the use of such a concept, but many European countries looked less convincing as contexts for this psychological attachment. However, despite the problems that are encountered in measuring it and hypothesising the very nature of the relationship between voter and party, it is clear that this anchor, *where it exists*, will reduce the likelihood of change.

From the rational choice perspective, of course, we saw that such a psychological attachment undermined the very basis of the vote decision-mechanism. Where voters remained 'loyal' to a party over time, if this did not derive from a rational calculation which pointed to the same party over time, then such loyalty should be interpreted as a rational cost-cutting exercise whereby the outcome was sufficiently beneficial to alleviate the need to engage in costly information-collection prior to the election: voters' utility from remaining with the same party was high enough to merit a 'blind' choice. This brings a fundamental opposition between the Michigan and rational choice traditions to the fore. In the former, the most stable voter is assumed to be the strong party identifier with ideological consistency and political information. Yet, from the rational perspective, the informed voter is the one most likely to engage in a utility calculation according to parties' policy positions and therefore is likely to be the one with sufficient information to motivate changing their vote, if necessary. The 'loyal' voter on the wings should not change.

Moreover, the voter at the centre for whom policy shifts are most likely to affect their voting choice is the one who should have the greatest incentive to be politically informed so as to make the right decision. However, as Downs noted, the voter at the centre is also the one who is most likely to be *least* affected by who wins if parties have converged and remain stable – the party differential will be minimal (1957: 244). So they too will have no incentive to collect political information – and so will not be in a position to realise if utility could have been maximised by changing vote.

It might also be objected that the strong identifier is more likely to be found in the same area as the 'loyal' rational voter, namely in a more extreme policy position. But as Robertson notes, '[A] strong Democrat is not necessarily an extreme Democrat.' (1976: 379) In other words, a strong identifier can equally be someone who is found in the moderate centre and within the area that parties compete for votes. Little research has looked at dimensionality to party identification, and the problems of implications of political information and knowledge suggest that we need to look elsewhere for insight into voting change. Party identification where it exists will act as an obstacle to voting change, but we cannot go much further beyond that from this perspective, whichever theoretical interpretation of identification and loyalty we use.

Social bases to stability and change

Moving one step back from the psychological attachment, then, which aspects of a voter's social profile may give an indication of her openness to change? Closely associated with the identification concept is age. Most analyses have confirmed that as voters get older they tend to become set in their voting ways. From the party identification perspective, this confirms the presence of a reinforcing feedback loop: as party identification predisposes vote, so the vote itself reinforces the strength of identification.

We need not invoke the identification model for age to be relevant. In the socialisation literature, some authors have noted that people's political views may now shift more frequently in later life than they did in the past due to exposure to a larger range of experiences (Sigel, 1989). However, the ageing process generally includes a stabilisation of social situation and of attitudes and preferences. Consequently, we would expect older voters to fall into a habitual vote. Conversely, young voters whose social situation is more likely to change and, from an identification point of view, whose loyalties may be less entrenched, will be more likely to change their vote.

As the rational choice perspective emphasises, the loyal voter who does not lose from their habitual voting choice is likely to rely on this as a simple indicator of how to vote in future years. Given that social position and status is less likely to change in latter years, so the vote is likely to continue to reflect this social status.[1] If there are changes in party supply which see this social grouping being abandonded by its traditional party, we might expect to see shifts among older voters. However, in terms of individual change, we would expect this to decrease with increasing age.

As we saw in Chapter 7, education is a strong predictor of turnout, acting amongst the higher strata both as a proxy for political information which facilitates participation and indicative in some countries of the possession of notions of civic duty. Traditionally, when levels of education were closely linked to social class, it would be more likely to find higher educated individuals voting for the Right, though of course such a link would to some extent be spurious: education *per se* was not responsible for this voting choice, but rather associated with it. That said, US models employing socioeconomic status have included education as a separate component of this index. The modern context has seen a shift, particularly given that New Left values – post-materialism and notions of the just society at more than just an economic level – have been widely seen as issues linked to a more nuanced, complex view of the world.

Consequently, Green parties in particular have been seen as appealing more to highly educated strata and, in a mirror image of this, the parties which have become associated with lower levels of education are Extreme Right parties with their simplistic programmes (Betz, 1994). However, if we look at education in terms of vote availability, we come up against the problem of political information. The informed voters more able to make a decision about who to vote for are, by some accounts, precisely the voters who are more likely to identify with parties and consequently not change their vote.

The last examples of social profile we should consider are the structural indicators such as class and religion. Can they give us a handle on availability? It seems unlikely, given the nature of the relationship between these variables and vote. Of course, in certain social and political contexts, a social class or religious group may shift its vote from one party to another. However, given the nature of social change, which is gradual, such a shift suggests either a wholesale policy shift by a political party, abandoning the social group which subsequently finds representation elsewhere; or a shift in the political demand of the social group, which is met by inert supply by the traditional party, with the same electoral result. Such shifts are of course fundamental to the results of elections and party success/failure. However, at the individual level, they imply a similar openness to stability and change amongst individuals with the same social profile which may well not exist. Why should all members of a single social group necessarily experience identical motivations, unless one is positing the highly unlikely case of one social determinant to all voting, with no other effects?

Of course, those open to cross-pressures, being without a clear social profile due to conflicting or absent social group affiliations, have been seen from the very earliest voting studies as more likely to change their vote. But again, although important, this is of little help to us at the individual level in hypothesising reasons for individual voting changes generally. To say, 'People without strong affiliations are more likely to change their decision' is of little explanatory help in explaining subsequently when and why they change. We could add that more influence derives from the short-term factors such as personalities and issues, but then we would be better off resorting to the individual-level explanations such as the rational choice theories, and once more we come up against the contradictions and paradoxes of who has political information and what they use it for. Overall, social indicators are clearly very useful as explanatory variables in vote choice, but as indicators of the mechanisms of change they are less helpful. Consequently we need to concentrate on the psychological profile of voters if we are to hypothesise about proclivity to change vote.

The belief system perspective

The traditional belief system

As we have seen in past chapters, the social psychological approaches such as the Michigan model have emphasised psychological elements such as identification to explain stable party choice. In doing so, they have also linked a voter's preference on issues and candidates to this party choice. However, we have not examined in detail the mechanism which accounts for this explanatory role for party identification in influencing these short-term factors. In their study of individual voters' ideologies, they found that there was a remarkable level of instability regarding their views on policies and the consistency of such views when related to party and elite ideologies.

This element of the Michigan model was developed most fully by Converse (1964). Taking the liberal-conservative continuum as a benchmark of political ideology in the United States, he measured the consistency of individuals' political attitudes on key policy areas by looking at the extent to which they followed the liberal-conservative continuum consistently. In other words, if someone expressed a liberal opinion on one policy, would they express liberal opinions on all policies? Secondly, would they express the same position on the policy across time? He argued that, if voters have a set of systematic and sophisticated political attitudes that helped them determine which political stances to take and whom to vote for, 'constraint' – the ability to predict one issue position from another – and consistency needed to be present (1964: 211–14).

However, his findings were a long way off proving that the electorate indeed possessed such ordered belief systems. Instead, he found that the majority had almost random political attitudes, which were unlinked to any liberal-conservative ordering and which fluctuated over time. Only a small handful had constrained belief systems. Introducing political knowledge as an additional critierion, he provided five categories of voter according to their level of belief system constraint:

- 'ideologues', politically knowledgeable, able to talk about politics at an abstract level and with constrained belief systems;
- 'near ideologues' who possessed constrained belief systems, but whose understanding of the liberal and conservative labels was limited;
- 'group benefit', who countenanced their support by reference to a party or candidate who represented the interests of a certain social group;
- 'nature of the times' who supported or criticised the incumbent government purely on the basis of the *status quo*, either for themselves or for the nation, but had no level of understanding of political labels or abstraction; and
- the 'no ideological content', who were the inverse of ideologues – politically ignorant and apathetic, and displaying unconstrained arrays of beliefs and sparse arrays at that. (1964: 218–19).

According to these 'levels of conceptualisation', he stated that '[W]e come a step closer to reality when we recognise the fragmentation of the mass public into a plethora of narrower issue publics.' (1964: 245). In other words, most voters have a handful of issues at most which matter to them, and which they can relate to the political process. Such evidence paints a harsh picture of mass involvement in politics, and this may partly be due to the definition of belief system that Converse uses. Such an analysis is based on the assumption that just as political ideologies and elites' beliefs form tight clusters along the liberal-conservative dimension, so they should for mass publics. But as others have argued (e.g. Kent Jennings, 1992), why should this necessarily be the case? Elite ideology has to follow a party programme in order to set out a consistently ordered collection of policy-positions. But the electorate at large have no need for such intellectually constructed and tailored programmes, and so, in policy terms, will rely only on the trickle-down of the salient policy positions.

The question that we can ask, then, is when salient policies do trickle down, do voters simply accept the positions on the basis of what their parties believe? Or do they have other benchmarks which can guide these? From looking at mass reactions to politics and policies, it would seem that voters do not always follow the party line, and indeed often criticise their party for its actions whilst in power. As Downs showed quite simply, governments in power disappoint voters by not matching their every preference, and so dissatisfied minorities will appear even if the government has taken the majority line on everything. Whilst this will not necessarily lose incumbents the election, for the reasons we considered in Chapter 4, it does mean that voters do have some guiding principle to their take on policy-stances.

Rational choice would call this 'preference structure' – we would suggest that the label 'belief system' can be retained, but amended from Converse and the Michigan School's use to reflect a less demanding and consequently more realistic use of the concept.

Belief systems and heterogeneity

> 'If all belief-disbelief systems were logical ones, some people would be said to have them, most would not. Our assumption is that *all* people have belief-disbelief systems that can be described in terms of the structural arrangement of their parts.' (Rokeach, 1960: 34)

The psychological literature, which Converse drew upon in his own work, makes the point that the belief system concept is only useful if we can arrive at a definition which encompasses everybody. Rather than starting with a 'logical benchmark' – the liberal-conservative dimension or, as we will use from now on, the Left–Right dimension – and then judging how well different individuals fit this pattern, it makes more sense to look more closely at how beliefs function within the belief system, and then use this as a predictor of how this can affect their voting behaviour.

One mainstay of psychological research has been that beliefs are individual elements which need to be linked to form a system. The link between beliefs may be formed by simple association, being learnt in the same context, or may be linked by consideration of two formerly separate beliefs. For example, an individual may believe in a penal system which concentrates on rehabilitation rather than retribution, and simultaneously believe that the death penalty is wrong. This second belief would be based upon the view that one should at least try to rehabilitate everyone, and reinforced by another belief, namely that the state should not act in an authoritarian and repressive manner, particularly in taking an individual's life. The same individual may subsequently be asked to consider whether racist or neo-fascist groups should be banned or allowed to exist, and decide that his instinct is to allow them to exist. On reflection, he may then realise that this is motivated and supported by a combination of the same beliefs, namely that it is better to try to eradicate such groups by educating individuals away from their racist views, rather than simply by suppressing them in an authoritarian manner.

However, individuals often hold beliefs which do not interlink so conveniently, and indeed are downright contradictory by most standards. The most common example is the simultaneous views that public services should be improved and that taxes need to be cut. Here, from a logical standpoint, improved public services require greater funding which will have to come from increased taxes; or tax cuts can go ahead if people are willing to accept cuts in public services – but one cannot have both. The key here, as Festinger notes (1957), is that beliefs may be *consonant* – one logically entails the other – or *dissonant* – one logically entails the obverse of the other – or *irrelevant* – one has no linkage with the other. In the public services/tax cuts example, individuals may hold apparently dissonant beliefs simply because they have not made the connection between taxes and government spending – the two beliefs are irrelevant to each other.

If such perceptions are possible, then on dimensions which are intellectually linked in party ideologies, such as the necessary complement of non-economic egalitarianism to economic egalitarianism in New Left thinking, it is very likely that many in the electorate will not see the relevance between the two. Hence, beliefs within a political belief system may well be irrelevant to each other. As we have noted in Chapter 5, there are a number of different political dimensions which can be used to measure individuals' political attitudes which are not necessarily related. In the American context, Zaller states that arrays of sub-system which do not match the overall ideological dimension of Left and Right are unusual, citing the small group of economically individualist but morally liberal libertarians (1992: 27). But, for instance in research on the UK, the economic Left–Right and libertarian–authoritarian dimensions are independent of each other (Heath, Evans and Martin, 1994). Similarly in France, economic and cultural liberalism have always been separated as two relevant sub-dimensions (Grunberg and Schweisguth, 1993). Much of the proximity modelling work carried out in the Netherlands also looked at two such dimensions (Middendorp et al., 1993). To contrast this with the Converse perspective, even if parties have a rigorously defined ideology – Left-libertarian for social democratic parties and Right-authoritarian for conservative and Christian Democrat parties for instance – this does not mean that their electorates will, or indeed more importantly, *should* share all these attitudes.

The possession of these independent dimensions of attitudes and beliefs derives from the nature of socialisation. As we have seen, the principal environments in which values and attitudes are passed on are the familial and educational spheres. But, unless these are explicitly political in nature because the attitudes being imbued are done so by one of Converse's ideologues, for example, there is no reason *a priori* that the sorts of values regarding economic position and financial matters will have any necessary corollary in terms of social and cultural values, i.e. non-economic matters. A party ideology may emphasise egalitarianism in economic and social sphere's – redistribution of rights as well as wealth – but there is no reason why a working-class voter should necessarily believe this. Indeed, the literature on working-class authoritarianism has demonstrated that such attitudes may be found in all social strata and regardless of attitudes characteristic of the economic Left–Right scale (Lipset, 1959b).[2] Similarly, there is no reason why a member of the middle class with Right-wing, free market ideals cannot hold more liberal or libertarian social ideals usually associated with the Left.

A spatial representation highlights how this ideological heterogeneity in voters' belief systems may relate to voting change and availability. If we take the example we used in Chapter 5, with two parties arrayed according to policies on prison reform and healthcare spending, we can add voter 3 (V3) who has a heterogeneous belief system (Figure 8.1). V3 believes in a more private-oriented healthcare system, but prison as rehabilitation. In terms of her personal ideology, they match neither party exactly, but share identical positions on them on one dimension. Assuming that her position on these issues reflects her general stance along the economic and non-economic dimensions, then we can make the following assumption: whilst economic matters motivate her voting then, *ceteris paribus*, she will vote for party P2, but if non-economic issues become more important, then she will be likely to switch to party P1.

Are such switches likely? And if so, under what conditions? Clearly, changes in voting could also be related to changes in the individual's political attitudes. However, as we have already seen, for most people, attitudes remain fairly stable across their lifetimes. They may shift in intensity but wholesale shifts from one set of attitudes to another contradictory set are rare. The shift in intensity may itself be sufficient to account for change from one party to another close by, as the directional model showed. For instance, if Left-wing agendas become radicalised, voters might move from a moderate social democratic or socialist party to a communist party which better suits the radical stance. However, the political context itself can shift the emphasis from one dimension to another for some voters, making one set of attitudes salient at one election when they were not salient at the next (Stone and Schaffner, 1988: 40).

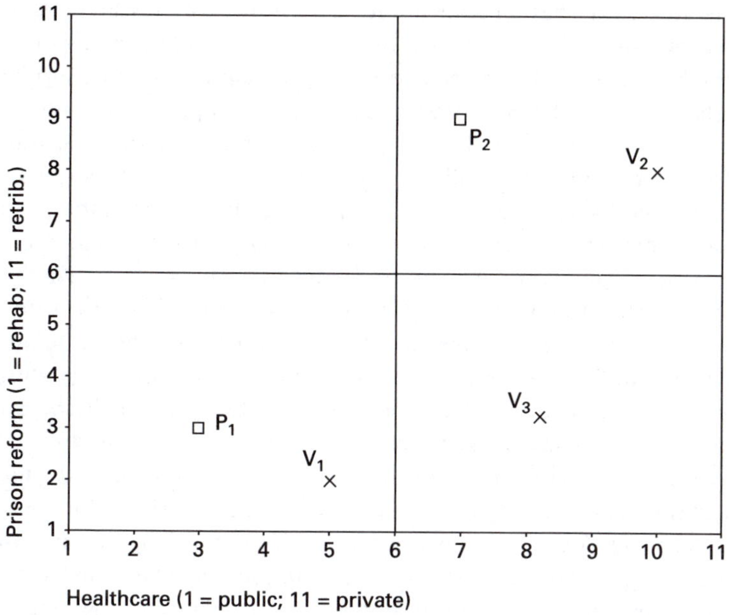

Figure 8.1 *Heterogeneous voter in two-dimensional policy space*

For example, in the 1993 Norwegian elections the European dimension and anti-European sentiment were salient due to the proximity to the referendum on joining the EC. The party which campaigned on this sentiment and against the Labour government's pro-European stance – the Centre party – consequently won a higher than normal proportion of the vote. Voters from other parties who had previously voted on 'normal' political issues switched for that election to the Centre. Some would characterise this as a protest vote, against the Labour government's stance on EC entry. However, given that it had clear ideological content, it seems more helpful as a vote explanation to link it to a simple shift in attitudinal priorities.

Similarly, in the 2002 French presidential and legislative elections, the main issue in the campaigns was that of law and order and insecurity. Previous elections had seen economic issues as the top priority. Partly as a result of this, the Right-wing opposition coalition which could claim ownership of law and order issues with its authoritarian stance trounced the Left-wing governing coalition which had ignored law and order and concentrated on economic matters. In such cases, some of the shifts in vote could be accounted for by individuals moving on the basis of the salient electoral issue of the time.

'Issue ownership' has long been put forward by many researchers: parties do not compete on the same issues, but instead promote the issues on which they think they have credibility and hence can garner the most support on (Robertson, 1976). That said, parties do not talk completely past each other in election campaigns: they do respond to each other's arguments, although they may put emphasis on different policies. Even Extreme Right parties (which in almost single-issue style campaign heavily on immigration and rely on xenophobic attitudes amongst their electorate), have an opinion on economic policies and criticise mainstream parties' policies accordingly. The importance lies in the priority they accord to such issues. The effect this may have on voters may reveal their availability in how they choose to vote. In terms of availability, we consequently have one potential working definition. The more heterogeneous a voter's belief system, the more likely she is to be available to more than one party within the system, *ceteris paribus*.

While the political supply and the voter's context remain constant, her vote will remain based upon a similar attitudinal dimension. Only once the context changes does change occur. Under this definition, we can conceptualise a change in voting behaviour which implies no change in the voter's own attitudes and social profile, but simply a change in context which pushes the voter to change the basis of her vote. How, then, can we look at this concept empirically?

Voter availability: theory and operationalisation

When we think about voting change, we are obviously primarily interested in those who change their vote between two elections, this being the simplest manifestation of the phenomenon. However, as Bartolini notes in his work on electoral competition, voters can also be thought of as being 'at stake' in elections, even if they do not necessarily change their vote (1999: 467). Thus, if we are to understand why people change their vote, it makes sense to take the conceptual step backwards and ask, 'Who *might* change their vote' as well as 'Who *does* change their vote?'.

He further suggests that looking at availability through the lens of voting change alone is a poor measurement (1999: 467). These are actual shifts, and are important in the electoral context, but they do not account for those who were available but who did not change. As Figure 8.2 shows, taken from Bartolini's article, the available electorate is a subset of the electorate, but at the same time individual voting shifts are a subset of the available electorate.

These individual voting shifts can then be aggregated into an overall net figure for changes within the system – aggregate volatility.[3] It is important

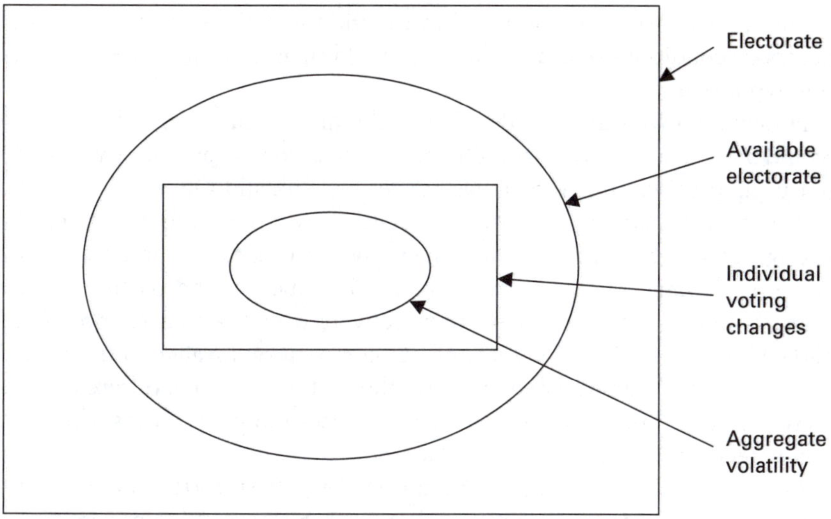

Figure 8.2 *Electoral availability as a subset of the electorate*
Source: adapted from Bartolini (1999:467)

to find those voters who are available but who do not change, particularly if we want to test this theory empirically.

There are three reasons for this. Firstly, one of the important aspects of availability is to discern where future defectors are to be found. We know that electoral competition is vital, inasmuch as it determines who wins. But where those votes come from is something which is usually relegated to retroprospective analysis. Availability potentially allows us to look for pools of votes ahead of time. Secondly, we must ask 'available to whom?'. In a two-party system, the only possible manifestation of availability is the party which the voter is not currently voting for. However, in a multiparty system there may be an array of different parties that the voter might potentially vote for. If we look only at the actual changes which occur, these will indicate one party which was available, but not all.

Thirdly, we would need to ascertain that the heterogeneity of belief system structure was present amongst not just those who moved from one party to another, but amongst the available non-movers. By the very nature of the belief system structure that we have offered, the heterogeneous array is a necessary but not sufficient condition of defection. By its static nature, it cannot cause vote change itself: another catalyst is required. This may be caused by the external context, but in the presence of stable context, we would expect to see a shift in some aspect of the defecting voters' perception of politics which was not present in their available but non-defecting counterparts. To ascribe this as the cause, and the belief system elements as necessary conditions of availability, we would then have an empirical test of the hypothesis.

How would we test this? Because of the individual change element, we would need to use survey data. The first work to look at availability (though not using precisely this term) was by van der Eijk and Oppenhuis (1991). In this they focused upon parties' success in winning potential voters by asking voters which parties they *might* choose in a forthcoming election, and then looking at the competitive performance of the parties in how many of these potential voters they converted into actual support. This allowed the separation of voters open to competition (available) from fixed on a single party (unavailable) and also the parties for which different pools were available. This approach, however, focuses more on parties' ability to win voters, rather than the voters themselves.

In the author's own work testing this (Evans, 2000, 2001), three specific questions were used to operationalise availability and 'defection' (vote change). Firstly, questions asking how the voter voted at two successive elections were used to isolate the stable voters from the defectors, in this case stable Left-wing voters from those who voted for a Left-wing party at one election and then an Extreme Right party at the next. Then a question asked whether the stable Left-wing voters could envisage voting for the Extreme Right party at some point in the future. Those that said yes were allocated to the available category, and those that said no were allocated to the stable category. Because of the nature of Extreme Right voting as a vote against the mainstream system as well as for the party itself, the hypothesised trigger for change was a high level of political dissatisfaction. And indeed, this turned out to separate the available voters from the defectors – but both had heterogeneous belief systems, with Left-wing stances on economic matters, Right-wing stances on xenophobic and authoritarian attitudes.

However, for other defections – for instance, those between mainstream parties with 'ownership' of different issues – an empirical proof could look for different issue saliencies between the available and defecting voters. Because it would be difficult to ascertain if issue saliency had changed between elections in a single survey, one would either have to make the assumption that such a change had occurred or, better still, panel data would allow such a shift to be studied directly. Indeed, the use of panel data in this case could alleviate other problems of operationalisation associated with such a hypothesis. Firstly, it relies on vote recall. Survey respondents can be asked how they voted at previous elections because it is a matter of fact rather than an attitude, attitudes being almost impossible to measure a long time afterwards. Unfortunately, voters will often not recall previous votes accurately (van der Eijk and Niemöller, 1983; van der Eijk, 2002). If they changed their vote, they will sometimes align their past votes with their most recent one, and hence in our model they would probably end up being excluded. Similarly, if voters have changed their political attitudes and party support since the most recent election, they may well report what their party support is now, rather than what it was at the time of the vote.

Secondly, we have no way of knowing the extent to which the attitudes which make up the economic, authoritarian and xenophobic dimensions have shifted for each voter between the elections. We have assumed that the attitudes remain fairly stable, to illustrate that voting change need not imply major belief change any more than it implies random and chaotic political beliefs. However, without the benefit of panel data, this is only an assumption but one which allows the model to be tested. Indeed, this characterises one of the problems of electoral research which relies on voting behaviour. Despite the prevalence of survey data, the bulk of this is cross-sectional in nature, and so the researcher is left with a snapshot of the election in question. Individual change becomes impossible to look at beyond recall of factual events such as previous vote, and even this is prone to error.

Lastly, for all the questions that we want to ask about voting choice, we can only ask a few, given the constraints of time and space in surveys,[4] and so the researcher is forced to find questions that can be answered given the data. Only those lucky and well financed enough to be able to carry out their own surveys are able to design surveys that ask what they want. We should also bear in mind the risk of expecting too much nuancing of respondents' replies. Surveys are designed for eliciting quick responses on simple matters. If we ask questions about how people have voted, would vote, might vote, which party they identify with, which rank-ordering of parties they would give, and so on, the risk is that the questions simply begin to tap the same few attitudes over and over again. In a multiparty system with eleven parties, the rank-ordering of the last few parties is unlikely to reveal much of interest either. Overall, then, we should all the while bear in mind the limits of survey data in revealing individual processes, whilst using it to full advantage where it is appropriate.

Individual traits as predictors of vote change

The above example is simply one of many that can be used to look at specific elements of voting change. However, it does emphasise the role that individual psychological traits can play in the vote process. Many of these elements have not received great attention in the voting literature because they are better tested in qualitative interviewing or the experimental setting. For example, Quattrone and Tversky's work on decision-making which we highlighted in Chapter 4 used the experimental setting to test whether individuals were risk-averse or risk-seeking – do they take the 'safe option' or not? – and whether they always distinguished between causal and diagnostic associations. Although these could have major effects on how people vote, it would be difficult to use such tests in a mass survey. In the US, the National Election Studies have allowed researchers to look in more detail at attitude formation and change regarding policy, and from this a large literature has grown on the political information short-cuts and judgement short-cuts ('heuristics') that individuals use to determine their stance on policies (e.g. Sniderman, Brody and Tetlock, 1991; Zaller, 1992). There has been some work in Europe looking at the role of political information in the UK (e.g. Andersen, 2003). However, there is a general lack of datasets allowing such theories to be tested more widely, and particularly cross-nationally.

This does not mean that such elements should be ignored completely, however. Just because we cannot test the interesting question or hypothesis does not mean that the question or hypothesis stops being interesting. For instance, we know that candidate personalities can have a strong effect on elections outcomes. Voters will be oriented towards candidates by their party, their ideology and their perceived competence, but in addition to this there will be subjective assessments which will derive from the voters' own personalities in how they rate a candidate. For instance, whatever the programme on offer from a candidate, the strength and single-mindedness with which this programme is presented and pursued may appeal to some voters more than others. Margaret Thatcher's hard-nosed and iron-fisted approach to implementing policy appealed to certain voters but repulsed others. François Mitterrand's Machiavellian and manipulative use of power similarly won admiration from some and condemnation from others.

Once ideology has been controlled for, differing perspectives are likely to derive from personality traits of voters. The seminal work *The Authoritarian Personality* (Adorno et al., 1950), which studied the basis to openness to authoritarian and in particular fascist appeal in certain individuals in society, showed that such individuals preferred strong, single-minded leaders to consensus-seeking liberals. But this was just one of a vast number of traits pertaining to dogmatism, xenophobia, sexual repression and the like which contributed to this personality. Although the openness to fascist appeals was the principal focus of the study, it is clear that such personality elements will also affect individuals' choices and views in mainstream politics.

The status of the beliefs themselves is also important in understanding attitudinal change. Similar to the dogmatic aspects studied in *The*

Authoritarian Personality, Milton Rokeach (1960), a psychologist whose work influenced Converse in his belief system formulation, performed research into 'open' and 'closed' minds. Individuals who were willing to take on board new information and amend their beliefs and behaviour accordingly were classified as open-minded; those who refused to accept new information if it conflicted with their existing beliefs, and clung tenaciously to these in their behaviour and decision were closed-minded. Again, whatever one's attitudes, party identification and social position, such elements are likely to affect one's perceptions of politics and the openness to change that one displays.

Lastly, beyond even the different information-digesting mechanisms that individuals employ, the emotional content of politics cannot be overlooked. As we already saw in Chapter 6, anger over the government's handling of the economy can have an independent effect on voters' choice. Alternatively, affect – the intensity of an attitude and closely linked to an emotional input – strongly determined the directional theory's prediction of vote (Chapter 5). Thus, emotions such as anger, pride, disgust and boredom have all been linked to political choice and participation. The extent to which we can nuance differences beyond positive and negative feelings towards politics is perhaps small. How much can we learn from separating nonvoters into 'disgusteds' and 'boreds', for instance – but there is no doubt that such feelings do play a part.

Finally, optimism and pessimism, threat and fear have all been linked to political choice and attitudes (e.g. Marcus and MacKuen, 1993). Economic voting incorporated views of next year's economy in the vote calculus, but equally our general feelings of what the future holds may influence our political choice. Anxious voters may seek out more information and be less ready to resort to habitual loyalties. When the future looks rosy, we may be ready to experiment with new ideas and policies, even vote for radical parties, secure in the knowledge that whatever they do probably will not derail things completely. But when the future looks dark, we may prefer to stay with the tried and tested – 'no experiments'.[5] In particularly dark times, one may even be prepared to accept a strong leader even if his programme is not one's favoured option.

Again, however, almost all of this work is limited to the United States where the tradition in political psychology is strongest. But there is no doubt that such work is vital in illustrating how individuals react to context, how their belief systems determine how they react and also how these very same systems may themselves be changed by such a context. In this sense, they also provide a link between social change and eventual electoral change, social position being the most widespread and common 'context'.

In this sense, the individual level provides the most auspicious perspective for considering the motivations and dynamics of political choice and changes therein.

Conclusion: the psychological nuance

In citing these psychological and personality aspects to voting, we are not arguing that they should be seen as wholesale alternatives to the theories which we have looked at over the last few chapters.[6] There are very good reasons for these theories becoming implanted in the voting literature, and that is because they provide robust explanations of the basis for party choice and electoral participation. Moreover, from an empirical point of view, these are theories which lend themselves to testing in a way that the psychological theories often do not. It is very difficult to conceive of how survey-based studies, for instance, could test personality effects beyond the more self-evident hypotheses, or indeed how one could build a theory of personality voting. On the grounds that one should only accept new theories when they provide a better explanation for events than their predecessors, we would be ill advised to throw out any of the previous theories and replace them with such an out-and-out psychological approach. Indeed, unless we subscribe to an entirely genetic view of personality, favouring nature in the 'nature–nurture' debate, social aspects must surely play some antecedent role in personality definition.

However, awareness of these individual characteristics can lead us to nuance our view of the voting decision. The benchmarks which we set on the basis of expertly informed political views are too high for the majority of voters. Instead of relegating voters to political ignorance and belief system chaos, the fact that we can discern underlying patterns in attitudes which are relevant to politics can give us a handle on their support for such issues and for their likely positions on future issues. As all well specified models of political information emphasise, what we learn depends on what we have learnt. Consequently, if a new situation is 'learning', then how we react to it depends on the views and information we already hold. But lastly, we must allow for the fact that the information will be treated differently according to the internal context of the receiver – it may be rejected; it may be accepted but suppressed; it may be rationalised to fit in with existing information; or it may be considered and allowed to influence the existing information, changing the latter. Exactly which psychological process pertains may have significant influence on the behaviour that follows.

Summary box

You should now be able to:

- explain the conceptual importance of studying voting change
- identify the key social and attitudinal indicators of vote stability
- understand the main problems which traditional theories pose to predictions of voting change
- explain the origins of the belief system concept in the voting literature
- critique the Converse belief system
- provide a more inclusive definition of mass belief systems
- explain the notion of voter availability and its purpose
- indicate personality and other psychological traits which may affect vote-choice.

Related reading

Adorno, T. et al. (1950) *The Authoritarian Personality*, New York: Harper and Brothers.

Bartolini, S. (1999) 'Collusion, competition and democracy', *Journal of Theoretical Politics*, 11: 435–70.

Converse, P. (1964) 'The nature of belief systems in mass publics' in D. Apter (ed.) *Ideology and Discontent*, New York: Free Press.

van der Eijk, C. and E. Oppenhuis (1991) 'European parties' performance in electoral competition', *European Journal of Political Research*, 19: 55–80.

Festinger, L. (1957) *A Theory of Cognitive Dissonance*, Stanford: Stanford University Press.

Rokeach, M. (1960). *The Open and Closed Mind. Investigations into the Nature of Belief Systems and Personality Systems*, New York: Basic Books.

Sniderman, P., R. Brody and P. Tetlock (1991) *Reasoning and Choice. Explorations in Political Psychology*, Cambridge: Cambridge University Press.

Stone, W. and P. Schaffner (1988) *The Psychology of Politics*, New York: Springer Verlag.

Zaller, J. (1992). *The Nature and Origins of Mass Opinion*, Cambridge and New York: Cambridge University Press.

Notes

1 The only exception to this would be where a party specifically appeals to pensioners, either as the basis for the party's foundation itself – for example, *Die Grauen* (the Greys), a pensioners' party in Germany – or a mainstream party campaigning on related issues.

2 A small but influential literature has argued over the extent of working-class authoritarianism, particularly in relation to middle-class authoritarianism. Whilst the extent and location of authoritarian attitudes has been disputed, the ubiquity of authoritarian values is clear.

3 For the most comprehensive consideration of volatility to date, see Bartolini and Mair (1990).

4 We will return to this problem in the conclusion.

5 And politicians know this – precisely this phrase (*Keine Experimente*) was used in campaigning by Konrad Adenauer and the CDU in Germany in the 1950s. The author is grateful to Tor Bjørklund for drawing his attention to this example.

6 Although many researchers do offer these theories precisely as alternatives, for instance cognitive alternatives to rational choice – see Marcus et al. (2000). The extent to which such work is an 'alternative' or a 'complement' is a moot point.

9

Conclusion

Over the previous eight chapters, we have presented the main theoretical elements relating to voting behaviour, together with their key methodological features and the general historical trajectory of their development. The six broad conceptual areas which we have analysed form the main 'schools of thought', principally the sociological and rational choice perspectives, together with derived analytical approaches, such as economic and spatial theories and models. Within the voting literature, we have cited those works which we feel best illustrate the above theories and approaches in the case of demand-side perspectives. In other words, we have very deliberately taken the voter herself as the point of departure.

There are some areas concerning voters' perceptions which we have spent less time on than we might, for instance candidate personality effects, the effects of political information levels on voters and how campaigns determine voters' choices. These are of course important potential determinants of voting choice. Because of this, we mentioned these where relevant to the specific theories in question. However, there does not seem to us to be a large and coherent body of work regarding such elements from a comparative perspective. We are not aware of any 'candidate personality theory' of voting for instance, beyond the largely self-evident hypothesis that voters will be less likely to vote for a candidate whose personality they dislike, *ceteris paribus*. Similarly, levels of political information are important in discerning voters' ability to choose between candidates and parties, and to make the 'correct' choice. But again, there is no broad corpus of work on political information *per se*. We can regard these more as intervening variables which vary the social and attitudinal effects on vote.

We have also deliberately excluded separate reference to the supply side – political parties – and to the rules of the games under which elections take place, namely the electoral and institutional system. We *have* considered these when inextricably bound up with the demand side – either to place the rational choice theory in its full context, or where the effect of individual perceptions on behaviour is determined by the institutional filter, such as the case of economic theories or of abstention. This is not to say that institutions are not important: they are crucially important in determining election outcomes, and indeed determining electoral choice amongst individuals. But we are concerned with those motivations immanent from the voters themselves, rather than their institutional context.

Some might criticise such exclusions, saying that one cannot study voters without studying the parties which constitute their choices and the system within which the electoral game takes place. We would agree that such a holistic approach is correct when trying to explain voting behaviour *in toto*. However, as far as this book as a teaching tool is concerned, such a broad take is not necessary. What we have tried to show is that such theories exist in their own right, and their principal elements and implications can be learnt without necessarily introducing the other components of the electoral equation. Certainly the vast bulk of the literature cited in the book does not refer to parties or electoral systems as variables – they are left to one side or simply acknowledged as other possible effects. Yet, strangely, to date we know of no English-language textbook on voting which takes such an approach, despite the same not being true of institutions or electoral systems. This, then, has been our principal aim.

As a tool meant only to communicate the main theoretical elements from this literature, what is left for a conclusion? Two topics should be considered. Firstly, what are the main elements that may be derived from all these theories? In the preceding chapters, we have drawn attention to similarities and divergence between the different theories, but we have not yet provided a summary of all voting theory's main assertions, whatever their theoretical perspective or analytical focus. However, as we shall shortly discover, the list which we provide can in no way be described as revelatory (except perhaps for readers with no knowledge of voting theories, and who have jumped straight to the conclusion). Indeed, one of the points of interest of voting studies half-a-century on from their initial blossoming is how little their basic tenets have changed. The theories are more nuanced, derived models are tested with greater sophistication using more copious and informative data. But there has been very little structural change to their foundations.

Secondly, then, what is the future for the study of voting? If the basic theoretical tenets have remained stable, what can future research add to our existing knowledge? As we shall see, if one is awaiting a revelation in terms of theoretical reasons why people vote the way they do, then one is likely to be disappointed. However, to interpret this as somehow the end of voting studies would be to take an extremely skewed view of what voting studies still have left to do. We will thus suggest some of the areas which are still ripe for future research.

The 'full' voting model

Given the different theoretical perspectives which we have covered, can we provide an overview of their findings which allows us to give a generalised insight into the motivations of voters regardless of time or context? A number of points can be highlighted:

- Voters have political proclivities derived from past experience and learning in political and non-political contexts which inform their party choice in elections.
- The foundations for such proclivities can be found in the most basic social indicators – age, gender and education, for instance. Such indicators provide a context for the socialisation process, as well as associated values.
- 'Politicised' social indicators – class/occupation, religion, linguistic or ethnic group, *inter alia* – provide attitudes reflecting political ideologies and which provide common reference points between voters and party programmes and, in cases of uncertainty, help decide which party corresponds most closely to the voter's political desires.
- Attachments to political parties, where they exist, provide a strong incentive to support this party, as well as potentially reinforcing the political positions provided by a voter's own proclivities.
- A voter's political desires will be affected by the political and economic context in which the voter finds herself.
- Where a voter's political desires cease to be fulfilled by a political party, the voter will change her vote or abstain.
- Where there is an absence of political desires, or political desires are satisfied by all or none of the parties, a voter will abstain.

It is immediately clear that, if one combines the earlier elements in the list – the later ones referring more to abstention and voting change – one sees a marked resemblance to the Michigan model depicted in Figure 2.1. This resemblance again brings to mind the notion that there is nothing new in voting, and we shall turn to this in the following section. However, this set of characteristics is also closely related to what many authors refer to as the 'full model of voting'. For instance, in his analysis of French presidential voting, Lewis-Beck characterises the French vote as based upon four principal variables – class, religion, Left–Right ideological position and economics. More generally, then, the vote can be said to be composed of cleavages, ideology and the economy (Lewis-Beck, 1988: 60). Similarly, as we draw upon the different theoretical elements to construct a model of vote, we find a parsimonious set of social and attitudinal predictors which, once controlling for the perceived economic context, will account for a large proportion of voting behaviour across time and location.

Thinking back to the Michigan model, the causal order of these elements is also clear – social profile and, disregarding party identification for the moment for the reasons highlighted in Chapter 3, derived from this the attitudinal components. Consequently, when we look at such full models in voting research, we often see researchers testing social effects first, and then subsequently introducing issues and attitudinal elements. Because the social effects are themselves responsible for many of the attitudinal positions of voters, the subsequent inclusion of these attitudes will 'wash out' a proportion of the social effects in a model.[1] Subsequently, this provides a good basic model for testing other variables which may determine vote, such as personality effects or political information, for example, controlling for social and attitudinal profile.

We have also seen the value of considering the possible variations which may occur on the basis of where voters live, for example the local and regional effects mentioned in Chapters 3, 6 and 7. Where possible, it is therefore also valuable to introduce aggregate level data in the shape of region, district or consituency to control for variations in political behaviour linked to this territorial aspect. In models testing a large number of country-cases comparatively and/or across time, it is also sometimes possible to include national level data such as unemployment figures or institutional indicators. Table 9.1 gives a summary of the levels and nature of variables that can be included in the full model.

We should remind ourselves that the statistical techniques used to operationalise these models are only as sound as the theory upon which they are based. We may find that such models fit the empirical data very well, but the only proof of causality we have is that which leads us to expect a relationship between, say, social profile and vote. As we saw in Chapter 3, many political scientists have been critical of the assumed link between class and vote, based upon the statistical models provided by political sociologists, precisely because of the assumptions that these latter make about voters' motivations and party intentions. Whether or not this criticism has been exaggerated, it alerts us to the possibility that statistical models may find associations but it

Table 9.1 ***The 'full model' of voting***

Level	Example	
Macro	National unemployment Institutions	
Meso	Region; constituency	
Micro (social)	Basic social controls:	Age Gender Education
	Relevant politicised cleavages:	Class/occupation Religion/religiosity Ethnic/linguistic group Agrarian Cultural
[Micro (partisan)]	[Party identification]	
Micro (attitudinal)	Left–Right placement/attitudinal dimensions:	Economic ideology Authoritarianism Ethnocentrism Post-materialism
Additional variables for hypothesis-testing	Economic attitudes Candidate popularity Political information Political dissatisfaction/protest Affective components	

is down to the researcher to argue for its causal importance both from a theoretical point of view and by further, related hypothesis testing.

A good example of related hypothesis testing would be that mentioned in Chapter 3, and encountered by Butler and Stokes and others, namely the role of trades union membership in Left-wing vote. We find an association between union membership and Left-wing vote, but is the interpretation that trades unions actively mobilise individuals to vote for these parties accurate? Or is it that those people likely to join a trades union are also more likely to vote for a Left-wing party? These are precisely the type of questions which need to be tested separately so that we can be confident that, if we include union membership in a voting model, we know that there is a direct causal relationship with vote which is not simply caused by class itself.

Thus, for all their technical sophistication, the researcher must always ask of statistical models, 'Can I be sure that the causal relationship I am inputing is theoretically sound?' It is also precisely questions such as these which provide one of the answers to the last fundamental question which this book wishes to consider, namely, 'Where can voting research go from here?'.

The future of voting research: different theory-testing or better theory-testing?

Perhaps a result of millennial malaise, one of the questions asked of psephology recently has been, 'Is there anything left to test?'. As we noted earlier, the foundations to most voting theory look remarkably similar to those used in the 1940s and 1950s by the Colombia and Michigan schools. Social context, policy positions as tapped by issues or attitudinal dimensions, possible party identification and contextual effects mattered then – and they still matter now. Perhaps the role of social context as traditionally conceived has declined, but none of the evidence claiming that social context has become entirely redundant is convincing. There has thus been a shift in the balance of social and attitudinal elements, but both still weigh upon the vote.

Even if we take the two perspectives which are often held to be most distant in their approach to voting – rational choice and sociological accounts – their ideal types may in some ways be strongly opposed, but in their more developed and empirically testable formats, their assumptions and findings are often similar or at the very least complementary. The ideal rational voter carefully calculates utility and votes accordingly; the 'sociological' voter may vote for a party because this is her natural party which her peer group and other social contacts all choose, and has been the party instilled into her since childhood as the 'correct' party to vote for. The former conceptualises vote as a consumer choice (although as we emphasised in Chapter 1, the researcher tries to ignore the choice element so that the rational calculation ascribes the vote), the latter sees vote as a derivative of identity almost akin to ticking a box on a census form.

Yet, the rational individual still needs a basis upon which to make the decision: past experience and learning affect how she perceives and calculates utility. The social context in which she finds themselves will also strongly determine how different policies weigh up in their effects. Similarly, no 'sociological' voter is so completely socially determined that the party receives their vote every election without any consideration of the benefits which derive from such a vote. These are not simply real-world considerations, either. It is theoretically unsustainable to posit an electorate of identical rational voters assigning identical utility values to all policy choices, and unsurprisingly rational choice does not do this. Similarly, it is unsustainable to posit 'sociological' voters lacking motive beyond their social group belonging – where does such a sense of belonging derive from, and, if we wish to include the party element, how are parties able to mobilise such voters if not by appealing to some calculation of benefit, however imperfect?

In both cases, the perspectives choose to focus on different parts of the voting process. Rational choice concentrates on the decision-making procedure, leaving the context of individual voters as implicit. Sociological approaches concentrate on the structural patterns amongst groups in society and takes the motivational elements largely as read. From the methodological perspective, of course, this often leads to irreconcilable differences between deductive and inductive approaches, although again the extent to which these approaches exist in their pure form is debatable. But once we go further and acknowledge that not only from a theoretical perspective such an ideal-type is unsustainable, but also that in real life most if not all voters actively combine elements of both in their vote-decisions, then the gap between the two again becomes smaller. The operationalisation of voting models mirrors this completely: as we move to the full model, so we include the various motivations which hold sway within the electorate.

Those affected by the 'millennial malaise' find the implications of this profoundly depressing. If two schools of thought with apparently such different perspectives are in some ways implying similar processes, even if they focus on different elements in the process and rely upon very different research traditions to test these, and if the Michigan model is still as valid now as it was in the 1950s, the way forward does not seem obvious. One probable reason for this feeling is deeply flawed, but understandable, namely the desire of all researchers to find something *new*. All scientific research, whether social or natural, is motivated in part by the wish to 'make a discovery'. In some branches of science, this is more likely than others. At the extreme, perhaps, astronomers would seem to have an easy time of it – point a large telescope in a certain direction in the sky, zoom in and find a star that no-one else has seen, or at least recorded. (But of course, simply finding a new star in astronomy will not rate very highly, if at all, as 'a discovery'.)

In voting studies, the problem seems to be precisely the opposite. We know why people vote the way they do, and we have known many of the elements behind voting long before the Colombia and Michigan schools formalised them. Not having a big discovery to make, as some people fool themselves that all scientists can do, our job lies elsewhere, namely in trying to *prove* that this is why people vote the way they do. It may not be as exciting as finding a star or synthesising a revolutionary drug or discovering a new sub-atomic particle, but from a scientific perspective it is equally as important.[2] Until one can exactly account for the process which leads from a set of conditions to an outcome, then in theory there is still work to be done. The question, then, is where in voting studies does there remain work to be done?

In a special edition of the journal *Electoral Studies*, entitled 'The Future of Election Studies' (2002), a number of national election experts asked precisely this question in reference to survey-based research stemming from the Michigan model. The editors' opening assertion might seem to subscribe to a version of millennial malaise – 'Election studies on the Michigan model are reaching the limit of what they can achieve, above all because the calls on questionnaire space have far outstripped our ability to include all desired questions without jeopardising the study.' (Wlezien and Franklin, 2002: 157).

The emphasis here is on the data collection involved in voting research, but this in itself has implications for the conceptualisation of such research prior to data collection. When we take into account the multitude of social indicator questions to adequately tap a respondent's background and current context; the host of voting questions, asking not just whether and how a respondent voted but also how they might have voted, when they decided how to vote, how they have voted in the past, how they rank the parties, and so on; the batteries of attitudinal questions to tap different dimensions; political satisfaction; state of the economy; and political information – surveys simply cannot cope with asking all questions that different researchers' full models might require.

However, such problems can be solved, for instance by linking together different surveys, aggregating individuals into cohorts and then linking this to census data (van der Eijk, 2002: 193). Greater space in the election survey can then be freed up to 'take care of core business' – as van der Eijk puts it – that is, to concentrate on accurately measuring the dependent variable, vote. Because of the wariness that researchers have of vote recall as an accurate account of how people really voted, this is a fundamental area where voting studies can still improve, and consequently improve our proof. We are unlikely to make revelatory new findings about voting as a result, but we can be more confident about testing our existing theories. Being confident that our dependent variable is largely free from measurement error is a major step towards feeling confident about the findings from our hypothesis-testing.

Other suggestions in the special edition provide avenues for research which improve our existing knowledge. For instance, Marsh suggests that more work needs to be done on electoral context. Research looking at neighbourhood effects suggests that these provide an 'experiential source' which may manifest itself as an independent effect on vote irrespective of individuals' own social profiles – we referred to such research in Chapters 3 and 6. However, can we assert that similar effects occur in larger territorial aggregations, such as regions? (Marsh, 2002: 210–11). What mechanisms in larger areas have a causal influence on vote? Moreover, even at the smaller neighbourhood level, and given geographical mobility, to what extent is it truly a contextual effect, as opposed to people of similar social and hence political profiles choosing to live in proximity to each other?

Zaller draws attention to an area which is growing in importance in voting research but which to date has perhaps suffered from being too subtle to detect in existing surveys, namely media effects and campaign exposure (Zaller, 2002). He argues from a statistical point of view that, even though we know from a real-world perspective that campaign exposure has an effect on how people vote, there has been no real formalisation of campaign effects because even surveys with thousands of respondents are simply not large enough to detect the effect. The counter-argument could of course be that the reason we are seeing no effect is that there is none. This would be a classic example of how our real-world assumptions do not bear out under rigorous scrutiny. However, he is right to argue that until the data are satisfactory – larger samples – we cannot satisfactorily reject it.

Lastly, Curtice draws attention to perhaps one of the most important areas for future research, namely endogeneity. He mentions the relationship between party identification and vote – does party identification influence vote or does vote influence party identification? (2002: 162) He also refers to the thorny problems of campaigns influencing attitudes (similarly to Zaller), and changes in party positions on policies and issues across time. These all emphasise the dynamic nature of elections. Parties and voters change their positions on issues, and on which issues to give priority to. Moreover in the case of voters, there are shifts not only in their attitudinal positions but also in their social positions, through social mobility, ageing and the like. Perhaps Converse's characterisation of voters as uninformed and randomly responding on most issues is somewhat harsh, as we argued in Chapter 8. However, much of the notion of stability could be a mirage produced by our over-reliance on cross-sectional data which, as we mentioned in Chapter 1, is static by its very nature.

Use of cross-sectional data is a second-best option in election studies, and indeed in social research of all kinds. Even if stability is the rule, we need to prove this by showing individual stability across time, rather than inferring it from cross-sections or extrapolating individual stability from aggregate stability between cross-sections. Longitudinal analyses using panel data, such as the British Election Panel Study, often reveal that, over one electoral period, there can be significant changes in the electorate's support for parties, their levels of political information and consequently on predictions of electoral outcome. Such data have also allowed new research into media effects on election results (Norris et al., 1999). Following Bartolini, our argument for more research into electoral change and particularly into the notion of electoral availability would rely upon tracking individuals across time in their voting choices to provide empirical proof of any formal hypotheses. Yet, to date, panel data is relatively rare though increasing.

Once again, however, such advances are unlikely to provide revelatory findings about the motives behind individuals' voting. Of course, this is always possible, but the most likely outcome is, as mentioned above, confirmatory.[3] We should expect to provide better, perhaps more nuanced, proofs of existing hypotheses as well as tracking how shifting policies, developments in social structure and the changing nature of national and international political arenas influence people's voting. But the desires and motivations which shape people's voting preferences will remain fundamentally the same – their position in society (whatever the structure of that society); their economic well-being, both relative and absolute; their views on acceptable behaviour, on the rights of others, on their values and mores generally; and their perceptions of candidates, parties and governments.

In this sense, Inglehart's post-materialist Silent Revolution is instructive. The promise of radical political change which many took this to herald never took place. Despite the appearance of New Political issues and the rejection of Old Politics by the post-materialists, over time the increasing integration of New Politics into the mainstream agenda and the realisation that espousal of New Political issues does not necessarily exclude the espousal of Old Political issues as well, may have shifted political discourse, but it has not redefined voting. Moreover, proponents of social dealignment should note that Green voters and other post-materialists have social profiles which predispose them to holding such views in the same way that social profile predisposes others to hold views on abortion, taxation and every other political issue. Those issues which truly cross-cut the electorate, and divide society along lines which are neither age, gender, class, religion or education defined are remarkable precisely in their rarity.

To take an unhappy contemporary example, the War on Iraq may have pitted Left against Left, and Right against Right, but it is precisely the abnormality of the issue which renders these cross-cutting divisions – fortunately, most issues do not follow this pattern. When new issues emerge which seem not to relate to existing frames of reference, the decline of the frames of reference themselves is a pre-emptive and fallacious leap to make. Over time, issues generally integrate into existing structures.

But finally, we should remember that, as we stated at the very start, the voting researcher's aim is to find patterns in behaviour. Even if one takes a deductive approach and starts from first principles of behaviour, one will need to find patterns in that behaviour as proof of these principles. Because these are only patterns, however, not rigid rules of behaviour which are never broken, there will always be exceptions and sometimes exceptions which are sufficiently widespread to provide surprises. In predictive terms, our parsimonious selection of variables will not always provide the right answer. Bush's victory over Gore in the 2000 US presidential elections; Jean-Marie Le Pen's defeat of Lionel Jospin in the first round of the 2002 French presidential elections; the Pim Fortuyn List's shock appearance and governmental inclusion in the 2002 Dutch legislative elections – all were outcomes that few or none would have predicted using empirical data any more than going on 'common sense' or instinct.

The outcomes are, of course, easily explained – a dull Democrat candidate, Ralph Nader, voting irregularities and the Supreme Court; a dull Socialist candidate, Socialist abstention, vigorous Left-wing competition and episodes of extremist-profiting violence before the campaign; and unresponsive, stagnant political centrism, a flamboyant and charismatic protest candidate and the 'bonus' of a sympathy vote after this candidate's assassination. For the reasons we explained in Chapter 1, we can include these in a retroprospective explanation, but it is difficult or impossible to include them in a prediction, either because events have not yet occurred or because it is difficult to estimate the likely effect of certain events ahead of the election itself.

To the extent that we cannot yet include such effects parsimoniously is in itself an illustration that there is still work to do. But we should not forget that, despite the surprise outcomes, this does not mean that the psephological rule book was thrown out of the window for these elections. In most cases, voters will have followed precisely the rules which the theories set out in this book provide. In many cases, the surprising result comes not from voters disobeying the rules, but from our inability to distinguish sufficiently between different motivations to say which rule will count for which voter. Whilst there remains such imprecision in our ability to discern explanatory variables until after the election, there will also remain work to be done to improve voting theory.

Notes

1 Often not all the effect will wash out – social variables remain significant vote predictors even once attitudes have been controlled for. How this should be interpreted depends upon the model in question, but generally it suggests that social effects do not only manifest themselves through the attitudes of voters but retain an independent effect. See, e.g. Evans (2003) on this.

2 Too often the qualifier 'human' is invoked as a reason why the social sciences cannot hope to achieve the rigour of natural sciences, and consequently such attempts at scientific enquiry are lost before they start. This misses the point: just

because the topic of study seems infinitely complex and often unpredictable does not mean that approaching it using basic consistent methods cannot help identify some order in the human 'chaos'. How much order can be identified remains one of the principal questions.

3 The most likely source of ground-breaking research is always when new areas or dynamics appear for study. In terms of areas, the developing democracies of Central and Eastern Europe are increasingly becoming the focus of more traditional hypothesis-testing. In the case of voting itself, the use of new technologies in voting may be the most likely source of such research in the future. Whether the medium of voting – home computer rather than polling-station booth – has an effect on voting behaviour remains a moot point, but one that in all likelihood will receive close attention in years to come.

References

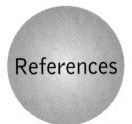

Adorno, T. et al. (1950) *The Authoritarian Personality*, New York: Harper and Brothers.

Aldrich, J. (1993) 'Rational choice and turnout', *American Journal of Political Science*, 37: 246–78.

Alford, R. (1963) *Party and Society*, Chicago: Rand McNally.

Alford, R. (1967) 'Class voting in Anglo-American political systems' in S. Lipset and S. Rokkan (eds) *Party Systems and Voter Alignments: Cross-National Perspectives*, New York: Free Press.

Allardt, E. (2001) '*Party Systems and Voter Alignments* in the tradition of political sociology' in L. Karvonen and S. Kuhnle (eds) *Party Systems and Voter Alignments Revisited*, London: Routledge.

Almond, G. and S. Verba (1963) *The Civic Culture*, Princeton: Princeton University Press.

Andersen, R. (2003) 'Do newspapers enlighten preferences? Personal ideology, party choice, and the electoral cycle', *Canadian Journal of Political Science*, forthcoming.

Andersen, R. and J. Evans (2003) 'Values, cleavages and party choice in France, 1988–1995', *French Politics*, 1: 83–114.

Andersen, R. and A. Heath (2002) 'Class matters: the persisting effects of contextual social class on individual voting in Britain, 1964–97', *European Sociological Review*, 18: 125–38.

Anderson, C. (2000) 'Economic voting and political context: a comparative perspective', *Electoral Studies*, 19: 151–70.

Babbie, E. (1998) *The Practice of Social Research*, Belmont (CA): Wadsworth.

Barnes, S. (1977) *Representation in Italy. Institutionalized Tradition and Electoral Choice*, Chicago: University of Chicago Press.

Barry, B. (1978) *Sociologists, Economists and Democracy*, Chicago: University of Chicago Press.

Bartolini, S. (1999) 'Collusion, competition and democracy', *Journal of Theoretical Politics*, 11: 435–70.

Bartolini, S. and P. Mair (1990) *Identity, Competition and Electoral Availability: the Stabilisation of European Electorates, 1885–1985*, Cambridge: Cambridge University Press.

Bellucci, P. (1991) 'Italian economic voting: a deviant case or making a case for a better theory?' in H. Norpoth et al. (eds) *Economics and Politics: The Calculus of Support*, Ann Arbor: University of Michigan Press.

Berelson, B. and W. McPhee (1954) *Voting: a Study of Opinion Formation in a Presidential Campaign*, Chicago: Chicago University Press.

Betz, H.-G. (1994) *Radical Right-wing Populism in Europe*, New York: St Martin's Press.

Blais, A. (2000) *To Vote Or Not To Vote. The Merits and Limits of Rational Choice Theory*, Pittsburgh: University of Pittsburgh Press.

Blais, A. and R. Carty (1990) 'Does proportional representation foster voter turnout?', *European Journal of Political Research*, 18: 167–81.

Blais, A. and A. Dobrzynska (1998) 'Turnout in electoral democracies', *European Journal of Political Research*, 33: 239–61.

Boy, D. and N. Mayer (eds) (1998) *L'électeur a ses raisons*, Paris: Presses de Sciences Po.

Budge, I. (1996) *The New Challenge of Direct Democracy*, Cambridge: Polity Press.

Budge, I., I. Crewe and D. Farlie (eds) (1976) *Party Identification and Beyond*, New York: John Wiley.

Bufacchi, V. (2001) 'Voting, rationality and reputation', *Political Studies*, 49: 714–29.

Burnside, R. (1999) 'Black voter turnout revisited: testing competing explanations of turnout among blacks', paper prepared for APSA annual meeting, Atlanta, Georgia.

Butler, D. and D. Stokes (1971) *Political Change in Britain: Forces Shaping Electoral Choice*, Harmondsworth: Penguin.

Campbell, A., P. Converse, W. Miller and D. Stokes (1960) *The American Voter*, New York: John Wiley.

Campbell, A. et al. (1966) *Elections and the Political Order*, New York: John Wiley.

Chong, D. (1995) 'Rational choice theory's mysterious rivals' in J. Friedman (ed.) *The Rational Choice Controversy*, New Haven: Yale University Press.

Conover, P. and S. Feldman (1986) 'Emotional reactions to the economy: I'm mad as hell and I'm not going to take it anymore', *American Journal of Political Science*, 30: 50–78.

Converse, J. (1986) *Survey Research in the United States*, Berkeley: University of California Press.

Converse, P. (1964) 'The nature of belief systems in mass publics' in D. Apter (ed.) *Ideology and Discontent*, New York: Free Press.

Converse, P. (1966) 'The concept of a normal vote' in A. Campbell et al. (eds) *Elections and the Political Order*, New York: John Wiley.

Crewe, I. (1986) 'On the death and resurrection of class voting: some comments on *How Britain Votes*', *Political Studies*, 34: 620–38.

Curtice, J. (2002) 'The state of election studies: mid-life crisis or new youth?', *Electoral Studies*, 21: 161–8.

Dalton, R. (2002) *Citizen Politics. Public Opinion and Political Parties in Advanced Industrial Democracies*, London and New York: Chatham House.

Dalton, R., S. Flanagan and P. Beck (eds) (1984) *Electoral Change in Advanced Industrial Democracies*, Princeton: Princeton University Press.

Denver, D. and G. Hands (1974) 'Marginality and turnout in British general elections', *British Journal of Political Science*, 4: 17–35.

Deschouwer, K. (2001) 'Freezing pillars and frozen cleavages: party systems and voter alignments in the consociational democracies' in L. Karvonen and S. Kuhnle (eds) *Party Systems and Voter Alignments Revisited*, London: Routledge.

van Deth, J. (ed.) (1998) *Comparative Politics. The Problem of Equivalence*, London: Routledge.

Dogan, M. (2001) 'Class, religion, party. Triple decline of electoral cleavages in Western Europe' in L. Karvonen and S. Kuhnle (eds) *Party Systems and Voter Alignments Revisited*, London: Routledge.

Doppelt, J. and E. Shearer (2000) *NonVoters. America's No-Shows*, Beverley Hills: Sage.

Downs, A. (1957) *An Economic Theory of Democracy*, New York: Harper and Row.

Dunleavy, P. (1979) 'The urban basis of political alignment', *British Journal of Political Science*, 9: 409–43.

Dunleavy, P. (1987) 'Class dealignment revisited: why odds ratios give odd results', *West European Politics*, 10: 400–19.

Duverger, M. (1954) *Political Parties*, London: Wiley and Son.

van der Eijk, C. (2002) 'Design issues in electoral research: taking care of (core) business', *Electoral Studies*, 21: 189–206.

van der Eijk, C. and B. Niemöller (1983) *Electoral Change in the Netherlands*, Amsterdam: CT Press.

van der Eijk, C. and E. Oppenhuis (1991) 'European parties' performance in electoral competition', *European Journal of Political Research*, 19: 55–80.

Electoral Studies (2000), special edition – 'Economics and elections', 19: 23.

Electoral Studies (2002), special edition – 'The future of election studies', 21:2.

Elster, J. (ed.) (1986) *Rational Choice*, New York: New York University Press.

Enelow, J. and M. Hinich (eds) (1984) *The Spatial Theory of Voting: An Introduction*, New York: Cambridge University Press.

Enelow, J. and M. Hinich (eds) (1990) *Advances in the Spatial Theory of Voting*, New York: Cambridge University Press.

Erikson, R. and J. Goldthorpe (1992) *The Constant Flux: A Study of Class Mobility in Industrial Societies*, Oxford: Clarendon Press.

Evans, G. (ed.) (1999a) *The End of Class Politics? Class Voting in Comparative Context*, Oxford: Oxford University Press.

Evans, G. (1999b) 'Economics and politics revisited: exploring the decline in Conservative support, 1992–1995', *Political Studies*, 47: 139–51.

Evans, G. (1999c) 'Economics, politics and the pursuit of exogeneity: why Pattie, Johnston and Sanders are wrong', *Political Studies*, 47: 933–8.

Evans, J. (2000) 'Le vote gaucho-lepéniste: le masque extrême d'une dynamique normale', *Revue Française de Science Politique*, 50: 21–51.

Evans, J. (2001) 'Les bases sociales et psychologiques du passage gauche-extrême droite: exception française ou mutation européenne?' in P. Perrineau (ed.) *Les Croisés de la Société Fermée*, Paris: L'Aube.

Evans, J. (2003) 'Ideology and party identification: a normalisation of French voting anchors?' in M. Lewis-Beck (ed.) *The French Voter: Before and After 2002*, Basingstoke and New York: Palgrave.

Farrell, D. (2001) *Electoral Systems: A Comparative Introduction*, Basingstoke: Palgrave.

Feldman, S. and P. Conley (1991) 'Explaining explanations of changing economic conditions' in H. Norpoth et al. (eds) *Economics and Politics: The Calculus of Support*, Ann Arbor: University of Michigan Press.

Ferejohn, J. and M. Fiorina (1974) 'The paradox of not voting', *American Political Science Review*, 68: 525–36.

Festinger, L. (1957) *A Theory of Cognitive Dissonance*, Stanford: Stanford University Press.

Fiorina, M. (1981) *Retroprospective Voting in American National Elections*, New Haven: Yale University Press.

Flora, P. (ed.) (1999) *State Formation, Nation-Building and Mass Politics in Europe*, Oxford: Oxford University Press.

Franklin, M. (1996) 'Electoral participation' in L. LeDuc, R. Niemi and P. Norris (eds) *Comparing Democracies: Elections and Voting in Global Perspective*, Beverly Hills: Sage.

Franklin, M. and E. Page (1984) 'A critique of the consumption cleavage approach in British voting studies', *Political Studies*, 32: 521–36.

Friedman, J. (ed) (1996) *The Rational Choice Controversy. Economic Models of Politics Reconsidered*, New Haven: Yale University Press.

Galli, G. et al. (1968) *Il comportamento elettorale in Italia*, Bologna: Il Mulino.

Goodhart, C. and R. Bhansali (1970) 'Political economy', *Political Studies*, 18: 43–106.

Gosnell, H. (1930) *Why Europe Votes*, Chicago: Chicago University Press.

Green, D. and I. Shapiro (1994) *Pathologies of Rational Choice Theory*, New Haven: Yale University Press.

Grofman, B. (1983) 'Models of voter turnout: a brief idiosyncratic review', *Public Choice*, 41: 55–61.

Grofman, B. (1985) 'The neglected role of the status quo in models of issue voting', *Journal of Politics*, 47: 230–7.

Grunberg, G. and E. Schweisguth (1993) 'Social libertarianism and economic liberalism' in D. Boy and N. Mayer (eds) *The French Voter Decides*, Ann Arbor: University of Michigan Press.

Grunberg, G. and E. Schweisguth (1998) 'Vers une tripartition de l'espace politique' in D. Boy and N. Mayer (eds) *L'électeur a ses raisons*, Paris: Presses de Sciences Po.

Habert, P. and A. Lancelot (1996) 'L'émergence d'un nouvel électeur?' in P. Habert (ed.) *Le nouvel électeur*, Paris: Vinci.

Harrop, M. and W. Miller (1987) *Elections and Voters. A Comparative Introduction*, Basingstoke: Macmillan.

Heath, A., G. Evans and J. Martin (1994) 'The measurement of core beliefs and values: the development of balanced socialist/laissez faire and libertarian/authoritarian scales', *British Journal of Political Science*, 24: 115–32.

Heath, A., R. Jowell and J. Curtice (1985) *How Britain Votes*, Oxford: Pergamon.

Heath, A., R. Jowell and J. Curtice (1993) *Understanding Political Change. The British Voter, 1964–1987*, Oxford: Pergamon.

Highton, B. and A. Burris (2002) 'New perspectives on Latino voter turnout in the United States', *American Politics Research*, 30: 285–306.

Hotelling, H. (1929) 'Stability in competition', *The Economic Journal*, 39: 41–57.

Hout, M., C. Brooks and J. Manza (1993) 'The persistence of classes in post-industrial societies', *International Sociology*, 8: 259–77.

Inglehart, R. (1977) *The Silent Revolution: Changing Values and Political Styles among Western Publics*, Princeton: Princeton University Press.

Iversen, T. (1994) 'Political leadership and representation in Western democracies: a test of three models of voting', *American Journal of Political Science*, 38: 45–74.

Jackman, R. (1987) 'Political institutions and voter turnout in the industrial democracies', *American Political Science Review*, 81: 405–23.

Jackman, R. and K. Volpert (1996) 'Conditions favouring parties of the Extreme Right in Western Europe', *British Journal of Political Science*, 26: 501–20.

Jennings. M.K. (1992) 'Ideological thinking among mass publics and political elites', *Public Opinion Quarterly*, 56: 419–41.

Jennings, M.K. and R. Niemi (1968) 'The transmission of political values from parent to child', *American Political Science Review*, 62: 169–84.

Journal of Theoretical Politics (1997), special edition – 'Symposium: the directional theory of issue voting', 9: 1.

Kahneman, D., P. Slovic and A. Tversky (1982) *Judgment Under Uncertainty: Heuristics and Biases*, Cambridge: Cambridge University Press.

Kalyvas, S. (1998) 'Democracy and religious politics: evidence from Belgium', *Comparative Political Studies*, 31: 292–320.

Karvonen, L. and S. Kuhnle (eds) (2001) *Party Systems and Voter Alignments Revisited*, London: Routledge.

Kinder, D. and D. Kiewiet (1979) 'Economic discontent and political behavior: the role of personal grievances and collective economic judgments in congressional voting', *American Journal of Political Science*, 23: 495–527.

Kitschelt, H. (1994) *The Transformation of European Social Democracy*, Cambridge: Cambridge University Press.

Knack, S. (1994) 'Does rain help the Republicans? Theory and evidence on turnout and the vote', *Public Choice*, 79: 187–209.

Korpi, W. (1971) 'Working-class Communism in Western Europe: rational or nonrational?', *American Sociological Review*, 36: 971–84.

Kramer, G. (1971) 'Short-term fluctuations in US voting behaviour, 1896–1964', *American Political Science Review*, 65: 131–43.

Kramer, G. (1983) 'The ecological fallacy revisited: aggregate- versus individual-level findings on economics and elections, and sociotropic voting', *American Political Science Review*, 77: 92–111.

Lane, R. (1962) *Political Ideology. Why the American Common Man Believes What He Does*, New York: Free Press.

Lane, J.-E. and S. Ersson (1990) 'Macro and micro understanding in political science: what explains electoral participation', *European Journal of Political Research*, 18: 457–65.

Langton, K. (1969) *Political Socialization*, New York: Oxford University Press.

Laver, M. (1997) *Private Desires, Political Action. An Invitation to the Politics of Rational Choice*, London: Sage.

Laver, M. and N. Schofield (1990) *Multiparty Government*, Oxford: Oxford University Press.

Lazarsfeld, P., B. Berelson and H. Gaudet (1968) *The People's Choice. How the Voter Makes Up His Mind in a Presidential Campaign*, 3rd edition, New York: Colombia University Press.

Leighley, J. and J. Nagler (1992) 'Individual and systemic influences on turnout: who votes?', *Journal of Politics*, 54: 718–40.

Lewis-Beck, M. (1988) *Economics and Elections*, Ann Arbor: University of Michigan Press.

Lewis-Beck, M. (1997) 'Who's the chef? Economic voting under a dual executive', *European Journal of Political Research*, 31: 315–25.

Lewis-Beck, M. and M. Paldam (2000) 'Economic voting: an introduction', *Electoral Studies*, 19: 113–21.

Lijphart, A. (1980) 'Language, religion, class and party choice: Belgium, Canada, Switzerland and South Africa compared' in R. Rose (ed.) *Electoral Participation*, London: Sage.

Lijphart, A. (1999) *Patterns of Democracy. Government Forms and Performance in Thirty-Six Countries*, New Haven: Yale University Press.

Lipset, S. M. (1959a) *Political Man. The Social Bases of Voting*, 1983 edition, London: Heinemann.

Lipset, S. (1959b) 'Democracy and working-class authoritarianism', *American Sociological Review*, 24: 482–501.

Lipset, S.M. and S. Rokkan (eds) (1967) 'Introduction' in *Party Systems and Voter Alignments: Cross-National Perspectives*, New York: The Free Press.

Listhaug, O., S. Macdonald and G. Rabinowitz (1994) 'Ideology and party support in comparative perspective', *European Journal of Political Research*, 25:111–49.

Lubbers, M. and P. Scheepers (2000) 'Individual and contextual characteristics of the German Extreme Right-wing vote in the 1990s. A test of complementary theories', *European Journal of Political Research* 38: 63–94.

McLean, I. (1982) *Dealing in Votes*, Oxford: Martin Robertson.

Macdonald, S., G. Rabinowitz and O. Listhaug (1998) 'On attempting to rehabilitate the proximity model: sometimes the patient just can't be helped', *Journal of Politics*, 60: 653–90.

Mackie, T. and R. Rose (1991) *The International Almanac of Electoral History*, London: Macmillan.

MacRae, D. (1958) 'Religious and socioeconomic factors in the French vote, 1946–1956', *American Journal of Sociology*, 64: 290–98.

Mair, P. (1999) 'Critical commentary: four perspectives on the end of class politics' in G. Evans (ed.) *The End of Class Politics? Class Voting in Comparative Context*, Oxford: Oxford University Press.

Mannheimer, R. and G. Sani (1987) *Il mercato elettorale. Identikit dell'elettore italiano*, Bologna: Il Mulino.

Manza, J. and C. Brooks (1999) *Social Cleavages and Political Change. Voter Alignments and US Party Coalitions*, New York: Oxford University Press.

Marcus, G. and M. MacKuen (1993) 'Anxiety, enthusiasm, and the vote: the motivational underpinnings of learning and involvement during presidential campaigns', *American Political Science Review*, 87: 672–85.

Marcus, G., W. Russell Neuman, and M. MacKuen (2000) *Affective Intelligence and Political Judgment*, Chicago: University of Chicago Press.

Markus, G. (1988) 'The impact of personal and national economic conditions on the presidential vote: a pooled cross-sectional analysis', *American Journal of Political Science*, 32: 137–54.

Marsh, M. (2002) 'Electoral context', *Electoral Studies*, 21: 207–17.

Maslow, A. (1954) *Motivations and Personality*, New York: Harper and Row.

Matthews, S. (1979) 'A simple direction model of electoral competition', *Public Choice*, 34: 141–56.

Meehl, P. (1977) 'The selfish citizen argument and the throw away vote argument', *American Journal of Political Science*, 71: 11–30.

Merrill, S. and B. Grofman (1999) *A Unified Theory of Voting: Directional and Proximity Spatial Models*, Cambridge: Cambridge University Press.

Michelat, G. and M. Simon (1977) *Classe, Religion et Politique*, Paris: FNSP.

Middendorp, C., J. Luyten and R. Dooms (1993) 'Issue-voting in the Netherlands: two-dimensional issue-distances between own position and perceived party position as determinants of the vote', *Acta Politica*, 1: 39–59.

Milbrath, L. (1965) *Political Participation*, Chicago: Rand McNally.

Miller, W. and J. Merrill Shanks (1996) *The New American Voter*, Cambridge: Harvard University Press.

Morris, D. (1999) *Vote.com. How Big-Money Lobbyists and the Media Are Losing Their Influence, and the Internet is Giving Power to the People*, Los Angeles: Renaissance.

Mueller, J. (1970) 'Presidential popularity from Truman to Johnson', *American Political Science Review*, 64: 18–34.

Nannestad, P. and M. Paldam (1994) 'The VP-function: a survey of the literature on vote and popularity functions after 25 years', *Public Choice*, 79: 213–45.

Nannestad, P. and M. Paldam (1997a) 'From the pocketbook of the welfare man: a pooled cross-section study of economic voting in Denmark, 1986–1992', *British Journal of Political Science*, 27: 119–36.

Nannestad, P. and M. Paldam (1997b) 'It's the government's fault! A cross-section study of economic voting in Denmark, 1990–1993', *European Journal of Political Research*, 28: 33–62.

Nie, N., S. Verba and J. Petrocik (1976) *The Changing American Voter*, Cambridge: Harvard University Press.

Niemi, R. (1976) 'Costs of voting and nonvoting', *Public Choice*, 27: 115–19.

Norpoth, H., M. Lewis-Beck and J.-D. Lafay (eds) (1991) *Economics and Politics: The Calculus of Support*, Ann Arbor: University of Michigan Press.

Norris, P. et al. (1999) *On Message: Communicating the Campaign*, London: Sage.

Olson, M. (1965) *The Logic of Collective Action*, Cambridge: Harvard University Press.

Overbye, E. (1995) 'Making a case for the rational, self-regarding "ethical" voter … and solving the "Paradox of not voting" in the process', *European Journal of Political Research*, 27: 369–96.

Paldam, M. (1991) 'How robust is the vote function? A study of seventeen nations over four decades' in H. Norpoth, M. Lewis-Beck and J.-D. Lafay (eds) *Economics and Politics. The Calculus of Support*, Ann Arbor: University of Michigan Press.

Paldam, M. and P. Nannestad (2000) 'What do voters know about the economy? A study of Danish data, 1990–1993', *Electoral Studies*, 19: 363–91.

Parisi, A. and G. Pasquino (1977) 'Relazioni partiti-elettori e tipi di voto', in A. Parisi and G. Pasquino (eds) *Continuità e mutamento elettorale in Italia*, il Mulino, Bologna.

Parsons, T. and N. Smelser (1956) *Economy and Society*, London: Routledge.

Pattie, C. and R. Johnston (1995) '"It's not like that round here": region, economic evaluations and voting at the 1992 British general election', *European Journal of Political Research*, 28: 1–32.

Pattie, C., R. Johnston and D. Sanders (1999) 'On babies and bathwater: a comment on Evans 'Economics and politics Revisited', *Political Studies*, 47: 918–32.
Pennings, P., H. Keman and J. Kleinnijenhuis (1999) *Doing Research in Political Science. An Introduction to Comparative Methods and Statistics*, London: Sage.
Percheron, A. and M.K. Jennings (1981) 'Political continuities in French families: a new perspective on an old controversy', *Comparative Politics*, 3: 421–36.
Perea, E.A. (2002) 'Individual characteristics, institutional incentives and electoral abstention in Western Europe', *European Journal of Political Research*, 41: 643–73.
Pierce, R. (1995) *Choosing the Chief. Presidential Elections in France and the United States*, Michigan: University of Michigan Press.
Popkin, S. (1991) *The Reasoning Voter*, Chicago: Chicago University Press.
Powell, G.B. (1980) 'Voting turnout in thirty democracies' in R. Rose (ed.) *Electoral Participation*, London: Sage.
Powell, G.B. and G. Whitten (1993) 'A cross-national analysis of economic voting: taking account of the political context', *American Journal of Political Science*, 37: 391–414.
Przeworksi, A. and G. Soares (1971) 'Theories in search of a curve: a contextual interpretation of Left vote', *American Political Science Review*, 65: 51–68.
Pulzer, P. (1967) *Political Representation and Elections in Britain*, London: Allen and Unwin.
Quattrone, G. and A. Tversky (1988) 'Contrasting rational and psychological analyses of political choice', *American Political Science Review*, 82: 719–36.
Rabinowitz, G. (1978) 'On the nature of political issues: insights from a spatial analysis', *American Journal of Political Science*, 22: 793–817.
Rabinowitz, G. and S. Macdonald (1989) 'A directional theory of voting', *American Political Science Review*, 83: 93–121.
Rattinger, H. (1991) 'Unemployment and elections in West Germany' in H. Norpoth et al. (eds) *Economics and Politics: The Calculus of Support*, Ann Arbor: University of Michigan Press.
Riker, W. and P. Ordeshook (1968) 'A theory of the calculus of voting', *American Political Science Review*, 62: 25–42.
Robertson, D. (1976) *A Theory of Party Competition*, London: John Wiley.
Rokeach, M. (1960) *The Open and Closed Mind. Investigations into the Nature of Belief Systems and Personality Systems*, New York: Basic Books.
Rokkan, S. (1967) 'Geography, religion and social class: cross-cutting cleavages in Norwegian politics' in S.M. Lipset and S. Rokkan (eds) *Party Systems and Voter Alignments: Cross-National Perspectives*, New York: The Free Press.
Rosenstone, S. (1982) 'Economic adversity and voter turnout', *American Journal of Political Science*, 26: 25–46.
Rosenstone, S. and J. Hansen (1993) *Mobilization, Participation, and Democracy in America*, New York: Macmillan.
Sanders, D. (1991) 'Government popularity and the next General Election', *Political Studies*, 62: 235–61.
Sanders, D. (2000) 'The real economy and the perceived economy in popularity functions: how much do voters need to know? A study of British data, 1974–1997', *Electoral Studies*, 19: 275–94.
Sanders, D. et al. (2001) 'The economy and voting', *Parliamentary Affairs*, 54: 789–802.
Sarlvik, B. and I. Crewe (1983) *Decade of Dealignment*, Cambridge: Cambridge University Press.
Sartori, G. (1969) 'From the sociology of politics to political sociology' in S.M. Lipset (ed.) *Politics and the Social Sciences*, New York: Oxford University Press.
Sartori, G. (1976) *Parties and Party Systems. A Framework for Analysis*, Cambridge: Cambridge University Press.
Sartori, G. (1994) *Comparative Constitutional Engineering: An Inquiry into Structures, Incentives and Outcomes*, Basingstoke: Macmillan.

Schattschneider, E. (1975) *The Semi-Sovereign People*, New York: Holt, Rinehart and Winston.

Schwartz, T. (1987) 'Your vote counts on account of the way it is counted', *Public Choice*, 54: 101–21.

Siaroff, A. (2000) *Comparative European Party Systems. An Analysis of Parliamentary Elections since 1945*, New York: Garland.

Siegfried, A. (1913) *Tableau politique de la France de l'Ouest sous la Troisième République*, Paris: Armand Colin.

Sigel, R. (ed.) (1989) *Political Learning in Adulthood. A Sourcebook of Theory*, Chicago: University of Chicago Press.

Simon, H. (1979) *Models of Thought*, New Haven: Yale University Press.

Smith, E. (1989) *The Unchanging American Voter*, Berkeley: University of California Press.

Smithies, A. (1941) 'Optimum location in spatial competition', *Journal of Political Economy*, 49: 423–39.

Sniderman, P., R. Brody and P. Tetlock (1991) *Reasoning and Choice. Explorations in Political Psychology*, Cambridge: Cambridge University Press.

Stone, W. and P. Schaffner (1988) *The Psychology of Politics*, New York: Springer Verlag.

Taylor-Gooby, P. (1986) 'Consumption cleavages and welfare politics', *Political Studies*, 34: 592–606.

Teixeira, R. (1993) *The Disappearing American Voter*, Washington DC: Brookings Institution.

Thomassen, J. (1976) 'Party identification as a cross-national concept: its meaning in the Netherlands' in I. Budge et al. (eds) *Party Identification and Beyond: Representations of Voting and Party Competition*, London: Wiley.

Tingsten, H. (1937) *Political Behaviour: Studies in Election Statistics*, London: P.S. King.

Topf, R. (1995) 'Electoral participation' in H.-D. Klingemann and D. Fuchs (eds) *Citizens and the State*, Oxford: Oxford University Press.

Weakliem, D. and A. Heath (1994) 'Rational choice and class voting', *Rationality and Society*, 6: 243–70.

Weatherford, S. (1978) 'Economic conditions and electoral outcomes: class differences in the political response to recession', *American Journal of Political Science*, 22: 917–38.

Westholm, A. (1997) 'The illusory defeat of the proximity theory of electoral choice', *American Political Science Review*, 13: 277–90.

Whiteley, P. (1986) 'Predicting the Labour vote in 1983: social background versus subjective evaluation', *Political Studies*, 34: 82–98.

Whitten, G. and H. Palmer (1999) 'Cross-national analyses of economic voting', *Electoral Studies*, 18: 49–67.

Wlezien, C. and M. Franklin (2002) 'Introduction – the future of election studies', *Electoral Studies*, 21: 157–60.

Wolfinger, R. and S. Rosenstone (1980) *Who Votes?*, New Haven: Yale University Press.

Wright, E. (1985) *Classes*, London: Verso.

Zaller, J. (1992) *The Nature and Origins of Mass Opinion*, Cambridge and New York: Cambridge University Press.

Zaller, J. (2002) 'The statistical power of election studies to detect media exposure effects in political campaigns', *Electoral Studies*, 21: 297–329.

Zuckerman, A. (1982) 'New approaches to political cleavages: a theoretical introduction', *Comparative Political Studies*, 15: 131–44.

Index